ROBIN BRIGGS

Early Modern France
1560–1715

Oxford New York
OXFORD UNIVERSITY PRESS

Oxford University Press, Walton Street, Oxford OX2 6DP

Oxford New York Toronto
Delhi Bombay Calcutta Madras Karachi
Kuala Lumpur Singapore Hong Kong Tokyo
Nairobi Dar es Salaam Cape Town
Melbourne Auckland Madrid

and associated companies in
Berlin Ibadan

Oxford is a trade mark of Oxford University Press

British Library Cataloguing in Publication Data
Data available

Library of Congress Cataloging in Publication Data
Data available
ISBN 0-19-289040-9

9 10

Printed in Great Britain by
J. W. Arrowsmith Ltd, Bristol

An OPUS book

Early Modern France 1560–1715

OPUS General Editors

Christopher Butler
Robert Evans
John Skorupski

OPUS books provide concise, original, and authoritative introductions to a wide range of subjects in the humanities and sciences. They are written by experts for the general reader as well as for students.

Contents

CONTENTS

List of Illustrations

Introduction

This book attempts to present an overall view of the history of France during the later sixteenth and the seventeenth centuries. Sober reflection suggests that this task is very nearly impossible; having now tried it I am tempted to remove the qualification, and assert that it is absolutely so. The over-simplifications, evasions, and plain guesswork that have gone into this brief essay will be painfully obvious to specialists in the many fields on which it touches. Readers with less background knowledge would also be well advised to treat my interpretations with the necessary scepticism. History of this kind cannot pretend to any great degree of exactitude, since too many important aspects of life during this period have left hardly any documentary traces behind. Getting the facts right is hard enough; finding the right emphases, above all the correct balance between the static and the changing elements in a past society, is prodigiously difficult. On occasion I have also allowed myself the luxury of direct or implied moral judgements on groups or individuals, which should at least allow readers to identify my own prejudices, but need not be taken too seriously. Those who reject my view of Richelieu or Louis XIV are welcome to do so—provided they remember Michelet's admirable maxim, 'Respect is the death of history'.

Some of the omissions in the book are deliberate, resulting from constraints on space and my own relative ignorance. Above all, I have excluded serious consideration of 'high culture'; music, literature, and the visual arts. This is regrettable, not least because the cultural milieu unquestionably influenced the attitudes of the ruling classes, but the subject could not be sensibly treated in the space available. Another important gap is any extended description of the 'human geography' of early modern France; this too would have made the book much longer, and there are already good studies on such lines. What I felt was most needed, and have tried to provide, was a survey identifying and linking the changes in social, economic, and political life during this crucial period in France's historical development. The pattern of the book is inevitably a compromise, since it has to be broken up into sections, which divide some of the topics whose interrelations I wish to stress. The chapter on the Wars of Religion is intended as a general introduction, giving the background without which much of the seventeenth century cannot be fully understood. The remaining three chapters are inter-dependent, and on some occasions carts get in front of horses. The reader who has difficulty with partial discussions of the *intendants* and royal fiscality in chapter 2, for example, should use the table of contents and the index to locate the fuller treatment in chapter 3. I have tried to give brief working descriptions of the institutions which play a large part in the story, but serious students will need a reference book like M. Marion's institutional dictionary, while beginners will find J. H. Shennan's short paperback helpful (see the bibliography for details).

Imperfect as it is, this book owes much to the example and advice of others. My intellectual debt to the *Annales* school of French historians will be obvious; among French scholars I must particularly mention Yves Castan, Pierre Goubert, Emmanuel Le Roy Ladurie, Robert Mandrou, and the late Jean Meuvret, with whom I have had illuminating discussions. Many other friends and colleagues in both France and England have helped me, notably Keith Thomas, who suggested both the idea of the book and many improvements in it, and Richard Bonney, who generously gave me access to as yet unpublished work on which I have drawn heavily, also making constructive criticisms of my original draft. As the book has grown I have been much helped by comments from Robert Franklin, and above all from my wife, who has read cheerfully through successive drafts, averting many stylistic and intellectual disasters. The work would have taken far longer without the support and facilities provided by All Souls College, and the help of its clerical and library staff. The task of getting the work into print has been made surprisingly agreeable by Carol Buckroyd and Robyn Swett of the Oxford University Press. Finally, I have been a great gainer from the Oxford Further Subject on seventeenth-century France, created by Menna Prestwich; my pupils have taught me far more than they can have guessed. The errors and inadequacies which remain are, of course, all my own work.

The maps, which are the result of collaboration between Richard Bonney and myself, were drawn by Julian Richards; the graphs were made fit for publication by the drawing office of the Oxford University Press in London. The graph on page 37 is taken from *Études d'histoire économique*, by Jean Meuvret, and appears by kind permission of the publishers, the École des Hautes Études en Sciences Sociales.

The French provinces at the time of Richelieu and Mazarin

(Stippled areas are those with provincial estates in 1661 and after)

The Crisis of the Monarchy

Most Frenchmen must have experienced the last four decades of the sixteenth century as a period of difficulties and dangers. The political and religious conflicts we know as the Wars of Religion may have been the work of relatively small minorities, but the destruction and disorder they brought proved both widespread and lasting. The effects of civil war combined with social and economic change to create golden opportunities for a lucky few, but deteriorating conditions and hardship for the many. The sharpest decline of all was that in the power and prestige of the monarchy. At the death of Henri II in 1559 the French king's authority in his own dominions still seemed as absolute as that of any of his rivals in Europe. In 1589 his last surviving son, Henri III, was murdered while laying siege to his own capital, with much of the kingdom in open revolt, and the line of the Valois kings came to an end. At this moment there was a real danger that the country would split up into a number of smaller units; it took all the abilities of Henri IV to re-establish the powers of the crown and the central government.

A breakdown on this scale of the internal structure of the largest unified state in Europe was a major event in international politics. Those long-lived and astute neighbouring monarchs, Philip II of Spain and Elizabeth I of England, could not afford to remain indifferent. Both had good reason to be fearful of the triumph of one or another faction, and both stood to gain from prolonging the period of French weakness. Their policies, together with those of the Protestant states of Germany and the Netherlands, complicated and deepened the conflicts in France. The civil wars were therefore the subject of intense interest, not only to professional diplomats, but also to the educated classes of much of Western Europe. The great contemporary histories of Davila and de Thou were widely read and translated when they appeared in the early seventeenth century, showing that this interest had continued beyond the end of the wars.

Unfortunately this promising beginning was never to be adequately followed up by later historians. The scrappiness of the documentary evidence has been one major problem, while the handwriting of the period is peculiarly atrocious, and many questions about the wars and their wider context remain unresolved. The sixteenth century as a whole has been the poor relation of French historical writing in the recent past. This book is primarily concerned with the seventeenth century, but many of its conclusions will show that an understanding of the earlier period is vital for any explanation of the evolution of the *ancien régime* as a whole. In the absence of satisfactory studies of sixteenth-century France some attempt to describe the major features of the period is essential, although it is bound to be rather tentative. Certain aspects of the more distant, medieval past are also highly relevant, but can be evoked more briefly.

The Renaissance Monarchy

Unlike their Anglo-Norman cousins, the medieval kings of France had built up their power slowly. The highly structured feudalism of England resulted from the exceptional circumstances which followed the conquest, allowing the imposition of a uniform system over a defined area. The French monarchs, in contrast, assembled their kingdom piecemeal, layer on layer. They accreted different customs, legal systems, and privileges, with little more to tie them together than the personal authority of the king. Under such conditions there was always a serious threat that the peripheral areas might break away, either to become independent or to attach themselves to neighbouring states. The long history of English involvement in France was a prime example of these dangers, which culminated in the Hundred Years War. In the early fifteenth century the combination of English military techniques and local particularism, as exemplified by the Dukes of Burgundy and other magnates, came close to destroying the French state. In the very process of survival the monarchy extended its power in one crucial respect: it acquired the effective power to tax at will. By a process of considerable obscurity Charles VII and his advisers managed to turn a limited and temporary concession by the Estates of 1439 into an established right. For the next three and a half centuries the monarchy was to collect the *taille*, the main direct tax, on this dubious footing. New taxes were still thought to require consent, and income from all sources tended to dribble in slowly and imperfectly, but the king's revenue was enormously increased, and the new wealth formed the basis of the political structure of the Renaissance monarchy.

The first call on this wealth was the creation of a sizeable standing army, the essential instrument of any powerful ruler. This was a great achievement for the crown, but the advantages were severely qualified, because most of the troops remained effectively under the control of individual magnates. Until the seventeenth century 'royal' troops were liable to be utilized by rebels against the king. The re-establishment of royal authority from the 1440s onward did not include any general measures designed to destroy provincial rights and liberties, the symbols of particularism. The monarchy sought to retain the loyalty of peripheral provinces by harnessing local patriotism, creating such important new institutions as the regional *parlements* to this end. This was part of a highly successful technique of ruling through the exercise of patronage. During the century between the end of the Hundred Years War (1453) and the death of Henri II the monarchy was generally able to get its way without resorting to coercion. The tax revenues, increasing with general prosperity in the late fifteenth and early sixteenth centuries, financed a massive spoils system, which gave new inducements for the magnates to remain loyal. Apart from money pensions, the great nobles were the beneficiaries of positions of power in the grant of the king, such as the provincial governorships. From Charles VIII's invasion of Italy in 1494 to the peace of Cateau-Cambrésis in 1559 the wars in Italy and against the Habsburgs were interrupted only by brief intervals of peace. Military service entailed prestigious commands for the magnates, and gave lesser nobles the chance to rise through serving the crown in battle. The wars also gave the kings useful pretexts for further increases in the tax burden.

Despite increased taxes, the long period of warfare inevitably placed a great strain on the royal finances. In part this was met by borrowing on the new money markets of Lyon and Antwerp, but such borrowings had eventually to be secured on revenues. Under François I (1515–47) a new expedient was developed, whose importance in French history rivals that of taxation at will. This was the first reign in which royal offices were sold in large numbers as a matter of course, and the practice would continue until the eighteenth century. The principle was a simple one: the king established a new court or tribunal to exercise judicial or administrative functions in a particular area, often by restricting the ill-defined jurisdictions of existing bodies. Posts in the new institution were then offered for sale, with the attraction of a small salary paid by the crown, supplemented by legal fees and various valuable privileges and exemptions. Apart from creating new institutions, the crown might also increase the number of posts in existing courts. Although the primary motive for the process was certainly financial, there were good reasons for supposing that France needed more royal judges and administrators in the early sixteenth century, and in view of the profits such jobs brought their holders there was a certain logic to the establishment of official venality. In many ways the system was an ingenious extension of patronage, since the new officials were dependent on the king and his council for support in the exercise of their powers, constantly challenged by rival institutions.

The wider implications of venality of office for the social, political, and economic development of France are almost incalculable, and will form one of the major themes of this book. In the present more limited context, it should be realized that the system was one important means by which royal power penetrated to the extremities of the realm. Power in the localities now depended not only on landholding and feudal dependence relations, but also on ability to influence the distribution of patronage from the centre. Nobles who enjoyed the king's favour might hope to secure positions for their followers; it was not uncommon for the king to allow such men to dispose of whole blocks of offices. In this way the new officials were absorbed into the clientage systems of the magnates, which were also being reinforced by the distribution of cash in the form of pensions and salaries. The Renaissance monarchs were aiding and abetting the extension of bastard feudalism as the basic form of political relationship in France. Depending as it did on the control of a strong king and the continuing availability of funds, such a situation was inherently unstable even if well managed. In practice François I and Henri II had little regard for the long-term effects of their policies, and failed to check the formation of dangerous power blocs under the control of great nobles; the only such concentration to be broken up was that of the Constable of Bourbon in 1521.

There were a number of reasons why the breakdown of this uneasy balance was slower than might have been expected. In the first place, Louis XII, François I, and Henri II were all effective rulers, whatever their individual failings, and were generally able to hold the loyalty of the magnates. The Italian campaigns long held out the promise of new wealth and new territories to divide up, and they brought one important and permanent gain. After his great victory at Marignano (1515) François I was able to impose his terms on the Pope. The Concordat of Bologna (1516) was to last until the Revolution, and it gave the kings almost complete control over the disposal of the higher positions in the French church. This meant another enormous extension of royal patronage, and also allowed the king to exploit the wealth of the church by a variety of means. The early sixteenth century was a period of rapidly rising population and economic expansion, which favoured the development of royal fiscality and the sale of offices to newly prosperous merchants. Finally, a series of fortunate deaths in the later fifteenth century had seen the end of many threatening magnate families, and the incorporation of Brittany and large parts of the Burgundian dominions into the main body of the kingdom.

With the sole exception of the Concordat these advantages proved ephemeral, and during the 1550s the situation changed with alarming speed. The royal finances were degenerating into near-bankruptcy, with revenues pledged two or three years ahead. In such circumstances the war with Spain could not be long continued, and any peace settlement was bound to be disappointing. The disastrous defeat at Saint Quentin in 1557 lost France her last chance of avoiding something like humiliation at the conference table, with the renunciation of her Italian ambitions. The economic and social changes which the monarchy had earlier exploited were creating tensions and conflicts it would not be easy to resolve, and which in their turn contributed to the new and alarming threat of religious strife. Even the Concordat had its reverse side; the secular interests of the king too often stood in the way of much needed reforms in the church, giving indirect encouragement to the spread of heresy. Henri II had proved an adequate figurehead, but even had he lived there was little evidence that he or his advisers possessed the ability to cope with the problems the peace would bring. His death in July 1559, as a result of a jousting accident in a tournament designed to celebrate the peace, marked a violent turning-point in the history of both his kingdom and his dynasty.

The Renaissance monarchy foreshadowed in many ways the 'absolute' monarchy of the next century. The kings used ostentation and display to reinforce their prestige, patronizing the arts and building on a grand scale. Their legists prepared sweeping *ordonnances*, intended to apply across the whole kingdom, and began to elaborate constitutional theories which stressed the royal powers. The central administration was still small and somewhat ramshackle, but the emergence of officials such as the Secretaries of State was evidence of increasing bureaucratization. By the end of the fifteenth century the Estates General had convinced the crown of their uselessness as a source of taxation, and in consequence they were not summoned between 1484 and 1560. The consultative nature of the early sixteenth-century monarchy has often been stressed, but this consultation was shrewdly stage-managed by the government. Assemblies of selected notables and town representatives proved a good means of raising money, and could be subjected to a variety of pressures. Impressive though this political system was, it did have one crucial weakness, which has already been stressed. The king had bought the loyalty of his greater subjects by a constant flow of largesse, and by allowing them a major share in his power. Like all medieval régimes, the 'new monarchy' made no effective provision for a weak king or a regency, so when either of these disasters arrived faction struggles were certain to get out of control. The greater the wealth and power of the central government, the more the magnates would aspire to seize these assets for their own benefit. As the civil wars were to demonstrate, a breakdown of this kind might prove very difficult to repair.

Social and intellectual changes

Many of the more technical aspects of demographic and economic developments will be discussed in the next chapter, but the crisis of the 1560s cannot be understood without reference to the important changes that were taking place within French society. Since the 1470s the population had been increasing fast, and it may have risen by as much as a third between then and the 1560s. The effect on the economic relationships between different social groups was dramatic. The fifteenth century had been a period of relatively abundant land and scarce labour, when wages were high and rents low. As the population began to press against the limits of available land and productive techniques this pattern was inexorably inverted. Few detailed studies of this phenomenon have yet been made, but the best examples, which are from such different areas as Mediterranean Languedoc and the Hurepoix (the region of cereal culture south of Paris), point in the same direction. Moderate sized holdings, commonplace in 1500, were disappearing fast, and a polarization was taking place between relatively large holdings and minute plots of land. The peasantry was suffering from general impoverishment with an enormous increase in vagrancy and begging. Employment was becoming harder to find, while the demand for work pushed wages down. Many of the poor sought work in the towns, with very limited success; poor suburbs began to spread outside the medieval walls.

Economic relationships were also under pressure from the inflation which was one of the main features of the century, and which was itself partly a product of the population increase. By modern standards the inflation was puny; grain prices barely doubled during the first half of the sixteenth century, and most other commodities rose more slowly. Even such a limited price rise, however, posed major problems for a society which did not fully understand what was happening, and had very inadequate machinery for adjusting to inflation. It took a considerable time for many landlords to realize that leases for long periods at fixed money rents were a very bad deal for them; for those who had exchanged feudal or seig-neurial dues originally levied in kind against fixed money payments there was no remedy. We know very little about the incomes of French nobles in this period, but it seems likely that many of them were failing to maintain their revenues, in real terms, just at a time when the temptations to overspend were becoming much stronger. It is clear that not all nobles were having such difficulties; those who saw the chance to exploit the situation and pushed up rents, perhaps also extend-ing their landed property, could realize major gains. The effects of the inflation on the privileged classes varied accord-ing to the skill with which individuals reacted, whereas at peasant level only exceptional good fortune allowed escape from the general deterioration in living standards. A small proportion of peasants did nevertheless benefit, building up their income from the sale of agricultural produce and assem-bling substantial farms. This rural élite showed some tendency to drift towards the towns, but many families stayed put, to become one of the key social groups of the *ancien régime*.

Between 80% and 90% of the population were country-dwellers, and production was overwhelmingly rural; much of the limited industrial activity of the period was dispersed in the countryside. France had a large number of towns, but only in exceptional cases like Lyon or Amiens were they sig-nificant centres of production. In general they were market centres for the surrounding *plat pays*, and the meeting places of royal courts. The merchants and lawyers who dominated town life were well placed to benefit from the price rise, and did not miss their opportunity. Most such men already possessed land outside the towns, and the sixteenth century saw their holdings expand rapidly, to the detriment of both the peasantry and the older nobility. This development emphasized the parasitic nature of the towns, and tended to aggravate the long-standing hostility between them and their agricultural hinterland. The urban élites were generally more self-centred in their culture and economic behaviour than their rural counterparts, and did not necessarily offer the protection and help expected from the traditional landlords, the nobility. Their penetration of the countryside might therefore be more than a change in ownership; it could alter the character of landlord–tenant relations in a manner the peasantry would find disconcerting.

Contemporaries had relatively little understanding of the forces which were changing their society, or of how far it was changing. Their social thought operated at the level of assumptions rather than of rational analysis, and these assumptions did not include any notion that change might be for the better. The object of almost all social legislation was to preserve the existing order of things. Rapid movements up and down the social ladder were regarded, even by those at the bottom, as a cause for complaint. Resistance, whether to the crown or to the local *notable*, was always justified by an appeal to the past against some infringement on customary rights. This situation added to the difficulties of governing the country, since political discourse often bore little relation to the facts it pretended to deal with. Assumptions and practice could be widely different without anyone seeming to notice; this was of particular importance in relation to the nobility. Noble representatives in various assemblies made vehement assertions about the hereditary qualities of their order, demanding the maintenance of privileges granted against past services. They blithely ignored the fact that many nobles were of very recent vintage, and the lack of any mechanism to check on pretensions to nobility. Such imperfect evidence as we possess suggests that many prosperous commoners were slipping across the obscure line which separated them from the nobility, and swelling the ranks of the order. In this respect, as in so many others, the sixteenth century was a period of increased social mobility.

These shifts in the balance of economic and social privilege seem to have been a national phenomenon, but their timing and importance clearly varied widely from one region to another. Change was probably quickest in the open plains and in the vicinity of large towns, where a more developed system of land tenure already existed, capable of adaptation to new circumstances. In the upland regions of the Massif Central, the Alps, the Jura, and the Pyrenees the traditional patterns were most durable. Here too the population increased, but the most obvious result was a great increase in emigration, seasonal or permanent, towards more favoured regions. Western and south-western France, from Brittany to Gascony, fell somewhere between the two extremes. With sufficient information it would be possible to produce a map of differential development, a patchwork quilt of tiny regions so complex as to defeat all generalizations. In the absence of such evidence the historian can still attempt to draw broad conclusions, but this must be done in the awareness that the reality was far more complex and contradictory.

While population increase and inflation were threatening the stability of the established social order, more insidious processes were working in the same direction. The appearance of the printed book was one of the great watersheds of cultural and intellectual history, and by the early sixteenth century the trade in books and pamphlets was well established. Combined with a very significant growth in literacy, especially among the privileged classes and the town-dwellers, printing brought an immense expansion of cultural horizons. Within a few decades a large proportion of the inheritance from classical antiquity had been made available as never before, while contemporary authors were discovering the potential audience for their writings. Erasmus showed the way, and France was to produce two of the great figures of the first age of printed literature, Rabelais and Montaigne. Their work, with that of lesser men, can still give some impression of the intellectual excitement characteristic of the period at its best; both were also subversive writers in some respects, questioning the established verities of religion and social behaviour. Printing gave a great impetus to educational and intellectual activity, and was a major factor in the explosion of new ideas during the sixteenth century. It seems likely that by the last decades of the century a vital threshold had been passed, in the sense that systems of censorship and control, by state or church, had been swamped by a flood of print. Political activity had become public in a new sense, subject to discussion and attack under the eyes of an ever-growing number of literate citizens.

In the very long run this cultural ferment was to lead into such recognizably modern movements of thought as the Enlightenment, but this was only after generations of assimilation. On close inspection even the most advanced thinkers of the sixteenth century reveal a great ambivalence; they shrouded their real originality from themselves as well as their readers by presenting their ideas in clothing borrowed from the past. The great heritage from the Graeco-Roman world was so rich and complex that its rediscovery brought as much confusion as illumination. The systems of Aristotle and his medieval followers might have lost much of their credibility, but replacements were very slow to appear; they would only emerge from the late seventeenth century onwards. During the intervening period the great majority of educated men apparently found it possible to tolerate the growing inconsistencies and gaps in their world picture; they cannot, however, have been entirely unaware of them.

The spread of Protestantism

The hesitancies and uncertainties of lay thought contrast sharply with the revolutionary changes in religion during the same period. The importance of printing both for the diffusion of the Reformation and for its very character has long been recognized. Mass-produced bibles and widespread literacy were preconditions for the new style of Christianity, with its emphasis on opening the scriptures to laymen. In France as in England the Protestant faith was slow to establish itself at first, but by the 1540s the pace of conversions was becoming rapid. By this date Calvin had given Protestantism a form which was well calculated both to win and to hold the loyalty of Frenchmen; his establishment of a base at Geneva gave him the opportunity to train ministers who would proselytize in France. The French Catholic church was in no state to take up the challenge, plagued as it was by non-residence and ignorance on the part of its clergy. In the 1550s Protestant missionaries were still remarking on the lack of religious enthusiasm among Catholic clerics and laity alike. This situation would have made it plausible for the monarchy to embrace the new faith, but the Concordat gave the crown too good a deal for there to be any economic incentive to break with Rome. François I and Henri II both persecuted Protestants, treating them as just another group of lower-class heretics, who could and should be exterminated by force.

The leaders of the first generation of French Protestants were largely drawn, as elsewhere in Europe, from among the regular clergy, notably the mendicant orders. Their early followers were mostly artisans and small tradesmen, but the movement had increasing success with groups rather higher up the social ladder, such as lawyers, notaries, doctors, and petty local officials. Eventually it began to penetrate the nobility, often beginning with the women and then, with their assistance, winning over husbands and sons. Calvin, who mistrusted the individualism of the early ministers, drew on the higher social groups for his new recruits to the ministry, and Geneva turned out increasing numbers of pastors who were far superior, both socially and intellectually, to their Catholic counterparts. The Protestant church had all the appeal of a young and vigorous institution, and for a time it seemed to have almost a monopoly of spiritual energy. The dead weight of accumulated abuses lay very heavily on the old church, giving rise to much popular anti-clericalism which the reformers were quick to exploit. The idea that benefices were a kind of freehold, ordination being simply the necessary qualification for holding them, had produced a clergy often barely distinguishable from the laity, except by its privileges. The teaching and charitable functions of the church were not being fulfilled, while the activities of religious houses and cathedral chapters as landlords became increasingly unpopular. It was easy for the early Protestants to see themselves as restoring the lost purity of religion, blaming the church for hiding the message of Christ.

Heresy cases came under the jurisdiction of the church, but France had no national Inquisition, and the *officialité* courts of individual dioceses proved a very inadequate means of persecution. By 1539 the crown had decided to transfer heresy trials to the *parlements*, with mixed results; Paris, Toulouse, and Aix saw more effective steps taken, whereas Dijon, Grenoble, Rouen, and Bordeaux dragged their feet despite royal pressure. During the 1540s only some 2,000 heretics were brought to trial, a derisory figure. Once heresy cases had been reserved to the *parlements* the officials in subordinate jurisdictions lost interest in hunting out Protestants, since they would not try the case or receive any legal fees. Such sins of omission were almost impossible to detect, let alone punish, and the inertia of the local officials combined with the operation of family connections and complicity to emasculate the persecution. The activity of the *parlements* was briefly interrupted between 1549 and 1551; the bishops had been upset by the loss of their rights of jurisdiction, and Henri II needed their financial help so badly that he returned to the pre-1539 position. Signs that Protestantism was spreading faster than ever led him to revert quickly to a policy of force, but this was probably counter-productive. Persecution made martyrs, whose faith impressed onlookers: this was particularly true in a society which placed considerable emphasis on a man's behaviour at the moment of death. The anti-Protestant campaign also had the effect of making Calvin the undisputed master of the Reformed churches in France, since his doctrine and organizational skills were those best adapted to a situation of extreme danger for the Protestants.

The success of the Protestants during the 1540s and 1550s was remarkable, but it was largely confined to the towns and their immediate vicinity. With rare exceptions such as the Cévennes, the countryside proved resistant; awareness of this, combined with the limited number of ministers available, led Calvin to concentrate his efforts on the towns, increasing the disparity. Widespread illiteracy, suspicion of strangers, and attachment to the traditional superstitions and cults of saints were all factors in excluding Protestantism from the rural world. This failure was not necessarily crucial, however, given the dominant position of the towns and the much greater success in winning over the lesser nobility, the holders of political power in the countryside. By the late 1550s Protestantism was approaching a crucial stage in its development. Operating in secrecy, the ministers had created substantial churches in almost all French towns; only Brittany, for reasons of both language and geographical isolation, was virtually untouched. The Protestant communities had suffered relatively little from the persecution, and had enjoyed tacit toleration in many areas. As their numbers increased, it became increasingly difficult to continue with clandestine meetings, so Geneva was inundated with requests for ministers. Manpower problems alone would eventually force the Calvinists to hold public worship, and reveal the extent of their success. Already Henri II was so alarmed by their activities that his attitude to peace negotiations was affected; one reason pushing the kings of both France and Spain towards peace was the need to devote their attentions to heresy within their dominions.

The Wars of Religion: the first conflicts, 1560–3

The death of Henri II revealed the true fragility of the French political structure. His eldest son, François II, was a youth of fifteen, and therefore technically of age, but obviously incapable of exercising power himself. During his brief reign of less than eighteen months the royal council was dominated by his relations by marriage, the duc de Guise and his brother the Cardinal de Lorraine. This ascendancy by one great magnate family was bound to create serious resentments among their rivals, particularly the great houses of Bourbon and Montmorency. The unequalled power of the clientage systems headed by the three families was recognized at the time, and has subsequently become a historical commonplace. This has perhaps led to some oversimplification on occasions, with the impression being given that France was neatly divided up between Bourbons in the south-west, Montmorencies in the centre, and Guises in the east. Apart from such important exceptions as Montmorency influence in Languedoc, that of the Guises in Brittany, or of the Bourbons in Normandy and Picardy, this geographical division gives a misleading picture of the position in the localities. There were many leading noble families which did not belong to the clientage systems of the three families, and even in the provinces where they were most powerful they had numerous opponents. This made the struggle for control of the royal council all the more vital, since local power balances might well depend on the operation of the patronage system.

Faction quarrels were inevitable without a strong king, but they were made much more serious by the appearance of religious differences among the magnates. The Guises were the great supporters of the policy of repression; the old Constable Montmorency generally shared this view, but his Châtillon nephews, notably Coligny, had become Protestants. The elder Bourbon prince, the king of Navarre, wavered on this issue as on every other one, but his brother, Condé, quickly emerged as the political leader of the Calvinists. The success of the Guises at court appeared to threaten intensified repression, and the Protestants quickly began to organize themselves as a military power. During the months after Henri II's death they openly defied the government by holding open-air services outside many towns, including Paris; their first national synod had met in May. Large numbers of nobles declared for the Reform, and inevitably began to displace the ministers in determining the policy of their church. In the short run the link between Protestantism and opposition to the Guises brought considerable gains, but many of the new converts were to prove fair-weather friends, and involvement with court factions had the ultimate effect of diverting the Protestants from their true interests. The early 1560s was the one period when Calvinism might have established itself on at least an equal footing with Catholicism, but the progress of conversion was to be so hampered by the equivocal policies of Condé and other noble leaders that the vital opportunity was missed. The great mistake was to think in terms of treaties, edicts, and other concessions by the crown, when it was *de facto* control in the localities which really mattered. The crown was clearly incapable of enforcing its own decisions, and lacked the resources for a national policy of coercion. While it is unlikely that an all-out Protestant offensive would have succeeded, there was at least a possibility that it could, and this was never to be the case again.

Paradoxically, the sudden death of François II in December 1560, which saved Condé from execution for treason, helped to lead the Protestants down this blind alley of co-operation with the crown. The dominance of the Guises had been greatly to the advantage of their opponents, since they were inevitably the target for widespread recriminations and resentment. The financial situation made it impossible to continue the patronage system on the old footing, large numbers of poor nobles found their employment in the king's armies gone, and the Cardinal de Lorraine, beset by would-be clients, was reduced to threatening to hang the next man who asked for a pension. Even the costly blunder of the attempt by Protestant zealots to seize the court at Amboise in March 1560 and exclude the Guises from power could not make their rule popular, and there seemed every prospect that they would succeed in uniting a large part of the political nation against them, much in the way Philip II did in the Netherlands. The new regime was very different: Charles IX was still a minor, and his mother, Catherine de Medici, became Regent, taking a position at the centre of the political stage which she was to maintain for almost thirty years. Catherine was a remarkable woman, tolerant, intelligent, and determined; her supple, often devious policies were to be relatively successful in maintaining at least the appearance of royal control. At the same time they had less fortunate effects on the country as a whole, since attempts to reconcile the irreconcilable tended to perpetuate conflicts, and prevent their final resolution. It would be absurd to blame Catherine for this, and her personal moderation and willingness to compromise were virtues many Frenchmen would have done well to imitate; if a strong moderate party had emerged earlier, a great deal less blood would have been spilt in vain.

Catherine brought the Protestant leaders back to court, where they enjoyed a brief period of ascendancy in the royal council. Religious persecution was effectively suspended from the beginning of 1561, and in January 1562 an edict prepared by the moderate Chancellor d'Hôpital granted something approaching freedom of worship. This rapid evolution in royal policy, which was received with predictable hostility by the fiercely Catholic elements among the lower orders in Paris and other towns, helped to create a degree of unity among those court nobles, led by the Guises, who were opposed to religious change. During the spring and summer of 1562 a series of local clashes developed into the first open war between Protestants and Catholics. These few months were to prove decisive in establishing the balance between the two faiths which would last for more than a century. In town after town across France the Huguenots, as the Protestants inexplicably came to be called, tried to take control of the municipal government, often with the aid of armed bands raised in nearby towns or by the local nobility. Many of the major cities, such as Lyon, Rouen, and Orléans, came under the control of the Huguenots; in others, notably Bordeaux and Toulouse, days of street fighting ended with the Catholics triumphant. A geographical pattern was beginning to emerge; north of the Loire the Huguenots might have many individual supporters, but only in Normandy were they able to form a serious power base. The heart of the Massif Central was also resistant to them, but their real strength lay in a great curve round its southern and western flanks. This area of Huguenot success ran from Lyon and its hinterland down the Rhône, through the Vivarais and the Velay and into Provence and Mediterranean Languedoc. By-passing Toulouse to the north and south, the Protestants were strong on the fringes of the Pyrenees and in Gascony, Guyenne, and western France south of the Loire. Much of the terrain they controlled was difficult of access, as well as being distant from the centre of government in Paris; it was studded with small fortified towns, and would be a very tough military proposition.

Even within the regions most favourable to them, the Huguenots had to contend with large enclaves of Catholic support. In the towns there was always a group of bourgeois which held to the old faith, and in the countryside the local nobility were similarly divided. In many towns the Catholics

soon regained control, arousing urban mobs against the Calvinist minority. Such mob violence was encouraged by the
provocative behaviour of the Huguenots, who emphasized
their break with tradition by despoiling churches, burning
relics, and desecrating tombs. By a curious but comprehensible psychological inversion, opposition to superstition and
'magical' religious practices seemed to require acts of dissocia-
tion which were themselves at once symbolic and semi-
magical. These episodes helped to make 1562 a decisive year
for French Protestantism. Until this moment it had been
possible for the Huguenots to appear as a loose confederation
of reformers, many of whose ideas might appeal to all reasonable men who wanted to see the abuses of the church reduced.
Now they had metamorphosed into a party of violent heretics,
who murdered priests, raped nuns, committed every kind of
sacrilege, and might at any moment attempt a general massacre of Catholics. Needless to say, most Huguenots were far
from approving of such behaviour; Calvin himself and many
ministers saw all too clearly that it would prove fatal to their
cause, but once the violence had begun it developed a momentum of its own. The next decades were to see a series of
horrible and inhuman killings and massacres, whose cumulative effect was to make co-existence between the differing
religions almost impossible, and which left the minority group
in any particular place living in constant fear for their lives.
Already in 1562 the Huguenots in Catholic towns were sometimes being slaughtered, men, women, and children alike, or
driven out *en masse*; Protestant violence was not slow to move
from image-breaking and priest-killing to similar procedures.

The first religious war proved as militarily indecisive as
most of its successors would be. The only pitched battle, at
Dreux in December 1562, was a hard-fought and bloody
shambles, ending marginally in favour of the Catholic royal
army. The Huguenots lost their fragile control over Lyon,
Rouen, and some of the major towns along the Loire, but
consolidated their position in the south and west. The appearance of both Spanish and English troops was an ominous
warning for the future; France's internal disputes could not
be isolated from European politics. By the end of 1562 the

king of Navarre and the Marshal de Saint-André, among the original Catholic leaders, were both dead, while Montmorency was a captive of the Huguenots and Condé of the royalists. The assassination of the duc de Guise by a Huguenot gentleman in February 1563 left the Queen Mother in unchallenged control of the Catholic forces, opening the way to a negotiated settlement. It also created a vendetta between the Guises and the Huguenot leader Coligny, whom they blamed for the murder, and this was to prove a great obstacle to any proper reconciliation between the noble factions. With the combatants running out of both the money and the will to continue hostilities, the Edict of Amboise (March 1563) brought the war to an end. The Edict conceded general liberty of conscience, and granted special rights of worship to nobles; otherwise the Protestants were allowed public worship in only one town in each *bailliage* or *sénéchaussée* (there were about 100 of these judicial districts at this time; their number later multiplied), and in those towns where they had been holding such services in March 1563. Such concessions were greatly disliked by most Catholics, but the Huguenots also had reason to be dissatisfied. The effect of the Edict was to confine them within the areas they had already taken over, and to make further conversions very difficult: the forward movement of the new faith had been checked, and would never reappear. In the future the Huguenots would be fighting for survival.

Reactions to the peace settlement among Catholics revealed divisions which were to persist throughout the wars. An extremist party, led by the Guises and supported by Philip II of Spain, favoured an out-and-out campaign to destroy Protestantism, including the physical elimination of the leadership if necessary. This party never enjoyed full control of the royal council, but its clear-cut policy was much more popular with the Catholic masses in Paris and elsewhere than the crown's efforts to maintain independence from Spanish tutelage and to avert widespread massacres of Protestants. The moderate policy found support among the higher officials, traditional servants of the monarchy, and among the many Catholic nobles who distrusted the Guises, were strongly anti-Spanish, and recoiled from the idea of further civil war. The upper levels of the political class had much to lose from anarchy within France, and showed a natural tendency to move towards a moderate position whenever the crown gave a lead in that direction. Until the 1590s, however, such ideas enjoyed much less credit among the lesser nobles, officials, and bourgeois; the ease with which members of these groups could be recruited in extremist causes was a powerful factor making for continued instability.

The second war and the Massacre of St. Bartholomew

Catherine de Medici and her advisers were very conscious that the peace was in constant danger; the crown lacked the means to enforce the Edict of Amboise properly, and its provisions became the source of endless friction at local level. Meanwhile the conflicts in the Netherlands were deepening, as Philip II refused to respond to his subjects' appeals for greater political and religious liberty. With the iconoclastic riots of 1566 and Philip's decision to send the Duke of Alva with an army of repression, a new and highly disruptive element was added to the political scene in Europe and in France. The Revolt of the Netherlands, and the Eighty Years War in which the kings of Spain tried to crush it, was to dominate international politics for decades to come. The Revolt, like the wars in France, would show just how hard it was, under sixteenth-century conditions, to conquer and hold down any substantial area. Philip II was the most powerful monarch in Europe, and the Spanish armies the best available, but against all expectation the rebels were to survive. Spain's dominating position in Europe, partly the product of Habsburg marriage alliances, rested above all on three foundations: the inflow of bullion from Spanish America, the proved quality and tradition of her armies, and the weakness of France. Franco-Spanish rivalry had been a constant feature of international politics for more than half a century, and potentially there was little doubt that France was the stronger power, with at least twice the population, and a more developed social and economic structure. Philip II and his ministers were well aware that if France could overcome her internal problems her natural policy would be to exploit the Revolt of the

Netherlands; effective French intervention would have made the Spanish position exceedingly difficult. This awareness of France as a potential threat was to lead Philip into increasing involvement in the civil wars, since it was so manifestly in his interest that they should continue, and because the Protestants would inevitably press for an anti-Spanish foreign policy.

The combination of internal instability with the threatening international situation proved fatal to the Queen Mother's efforts to maintain the peace. Taking an intelligent initiative, she promenaded the young king around much of France between 1564 and 1566, seeking to reinforce loyalty and damp down local disputes. The good effects of this policy were destroyed by her meeting with Alva and other Spanish emissaries at Bayonne in 1565: the Huguenots, already fearful of the intentions of the crown and worried by developments in the Netherlands, jumped to the conclusion that the courts of France and Spain had agreed on plans to eradicate heresy. Huguenot fears were increased by the apparent return to favour of the Cardinal de Lorraine, the leading advocate of extreme policies, and one of those who placed the need to restore religious uniformity above the traditional hostility to Spain. Anticipating the revocation of the Edict of Amboise, the Huguenots set off a new round of warfare with an abortive attempt to seize the court at Meaux in September 1567. With only a brief interval in 1568, this conflict was to last until the summer of 1570. During these years, with moderate councillors discredited, the crown reverted to the policy of the Guises and sought a military solution; the king's younger brother, the duc d'Anjou, rose to prominence as lieutenant-general of the kingdom and an advocate of extreme policies. The major battles of the war, Jarnac and Moncontour, were Catholic victories, but they proved strategically barren, while the Protestant leader Coligny replied with a brilliant fast-moving campaign. Even the killing of Condé after Jarnac was of little advantage to the Catholics, since his son and the young king of Navarre took his place as the nominal leaders of the Protestants. As usual the monarchy ran out of funds, and by the summer of 1570 the king and his mother were ready to abandon the Guises, make peace and revert to moderate policies.

The Peace of Saint-Germain was another version of the Edict of Amboise, with the addition of four *places de sûreté*, fortified towns the Huguenots were permitted to garrison for a period of two years.

Taking into account the appalling problems it had faced in 1559, the monarchy had maintained its position reasonably well during the awkward years when the king was an adolescent. Although there were still considerable differences of opinion among the adherents of both creeds, the experience of civil war had reinforced the moderate tendencies on both sides. The crown and its officials made real efforts to enforce the peace provisions on toleration, and the Huguenot leaders returned to court. That the situation should have gone from bad to worse over the next twenty years was above all a comment on the character and behaviour of Catherine de Medici's three sons, Charles IX, the duc d'Anjou (later Henri III), and the duc d'Alençon. All were to prove weak and incompetent, while their rivalries helped divide the nation. At most times during the following years a strong king would have been able to restore the position, but the last Valois never began to measure up to the job; none of them even managed to produce an heir. As a result the kingdom and its people were allowed to drift towards catastrophe, with the progressive breakdown of law and order emphasizing the vacuum at the centre of affairs.

The results of royal weakness were seen with brutal clarity in the Massacre of St. Bartholomew's Day (August 1572), which was at once a royal crime and a disaster for the monarchy. Since 1571 Charles IX had been toying with plans for intervention in the Netherlands, and it was generally expected that he would try to unite his subjects by the classic means of foreign war. The long-standing notion that the young king was under the influence of Coligny has recently been disproved; in fact the Huguenot leader seems to have disliked the plans forced on him by a number of the younger noble members of his party. During the spring and summer of 1572 the timing of the proposed intervention went disastrously awry, largely because the capture of Brill and other towns in Holland and Zeeland by the Sea-Beggars came before anyone was ready to take advantage of them. Semi-official attempts to send small forces into the southern Netherlands during the summer were easily dealt with by Alva, although it was the menace of French invasion which prevented him reacting to the actions of the Beggars in the north, and thereby made the success of the Revolt possible. In retrospect it is clear that the French position was extremely strong, for the Spanish commanders were desperate to avoid open war, and even the intervention of a Huguenot army with the covert permission of the king would not necessarily have led to formal hostilities. The Queen Mother and Charles's Catholic councillors, over-impressed by Spanish power and cowed by Alva's blustering, became determined to withdraw from the dangers of involvement in the Netherlands, the king wavered, and French policy collapsed into an undignified mess. Charles IX pressed on with the plan for a marriage of reconciliation between his sister Margaret and Henri of Navarre, which was celebrated on ₁8 August; large numbers of Protestant nobles came to Paris for the celebrations. Coligny was preparing to leave court and lead an army into the Netherlands, but on 22 August he was wounded in an attempt on his life, probably instigated by one or another of the pro-Spanish Catholic leaders. With extraordinary imprudence the Huguenot nobles threatened the king and the royal family with revenge; the threats were given substance by the presence of Huguenot forces near Paris, preparing to march to the Netherlands. In what seems to have been a panic reaction, the Queen Mother and her associates persuaded the king that the Protestants were planning a coup, and that he must strike first; the result was the massacre.

The court's intentions were limited to the elimination of a relatively small group of leaders, notably Coligny. The execution of this plan in the early hours of 24 August set off an unintended chain reaction: the Paris mob ran amok, killing perhaps two thousand Protestants over the next two days. Lesser massacres occurred in about a dozen other towns as the news spread, despite royal attempts to prevent this. The king of Navarre and Condé, held prisoner, were forced to abjure and become Catholics. Making the best of a bad job, the court claimed that the massacre had been a deliberate act, fully justified by the conduct of the Huguenot leaders over the previous decade. There was no point in saying anything else; the crown had burnt its boats, and could only take up the policy of the extremists, trying to eliminate the heretics by force. The Huguenots, who would never trust the Valois kings again, abandoned their efforts to win the court over to policies of toleration. They concentrated grimly on defending their provincial strongholds, while their theorists began to elaborate ominous theses about the right of the lesser magistrates to resist a tyrannical king. Moderate Catholics found themselves in something of a dilemma, now that the crown had lost the centre position and become the prisoner of the extremists; a *politique* party soon emerged, as a group seeking a negotiated settlement including some element of toleration. A number of major nobles, opposed to the Guises and favouring such a compromise solution, dissociated themselves from the court. They included the youngest of the royal brothers, Alençon, and Montmorency's younger son Damville, governor of the key province of Languedoc. Even without their opposition, the royal forces would probably not have been able to conquer the Huguenot strongholds. The armies of the period were small, ill-disciplined, and fragile; their supply systems were in perpetual chaos, while epidemics and desertion could destroy even victorious armies in a few weeks. By the time Charles IX died in 1574 it was plain that the massacre had solved nothing; it had merely rendered the divisions within the kingdom more bitter, and brought a severe diminution of the crown's moral and political credit.

Henri III and the Catholic League

The new king, Henri III, had to make his way back from Poland, where he had recently been elected king; his return did nothing to remedy the situation, particularly as the favour he showed a small clique of his personal followers created new tensions at court. He failed to satisfy the ambitions of Alençon, who continued to plot against him, while in Languedoc Damville had made an alliance with the local Huguenots, thereby establishing a virtually independent principality. It was proving all too easy for local leaders to divert nominally royal taxes into their own treasuries, and on this basis civil war might continue almost indefinitely. A major alliance of Huguenots and *politiques* came into being, and with the aid of an army of German mercenaries the king was forced into a humiliating surrender. The Peace of Monsieur in 1576—so named because the heir to the throne Alençon was the nominal leader of the rebels—was the most favourable settlement the Protestants were ever to obtain. It was an illusory success, since the treaty proved as unenforceable as most of the other 'settlements' of the wars, but its reception showed how wide the divisions among the king's Catholic subjects had become. It was increasingly clear that the Protestants had lost any hope of converting the nation as a whole; the issues were therefore whether the minority should enjoy some limited toleration, and how France should conduct her foreign policy. There was no hope of agreement among the Catholics on these issues; only a strong line by the crown could have restored some stability to the situation, yet Henri III was temperamentally incapable of taking it. Now that he was king his considerable intelligence told him that a middle course was the right policy, but he was debarred from following it effectively by his lack of application and the legacy of his past extremism.

The concessions made to the Huguenots caused widespread dismay among the Catholic zealots, and a new force appeared on the scene in the shape of a general Catholic League. This was an essentially conservative party based among the nobility, under the leadership of the young duc de Guise, committed to the restoration of religious uniformity. The king was to be preserved in his authority according to his coronation oath and without prejudice to the rights of the Estates; the provinces were to have their ancient rights restored; all members of the League were to swear obedience to its head without regard for any other authority. Taking a leaf out of the heretics' book, the Catholic extremists were learning to play dangerous constitutional games, which plainly threatened the royal authority. Henri III only managed to stave off the danger by renewing the war against the Huguenots and declaring himself the head of the League; this latter step was not at all to the taste of the Leaguers, who preferred to disband the organization. Limited royal successes in 1577 led to the Peace of Bergerac at the end of the year, which virtually returned to the old terms of Amboise, and also dissolved all Leagues. The kingdom was far from being generally pacified, but the next eight years were to see only one brief resumption of general hostilities. Henri III made poor use of this opportunity; it was inevitable that heavy taxes must be levied to pay off the war debts, but his extravagance increased them further, giving an obvious target for popular resentment. The more bizarre features of the king's personal behaviour, mixing debauchery and ostentatious religious fervour, won him few friends, while the appearance of a new group of royal favourites, the *mignons*, added to the faction rivalries at court. In foreign policy France did nothing to exploit Philip II's difficulties, beyond allowing Alençon—still on bad terms with his brother—to embark on a notably unsuccessful private venture in the Netherlands.

The death of Alençon (or Anjou, as he became towards the end of his life) in 1584 set off the last and climactic period of the civil wars, the Catholic revolt which was in a sense the counterweight to the Protestant rebellion of 1560-77. Henri III seemed virtually certain to remain childless, and the heir apparent to the throne was the Huguenot leader, Henri of Navarre; even moderate Catholics could not be expected to welcome this prospect. The Catholic League now reappeared in a different form, inspired by a small Parisian group of clerics and lesser bourgeois, who built up a party among the artisans, the guilds, and the municipal officials. This League was much more dangerous than its predecessor, because it mobilized the fanaticism of the lower orders in the towns, combined it with the social ambitions of many lesser men, and turned the resulting passions against the moderate royalists who so often dominated the municipal oligarchies. The noble League of 1576 was revived all over Catholic France, and early in 1585 its leaders published a manifesto at Péronne, in which they put forward a programme for remedying the ills of the kingdom in the name of the Cardinal de Bourbon, their claimant to the throne. Immediately the Leaguers seized control of most of the towns and provinces of northern and central

France; the king could only agree to their demands and take steps to carry out their policy. In July 1585 he forced an edict through the *parlement* of Paris which revoked all the concessions made to the Protestants, and called on them to abjure or leave the country. In September of the same year the new Pope, Sixtus V, gave unintentional help to the king of Navarre by declaring him deprived of his rights to the throne, and releasing his existing subjects from their duties; this Bull aroused all the old Gallican opposition to Papal claims, and proved a major embarrassment to the League.

The resumption of warfare was slow, as both sides tried to muster their resources, the king by taxing the church and the Protestants by playing on the fears of their co-religionists in Germany and England. In the first major campaign of the war, in 1587, the king tried to discredit the League by sending Guise with inadequate forces to confront a German invasion, while he waited in reserve with the main army, and sent his favourite Joyeuse against the Huguenots. This ingenious plan misfired totally. The Germans decided to retreat again, giving Guise the chance to win some easy if insignificant successes against their rearguard, while Joyeuse disregarded royal orders, attacked the king of Navarre, and was routed and killed at Coutras (October 1587). The prestige of Guise and the League rose ever higher, while that of the king sank dismally. Growing League exasperation with Henri III was exacerbated by the execution of Mary Queen of Scots; he was unjustly blamed for acquiescing in this, and the Paris preachers denounced him for collusion with the 'English Jezebel'. Spanish influence over the League was maintained by the ambassador Mendoza, who subsidized its operations and manipulated its leaders, seeking to ensure that France would be powerless to intervene when the Invincible Armada arrived to reconquer England for the Church. During the early months of 1588 there was growing agitation in Paris, with the moderates and royalists losing ground daily; in May Guise defied royal orders and entered the city. The king tried to stage a coup and regain control of Paris by force of arms, but in the famous Day of Barricades (12 May 1588) the population drove out his Swiss guards, and he fled to the west. The capital was now under the control of the popular League through the organization known as the Sixteen, but the noble leaders were still anxious to reach a working agreement with the king; for all Henri III's failings, the monarchy commanded great residual loyalty, and few could imagine any viable political alternative. Henri seemed to give in, and agreed to summon the Estates General to Blois in the autumn: Guise became lieutenant-general of the kingdom, and the Cardinal de Bourbon was recognized as heir-presumptive.

Before the Estates, predictably dominated by supporters of the League, could meet, the whole political climate was altered by the failure of the Armada, whose defeat by the English had burst the bubble of Spanish invincibility. The king, bitterly resentful of his repeated humiliations, was in no mood to make things easy for his persecutors, and even Guise found the Estates difficult to manage. They were ready enough to call for the eradication of heresy, but not to pay for the armies this would require; instead they demanded reductions in taxation, and measures against the financiers. As Christmas approached a stalemate seemed to be setting in, but Henri III feared that Guise would soon take a new initiative against him. At last the king turned on his enemies: on 23 December he had Guise murdered, and the following day his brother, the Cardinal de Guise, suffered the same fate. The Cardinal de Bourbon and other League leaders were imprisoned, and in January the stunned members of the Estates dispersed; Catherine de Medici, for so long the advocate of temporizing policies, had died at the beginning of the year. The murders at Blois were the occasion for a major realignment of forces across the kingdom, with the crown and many Catholic royalists irrevocably committed to repressing the League. Whatever the morality of the act—and it is difficult to feel much sympathy for Guise, whose personal ambitions had cost so many lives—it went a long way to extricate the monarchy from the false position it had been in since the Massacre of St. Bartholomew's Day. The new crisis might be the severest of all, but at least it held out the prospect of a decisive settlement, with the crown seeking to unite moderate men of all parties against the extremists.

Henri IV and the victory of the politiques

The immediate result of the murders was to produce declarations of fury and defiance from the League; the popular preachers called for tyrannicide and the extermination of the heretics, while Guise's brother Mayenne took command of a rebel area stretching from Burgundy and Champagne across northern France to Brittany. South of the Loire the League was less strong, but a number of towns declared for it, and there were centres of League power in Toulouse and Marseille. Henri III had no choice but to make an alliance with the king of Navarre and the Huguenots. The two kings mustered a powerful army and marched on Paris, to which they laid siege in the summer of 1589; the city seemed doomed when a fanatical monk, Jacques Clément, avenged the Guises by assassinating Henri III. The frenzied and rather indecent rejoicings of the Parisians seemed justified when Henri IV, unable to hold the coalition of *politiques* and Huguenots together, had to abandon the siege. This was a misleading omen, for the new king was a formidable figure; a brave and skilful soldier, he also possessed a remarkable sense of political timing. He showed his astuteness by declaring his intention to preserve and protect the Catholic religion, but delaying his own conversion, despite heavy pressure from his Catholic friends. He knew that an immediate abjuration would look insincere and convince no one, while he needed to retain the loyalty of his Protestant followers, the core of his army. The value of the army was quickly demonstrated in the autumn of 1589; when Mayenne pursued the king into Normandy he was driven off in several engagements around Arques, the first of a series of victories which encouraged men to rally to the royal cause.

The following spring a much greater victory over Mayenne's army at Ivry allowed the king to resume the siege of Paris. In this extremity for his allies Philip of Spain decided to intervene, ordering the reluctant Prince of Parma to break off his assault on the United Provinces and march into France. Parma's army relieved the city, but the king handled the situation with great skill. He knew that the Leaguers expected great things of the Spanish veterans and their general, the most prestigious military combination in Europe. Henri set out to frustrate these hopes; he drew Parma into a war of manoeuvre, refusing any set-piece battle, and at the end of an indecisive campaign the Spaniards withdrew with the royal army snapping at their heels. To have confronted Parma on equal terms was another moral advantage for the king, while the League had alienated moderates and patriots by bringing in foreign troops. During 1591 the royalists captured a number of important towns, and the divisions among the Leaguers became more and more evident. The popular leaders in Paris, faced with increasing resistance from the upper ranks of urban society, struck at the *parlement* by executing the *premier président* and two *conseillers* for collusion with the royalists. This act seems to have horrified even most Leaguers, and Mayenne felt obliged to react; four of the ringleaders were summarily hanged, others fled or were imprisoned. The power of the demagogues and preachers in Paris never recovered from this setback; the hardships of the war, the appearance of Spanish troops, and the violence of their rule had alienated many of their erstwhile supporters even among the lower classes. In other Leaguer towns similar tendencies were apparent, and the king's opponents were being increasingly isolated as small groups of religious fanatics and political careerists. It had been easy for ambitious lawyers and merchants, who felt that their path upwards was blocked by the existing oligarchies, to mobilize opinion against the authorities; once they had attained power these men could offer little to the masses beyond a continuation of the war, with all its miseries. To make matters worse, the early 1590s were to see exceptionally bad weather conditions, leading to poor harvests and soaring grain prices. The difficulties of the poor were increased by the operations of the armies and garrisons; the wars of the League covered more of the national territory than any of the earlier conflicts, and had splintered into innumerable local power struggles. The troops lived off the countryside, interrupting normal agricultural work and cutting towns off from their sources of supply. In such circumstances the cries for peace grew ever stronger, but the Leaguer leaders could not afford to listen to them.

The death of the Cardinal de Bourbon in 1590, still a prisoner although proclaimed as Charles X by the League, presented Mayenne and his associates with an insoluble problem over the succession. There was no other plausible candidate as a figurehead, so the League would have to find some way of electing and legitimizing a new king. In another of those moves by foreigners which showed a complete ignorance of the basic facts of French politics, Philip II's envoys pressed the claims of the Infanta of Spain, granddaughter of Henri II, and tried to dismiss the Salic Law, which barred women from the succession, as an obsolete French prejudice. To add weight to this ill-conceived initiative Philip ordered Parma back into France, to prevent the capture of Rouen by a combined royal and English army, and to protect the meeting of an Estates General summoned by the League to settle the succession problem. Henri IV repeated his tactics of 1590 in the 1592 campaign, with greater success; Parma narrowly escaped being trapped in Normandy and had to retreat in some disarray, although Rouen was relieved in the process. This abortive campaign turned out to be Parma's last, for he died soon after his return to the Netherlands from the consequences of a wound received in France. Wiser than his master, he had always recognized that intervention in France was a dangerous gamble; his efforts had only propped up the League temporarily, at the cost of serious reverses in the Netherlands. When the Leaguer Estates finally met in 1593 they proved to be a fiasco, since even the hundred-odd delegates who struggled across dangerous territory to Paris were determined to resist undue pressure from foreigners, agents of Spain or the Pope alike. Meanwhile the leaders of the party, increasingly uncomfortable about the future, began negotiations with the royalists. The king watched the situation carefully; recognizing his opportunity, he abjured the Protestant faith in July 1593, and cut the ground from under his enemies' feet. The extremists could still claim that his conversion was insincere, and would only be valid when he was absolved by the Pope, but nothing could stop the steady stream of desertions to the royal camp.

Henri pressed home his advantage with a formal coronation at Chartres early in 1594, and soon Paris was surrendered to him by its governor, despite the presence of a small Spanish garrison. Here as elsewhere Henri was generous to his opponents; there were handsome bribes to the leaders, while the rank and file were excused any past offences. A general collapse of the League followed the fall of Paris, as its commanders hurried to take advantage of the king's liberality. Over the next year or two the crown pledged many millions of livres to regain control over its own patrimony; in so doing it was effectively assuming responsibility for the debts of the League, most of whose richer members had virtually bankrupted themselves for the cause. The last pockets of resistance were on the periphery of the kingdom, notably those led by Joyeuse (brother of Henri III's *mignon*) at Toulouse, Mayenne in Burgundy, and Mercœur in Brittany. In all these cases, however, the surviving Leaguers were fast losing any local support, and their surrender was merely a matter of time. In 1595 the king felt strong enough to declare war on Philip II; although in military terms the results were rather mixed, this was another shrewdly judged move to unite France behind a monarch who knew how to exploit his own prowess on the battlefield. War with Spain did not prevent the Huguenots from moving into open revolt against their old leader in 1597, a crisis which emphasized the need for peace and a new formal religious settlement. Fortunately by 1598 the king of Spain, near to death and in desperate financial difficulties, was ready to make peace on the terms of 1559, while the duc de Mercoeur had to abandon his ambitions to create an independent state in Brittany. The choice of Nantes, once a stronghold of the Breton League, as the town where the king issued an edict of toleration, was a symbol of the restoration of the monarchy. The Peace of Vervins, which ended the Spanish war, and the Edict of Nantes were both signed in the spring of 1598, bringing France's long agony to a close.

The signature of an edict was not in itself of much consequence, as repeated experience had shown. It was to take several years to restore a reasonable degree of law and order to some areas of France, where brigandage had become a way of life for local nobles and bands of ex-soldiers. The Edict of Nantes met stiff opposition from the *parlements*; they were prepared to swallow the concessions on freedom of worship in a limited number of towns, but objected to some of the guarantees offered to the Huguenots. The religious settlement was a development of the various previous attempts; the Protestants were granted a large number of *places de sûreté*, and special *chambres de l'Édit* were created to hear cases involving Protestants which came before the *parlements* and other sovereign courts. Various concessions had to be made to the *parlements* before they would register the edict, but all had done so by 1600 except Rouen, which observed its terms while managing to avoid formal registration until 1609. The edict was unpopular with everyone, accepted merely as an unpleasant necessity by Catholics and Protestants alike. The existence of considerable areas controlled by the Huguenots, with their own troops and fortresses, and of assemblies which negotiated with the king, were implicit diminutions of the royal authority which Henri IV himself found irksome. Perpetual friction over the observation of the terms was inevitable, and was always likely to produce further violence.

Henri IV's personal prestige and ability were certainly badly needed if the monarchy was to re-establish its position, for the long wars had helped to erode the old bases of royal power. Years of virtual independence had allowed towns and provinces to reinforce or reclaim local rights which limited central intervention, while smaller communities had come more than ever under the equivocal 'protection' of the local nobility. Large numbers of offices had been created and sold during the wars, with serious consequences; apart from causing disputes within and between royal courts, many of the holders belonged to factions or clienteles which it would be difficult to satisfy or control. The state of the finances was deplorable, and the disorder of the wars had favoured corruption and speculation on a grand scale. Local magnates like Damville in Languedoc and the duc d'Épernon in Angoumois had entrenched their own power at the king's expense. Awareness of these problems was to combine with the natural inclinations of the king and his closest advisers to direct the monarchy into policies of centralization and deliberate state-building, which would largely take the form of chipping away at the vast complex of privileges and liberties which restricted royal power. In certain ways the experiences of the later sixteenth century actually made this task easier; the League became a kind of bogey in the minds of most men of property, symbolizing the dangers of extremism, rebellion, and social disorder. During the century to come the kings would play repeatedly on the fear of a return to anarchy. The Huguenots and the Leaguers had produced a quantity of political theorizing in justification of their resistance, calling on every available argument to diminish the king's personal power; the final effect was chiefly to discredit a whole range of ideas which would otherwise have been attractive to defenders of the established order against royal initiatives. The Estates General, summoned several times during the wars, had come to appear not only useless but dangerous, and Henri IV took good care never to fulfil his promises to convene them. The future belonged to the monarchy, although few of its subjects could have realized this as the new century began.

2

Economy and Society

Population and subsistence crises

If the rise in both population and prices during the sixteenth century had advantaged the few at the expense of the many, the full impact of this process was only to be felt in the next century. In broad terms historians seem agreed that a great upward movement of economic activity and production, which had begun in the aftermath of the Hundred Years War, was faltering by the later decades of the sixteenth century. In many ways the situation resembled that of the century before the Black Death, with a rapidly rising population outstripping the productive capacity of the land, and creating pressures which actually tended to reduce agricultural yields in the long run. The combined effects of plague and prolonged war had provided a brutal solution to the earlier period of crisis, but it had been merely a matter of time before the fundamental problem reappeared, with demand exceeding the inflexible capacity of the old rural economy. There are immense difficulties in estimating the total population of France at any time before the eighteenth century, but there are good reasons to suppose that it was actually higher in 1600 than in 1700; in certain regions the peak could even have come as early as 1560. During the seventeenth century as a whole the population probably oscillated around the level of 18–20 millions, making France one of the most densely peopled countries in Europe. This relative equilibrium was maintained only by savage natural factors, notably very high infant mortality, periodic epidemics, and recurrent harvest crises. The practice of some elementary birth control measures cannot be ruled out, but is unlikely to have had much effect; the only real way to reduce natural fertility, apart from sexual restraint, was for women to marry later, and there are signs of a trend in this direction. Such a reaction to hardship would have been very likely in a period when the pauperization of the mass of the people, already marked in the later sixteenth century, was being taken to new levels.

Apart from the concentration of land in the hands of the privileged élites, worsening conditions for the peasantry accentuated the existing fragmentation of their holdings into tiny units, quite inadequate to support a family. Most peasants were buyers of food, who suffered from the rise in agricultural prices, and were living on the edge of starvation in many years. The pattern of demand was heavily in favour of cereals, and excessive concentration on arable farming produced a vicious circle of declining or static production. The lack of beasts meant that there was inadequate manure, and a shortage of animals to work the land properly, so that yields were poor; this low level of production kept up the pressure to grow cereals, even where the soil was unsuitable. Despite these unfavourable conditions, France was a fertile country, capable of feeding her population adequately in an average year. Many years, however, were far worse than average; yields could vary enormously, from perhaps 50% of average in a bad year to 150% in a good one. The climate was crucial, and it seems to have been peculiarly capricious in the seventeenth century, working together with the structural problems jo agrarian society to produce the great era of the *crise de subsistence*. A really bad harvest, or more probably a sequence of mediocre and bad harvests, would push grain prices up to peaks of two, three, or more times their normal level, if any grain was coming on the markets at all. The machinery of informal local charity, on which many of the poor depended to some extent during the difficult months before the harvest, could not cope with such conditions, and large numbers of people would be virtually starving. Malnutrition and the associated epidemics then resulted in heavy mortality, particularly among children and old people, while conceptions would fall away to almost nothing for the duration of the crisis. A village might expect to lose 10% to 20% of its population

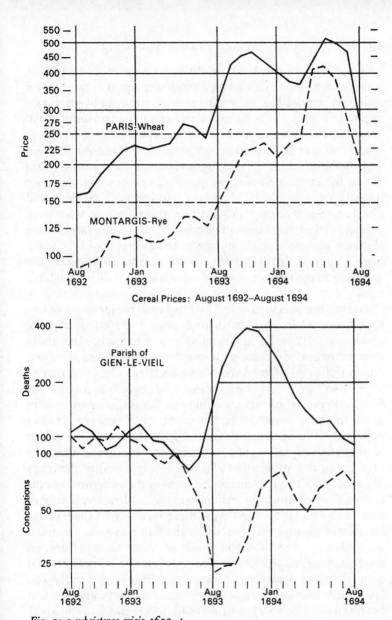

Fig. 1: a subsistence crisis 1692–4

Conceptions and deaths, August 1692–August 1694, at Gien, a small town near Montargis, south of Paris. Given as percentages of the mean figures for 1690–92, on a three-month moving average.

from Jean Meuvret: Etudes d'histoire économique

in a bad year of this kind, and it was repeated blows on this scale which were fundamental in keeping the population relatively stable. It is necessary to distinguish between major crises, affecting much or all of the country, and more local episodes; the latter might be equally important in the context of a particular region, given the state of the transport system and the impossibility of moving substantial quantities of grain except by water. The effect on population was a complex one; initially there would be a recovery, linked with an increased number of marriages among those young adults who were generally most resistant to the crisis. If the death rate among children had been high, however, the effect would be felt a decade later, with a sharp drop in the number of young people reaching marriageable age and ultimately a fall in the birth rate.

During the period covered by this book, major crises of this type occurred in 1596–7, 1630–1, 1648–53, 1661–2, 1693–4, and 1709–10. The list is inevitably somewhat arbitrary; there were other episodes scarcely less severe, and not even the great crisis of 1693–4 affected the whole country. The mortality of 1693–4 was probably the heaviest, and there was a tendency for the demographic effects of harvest failure to become more acute in the second half of the seventeenth century. It does appear as if in northern France at least the combined effects of the 1648–53 and 1661–2 crises were so grave that the population did not return to its previous levels until the reign of Louis XV. The famous descriptions of the miserable condition of the peasantry by writers such as La Bruyère, Vauban, and Locke fit all too well with these facts, emphasizing that for most of his subjects the reign of the Sun King was an epoch of hardship, often of despair and untimely death. Detailed analysis, year by year and region by region, naturally reveals a much more complicated picture; within a generally unfavourable climate there were periods of recovery and relative prosperity, while every area escaped one or more of the great national crises. Important though these variations are, notably those between the south and the rest of France, they are really only differences in the incidence of phenomena which were common to the whole country over the long term.

Landholding, prices, and agrarian depression

Stagnation or slight decline in France's population between 1600 and 1715 must be linked with parallel movements of both production and prices. Some technical reasons for decreasing agrarian production have already been suggested, mostly connected with soil exhaustion; there were also human problems which were worsened by the repeated crises. Undernourished and badly clothed, the peasantry lacked energy for the performance of their regular tasks, let alone the enterprise to bring about improvements. Perhaps most serious of all, the small rural élite of independent peasants and substantial tenant farmers, the men who provided the link between the absentee landlords and the countryside, were coming under pressure. Apart from their own land, the capital resources of these men were heavily concentrated in animals and equipment; this was true of prosperous sharecroppers in the south and west as well as of the *laboureurs* in the northern plains. There is some evidence to suggest that from the middle of the century an unusual number of such men were running into debt, and finally slipping back into the mass of the peasantry. Given their crucial role as providers of work and loans for the local community, and as managers for the privileged classes, their problems were bound to have grave implications for the functioning of the rural economy. Once their small accumulations of capital had been broken up it was very difficult to replace them; a holding sufficient to support a family cost something like a century's wages for a day-labourer, and a large collection of animals was in the same area of relative values. The position of those who inherited such wealth was inherently very strong, so it is unlikely that their numbers declined on any great scale; the check to their position was extremely important, however, since they represented the most dynamic element in French agriculture, and an increase in their prosperity would have been the likeliest way to stimulate production.

The situation of richer peasants was closely bound up with the phenomenon of harvest crises and the linked pattern of rural indebtedness. A bad year compelled many peasants to borrow simply to survive, giving the better-off an opportunity to exact cruel rates of interest; this was particularly true of loans in kind, where a sack of grain in May might be treated as the equivalent of two sacks in October. Over time this kind of operation allowed a crushing burden of debt to build up, and the creditors might eventually accept land in payment, or establish perpetual *rentes* as the condition for prolonging the loan. This mechanism allowed the concentration of land, or its profits, in the hands of the rich, emphasizing the pauperization of the peasantry. The peasantry were losing land fairly steadily during the seventeenth century, especially in the areas near towns or waterways, where production for the urban markets was least hampered by transport costs. By general European standards they remained relatively well-placed, however, since they still retained direct possession of something approaching half the cultivated area of France. As long as the harvest crises were not too serious or prolonged, the rural élites had been among the beneficiaries of the system, since they had possessed reserves with which they could make well-placed loans. By the middle of the seventeenth century this position was changing, for the more marginal members of the élites at least. The combination of increased rents and taxes with falling grain prices had diminished their profits to the point where they too had to borrow in a bad year, so the greater frequency and intensity of the crises was all the more serious. Scarcity and high prices now worked more than ever in favour of the privileged groups in the towns, and there is little doubt that a good deal of hoarding took place in order to speculate on the grain market; the behaviour of urban mobs often showed an awareness of this practice, when they forced the sale of stocks held by merchants or religious houses. In a system where the *rentier* already took a high proportion of total production, the additional load of debt was not capable of infinite expansion, and in the end it was bound to create major problems even for those who had imposed it. Proprietors who found it impossible to replace their tenants satisfactorily might prefer to let arrears of rent pile up, rather than risk an eviction which might leave the property damaged or abandoned.

Some at least of the difficulties arose because the economy

was so slow to adjust to changed circumstances. Just as their predecessors had often failed to take advantage of the sixteenth-century inflation, so later landlords tried to maintain unrealistically high rents in a period of falling prices, worsening the situation of the men on whose solvency they were ultimately dependent. The failure of wage rates to keep pace with inflation had diminished the purchasing power of the masses, and this was one of the major reasons for the eventual slide into depression. In both these ways the immediate greed of the proprietors worked against their own long-term interests, to help precipitate a partial collapse of the rural economy in the later years of Louis XIV's reign. The process was a long-drawn-out one, lasting over decades, and this must have helped to obscure its nature for contemporaries, while making its effects more lasting. In northern and central France the turning-point, for prices at least, occurred between 1630 and 1650; the first third of the century had still been a period of inflation, if on a reduced scale, but was to be succeeded by a hundred years of static or falling prices, with only limited interludes. In the south the pattern is similar, but here the depression began earlier, around the beginning of the century, and also ended at an earlier stage, in the first decade of the eighteenth century. With one or two possible exceptions, notably southern Provence, the whole of France was suffering from a deepening recession from the 1660s to the 1690s. These price movements were not purely an internal affair, but form part of important changes which were taking place across Western Europe, with the moderation of the inflationary pressures of the sixteenth century. Everywhere we find a trend towards depressed prices setting in some time during the first third of the century, although the ultimate experience of individual countries was not to be identical. The Mediterranean regions of France followed much the same evolution as their neighbours, whereas the northern part of the country failed to develop in the same way as roughly comparable areas in the Netherlands and England. The Maritime Powers of north-western Europe were not only the leaders in international trade; despite the stabilization of prices, their agricultural production seems to have increased through the seventeenth century, with important

changes in the direction of greater efficiency. In comparison
France was slipping back, because the structure of her rural
society and economy had proved incapable of adjustment to
changing circumstances.

Many of the reasons for this state of affairs have already
been given, but they are far from constituting a complete
explanation. What remains especially puzzling is the failure of
the proprietors to invest in the kind of agricultural improvement which was becoming commonplace in both England and
the Dutch Republic. There are some French examples, but
they are rare and geographically limited, in sharp contrast to
the eagerness with which the rich bought up the land itself.
The most plausible reason for the lack of such investment is
perhaps the very success of the landlords in extracting substantial returns from their lands without destroying the traditional forms of rural society. Coupled with the relatively
constant availability of land for purchase, this may have discouraged longer-term investment; there was much to be said
for buying another piece of property with a guaranteed return,
rather than taking a chance on the yields from improvements.
There are grounds for supposing that great French aristocrats
were alienating landed property more readily than their
English counterparts, and the land market also reflected the
continued presence of the peasantry as holders of a substantial
fraction of the total surface. The vulnerability of the small men
provided good pickings for the rich, through the mechanism
of debt and foreclosure, or, in a good half of France, through
the notoriously unprogressive system of sharecropping (a
method of leasing land under which a fixed proportion of the
annual produce is taken by the landlord). Most important of
all perhaps were the habits of mind which the situation
encouraged; the extraordinary lack of writings on agricultural improvement after those of Olivier de Serres at the very
beginning of the seventeenth century is very clear evidence of
this mental rigidity, although this too is easier to identify than
to explain. It may be that this lack of interest in the techniques
of farming is another facet of the domination of the towns and
their values, although most proprietors spent some time attending to their lands in person, and cannot have been entirely

ignorant of the detailed problem of exploiting them; leases and similar documents often show them laying down elaborate restrictions on the tenant's freedom of action, usually to prevent him damaging the long-term profitability of the holding. It is tempting to argue that another reason for limiting investment in improvements was the alternative possibility of purchasing offices, taking a share in the taxation system, or lending money to the government; such factors cannot be dismissed, but similar opportunities for investment outside agriculture existed in other countries without producing the same results. Whatever the ultimate reasons, the actual state of French agriculture by the later seventeenth century made a bitter contrast with the boasts of economic propagandists, assuring the king that his dominions were the fairest and richest in Europe.

Money, wages, and living standards

Some reference has already been made to the general movement of prices, and here we strike a peculiarly difficult technical problem. The interpretation of the excellent statistical series for our period depends crucially on the distinction between nominal and real value—yet there is no truly satisfactory way of producing a single index for real value. It may not be immediately obvious why it is inadequate to calculate in straightforward money terms; apart from a short period in the later sixteenth century when the government tried to use the écu (= 3 livres) as a money of account, prices were always reckoned in livres tournois. The trouble is that the livre declined in real metallic value during the century by some 30%, and this factor cannot be disregarded in an age when money had an intrinsic value related to its bullion content. Most recent historians have preferred to convert prices into the silver equivalents of the livre at different dates, but this procedure is also open to grave objections. Numerous factors prevented the internal economy from responding fully to the periodic changes in the bullion value of the livre, so the effect of these devaluations was very muffled and limited. The kind of rigidities involved are fairly obvious; in the absence of machinery for adjusting wages, rents, or other internal transactions at any but the most leisurely pace, established levels tended to persist in defiance of apparent economic logic. Grain prices were the crucial element in the market economy for most people, and there are quite compelling arguments for indexing both wages and taxation against them, but this leaves the problem of measuring the true change in the level of the grain prices themselves. The nature of the difficulty is such that no one answer will do; the prices have to be considered in relation to a whole range of other variables, according to the particular context. What does seem clear is that a graph plotted in terms of nominal prices shows a quite unreal increase in prices during the whole century, and one in bullion terms gives a greatly exaggerated decline. The arguments already put forward about the movement of agricultural prices rest on the premise that in relation to most of the relevant variables, grain prices show a modest decline after 1630, but this is not demonstrable in any precise statistical form..

The complexities arising from a monetary system in which the means of exchange had real value were even more of a nightmare for contemporaries than they are for modern historians. Three metals were in use, gold, silver, and copper. The ratios between them were never stable, particularly that between gold and silver, and this offered many occasions for the well-informed or dishonest to profit, notably in the course of international trade. All governments, preoccupied with the need to prevent the drain of good coinage to their neighbours, were constantly fiddling with the exchange rates and the weight and fineness of coins. This situation generally discouraged outright debasement, since governments were aware of the dangerous implications this would have for their international position, but it added to the general confusion. Just to complicate matters further, the French *livre tournois* was a money of account, not a specific coin. Much of the money in circulation in France was foreign, especially Spanish, and the result was a chaos of different values and rates of exchange. The government might decide at any time to call down or mark up such actual coins as the *écu*, *louis*, or *pistole*, and frequently did so. The whole system was inevitably bedevilled by illicit coining and clipping, and by the way in which the more sophisticated hoarded the better coin. The existence of the copper coinage posed additional problems, since it was even more difficult to establish its relative value, yet many peasants paid their taxes and rents with these modest coins. Attempts to regulate the value of copper coins, or to restrict their use in larger transactions, sometimes led to important popular revolts, notably during the 1640s. The wealthy did not react in such extreme ways, partly because they generally found means of taking advantage of the shifts in the value of coin, which any man of even modest wealth had to watch all the time. The art was to spend bad coin, or get a premium for good, while somehow getting paid in good coin oneself. The great losers were those whose dependent positions deprived them of any real bargaining power, the peasants and artisans, and the royal treasury, which lacked effective means of controlling the sharp practices of its own agents. It is arguable that Colbert, anxious to preserve the real value of the taxes, and to help foreign trade, pursued a deflationary 'stable money' policy which added to the post-1660 depression by leaving the countryside very short of small coinage.

The precise importance of money in the French economy is very difficult to estimate. Many transactions were carried out in kind, especially at the village level, and it may be true that a permanent shortage of coin was one of the factors which tended to restrict economic development; seen in this light the bullionist commercial policies of ministers like Colbert may make rather better sense than is sometimes admitted. Royal agents in the provinces often stressed the need to protect local trading patterns if the people were to have enough cash to pay the taxes, and the government found this argument compelling. Apart from the taxes and those rents or other charges not paid in kind, the village economy required a certain amount of coin in circulation to maintain the system whereby the mass of peasants hired out their labour to the richer men, whose excess production they subsequently purchased. Day-labourers received part of their payment in kind, since it was normal to provide them with at least one meal, and this makes calculation of agricultural wage rates almost impossible. Nominal wage rates are in any case irrelevant unless one has some idea how much employment was actually available; almost all pre-industrial economies seem to have existed in a state of permanent underemployment, largely seasonal, and seventeenth-century France was no exception. The existence of communal land, the possession of a small plot for intensive cultivation, and customary rights such as gleaning were all of vital importance to the peasantry in their constant battle for survival. Only at certain limited periods, above all harvest time, could they be reasonably sure of finding regular work. As far as can be detected, the great period of falling agricultural wages was the sixteenth century; the second half of the seventeenth century may even have seen a marginal improvement—but this was probably negated by a drop in employment. Even if a man had been able to find regular work, he could still not have fed a family without his wife's contribution, and the resulting surplus of female labour meant that women's wages were only half those paid to men. The family unit depended on the efforts of all its members, apart from very young children; it is no surprise to find that in a period when many if not most marriages were broken relatively soon by the death of one partner, the survivor normally remarried in a matter of months. The precarious balance of the family economy could be broken at any time by personal disaster, such as accident or illness, or by one of the *crises de subsistence*; a bad harvest reduced employment at the moment when it was most needed.

The situation just described was a general one, but the reactions to it naturally varied from region to region, and hardship was never equally spread. The poorest areas were probably in the uplands of the Massif Central and the Alpine and Pyrenean fringes; here much of the male population would spend part of the year away from home, looking for work in the fertile plains, or perhaps migrating as far as Spain. Brittany and western provinces such as Poitou also seem to have been notably poor, although their inhabitants were less prominently mobile. The importance of animals in the economy of the uplands was reflected in the numbers of shepherds, drovers, and muleteers who moved with their beasts. The most numerous specialized group, however, was that of the wine-producers or *vignerons*; the intensive cultivation demanded

by the vines allowed them to combine work for larger enterprises with the exploitation of a small vineyard of their own.
Wine was the only cash crop of much significance apart from
grain, and its popularity with the peasants fluctuated along
with the relationship between the prices of the two commodities. Since wine was a relative luxury the hard times of the
later sixteenth century had seen a disastrous slump, and while
prices remained relatively stable during the seventeenth century the gap tended to widen, with only temporary or local
exceptions. The *vignerons* were a notoriously cohesive yet vola-
tile professional group, often numerous around the larger
towns; the drop in their incomes made them more determined
to resist new taxes, and they became one of the centres of
lower-class disaffection. Low prices discouraged wine production in unsuitable areas, but much of the wine was of poor
quality and not worth transporting, so vines were still cultivated in surprising places during this period. Most wine was
naturally produced away from the cereal growing plains of
northern France, the area which contemporaries described as
the *pays de grande culture* to contrast it with the *petite culture*, or
more varied agriculture, of the greater part of southern and
western France. These regional distinctions can be multiplied
almost indefinitely; they represented a series of compromises
between the natural possibilities of soils and climate, and the
complex social and economic structures built up over centuries of semi-autonomous development.

The local community, the landlords, and the state

There was one particular factor which maintained this
diversity, while itself being common to the whole country. The
village community had demonstrated remarkable coherence
and strength during its long past, putting up continued resistance to excessive demands from outside, whether they originated from the *seigneur*, the church, or the king. Although the
whole legal and governmental system was heavily biased in
favour of the propertied classes, the sheer persistence of the
peasantry in defending their rights, real or assumed, had often
brought considerable success. This could only have resulted
from a degree of unity which was itself part of a pattern of

solidarities very different from that of modern societies. While most people lived in nuclear family units, their primary loyalties were to their lineage—the extended family—and to the community. Country-dwellers might extend their horizons to include the *pays*, a group of perhaps ten or twenty villages associated by similar geographical features and local traditions; only exceptionally would they think in terms of their province, still less of France as a whole. The enormous majority of marriages were between members of the same village or two immediately adjoining villages, and emphasized the closed character of the rural world. Any stranger, immediately identifiable by speech and dress, would be the object of suspicion if not fear, and in practice population mobility was only possible within very strict limits. Seasonal migration, already discussed, was one of the most important, but did not represent a real break with local roots; movement to the towns was another, and here the immigrant would expect to find help from other members of his original community who had preceded him. The real vagrant, who took to the road and lost touch with his origins, had placed himself in a desperately exposed position, so in general it was only complete destitution which led people to take this extreme course. The economic conditions of the seventeenth century produced a large number of these tragic victims, far outstripping the efforts of municipalities and charitable foundations to control and help them, but they were still a tiny minority even of the poor. Most Frenchmen still lived and died within sight of the church where they had been baptized.

Self-help within the community was the essential condition for the very survival of the mass of the peasantry during this bleak period in their collective history. Without reciprocal services and loans the whole agricultural system would have collapsed, while village ceremonies, festivities, and dances provided a certain minimum of distractions, as well as asserting the cohesive spirit of the locality. One should be careful to recognize that this social order made heavy demands on the individual, and was far from being an idyll. Privacy was almost unknown, and those who stepped out of line in some way might be subject to brutal and long-lasting reprisals; a certain degree of licensed violence was tolerated, as in the strange ritualized battles between neighbouring villages, or the numerous feuds between families. The village assembly was far from being a primitive democracy, since even if the poorer peasants were present their voice counted for little, while during the seventeenth century there was a marked tendency for the assemblies to become more restrictive in their membership, and to pursue only those policies which suited the few prosperous men. This process was greatly strengthened by the growing intervention of the authorities, and notably those agents of the absolute monarchy, the *intendants* and their *subdélégués*. At every opportunity they sought to limit participation to the upper elements in village society, rightly considering that those who had most to lose would be easiest to coerce. Still more devastating for the communities, the *intendants* took advantage of their increasing indebtedness to assume control of their finances, thereby depriving them of almost all liberty of action. There is no more conclusive demonstration of the power of the absolutist state than this erosion of the local communities, something no previous regime could have attempted. In the future the main defence of local independence against the government and its local representatives would be the small number of the latter, which was the real limit on their intervention at village level.

The communities' debts were the result of their efforts at self-protection, against those outside bodies or groups which took a share of their production, through taxation, tithes, or the various forms of feudal and seigneurial dues. There were endless opportunities for dispute over the detailed application of the rules, and redress could be sought from the courts or from the royal administration. Bringing a lawsuit was expensive, and the courts generally favoured the landlord or the church, a tendency which was accentuated as the judges became more firmly established in the upper levels of society, often receiving direct or indirect benefit from such levies themselves. Borrowing to pay the costs of legal action and to meet the local tax bill when it exceeded the amount that could be raised from individuals was obviously a short-term policy, justified by the hope that better times lay ahead; when they failed to arrive the burden on future generations became a very heavy one. In this situation the *intendants* and their subordinates intervened vigorously; they compelled the communities to pay off existing debts where possible, preventing them incurring new liabilities, and it was through the *intendant* and the royal councils that relations between the communities and the feudal and ecclesiastical exploiters increasingly came to be controlled. The new administrative machinery created between the time of Richelieu and of Colbert was drawn unwillingly but inevitably into this role, which it was exceedingly difficult to perform without becoming generally unpopular. Clearly one of the government's intentions was to preserve the taxpayers from excessive spoliation by rival expropriators of wealth, noble, bourgeois, or clerical. The sheer complexity of the relics of the feudal past within which the rural economy was still trapped defies description, but there can be no doubt that they imposed yet another heavy burden on the peasantry. The *seigneur* generally possessed the right to levy a whole range of duties, from a form of secular tithe to charges for the use of the mill, and maintained a court of first instance through which he could enforce them. Ordinary landholders did not enjoy a full freehold; if they sold land they had to pay a part of the proceeds to the *seigneur* as *lods et ventes*, while there were often provisions enabling him to purchase such land himself if he could match the price offered.

Already complicated by innumerable regional differences, of which perhaps the most important was the principle adopted in the south, under which the burden of proof lay with the *seigneur* (in the north the landholder had to show good legal title to escape the customary levies), the system was highly arbitrary in its incidence. Some villages were fortunate in having the seigneurial rights divided up among so many individuals that none of them found enforcement worthwhile; such subdivision was common, and difficult to reverse. Everywhere the local community sought to erode the levies, and this persistent pressure usually had some effect, if only by making collection laborious and expensive. The preservation of seigneurial revenues was only possible by the practice of periodic legal enquiries, which have sometimes been described as a form of 'feudal reaction'. Originally perceived as a late eighteenth-century phenomenon, this now looks more like a constant process dating back at least to the middle decades of the seventeenth century, by which the *seigneurs* regained temporarily lost rights. It is possible that such activities were more intensive in times of economic difficulty for the privileged, but this has yet to receive statistical confirmation. What does seem clear is that resentment of the dues increased sharply in the later seventeenth century, as the relationship between *seigneur* and community changed; for reasons which will be explained later, the degree of protection that could be expected from the *seigneur* diminished greatly, so the levies lost any plausible justification in terms of services rendered.

The same criticism could very often be levelled at the tithe, since much of its returns left the locality to swell the revenues of distant abbeys or bishops, leaving the *curé* with only a fraction for his subsistence and his charitable activities in the village. This had been a major point on the side of the Protestants, and had encouraged the widespread evasion or refusal of tithes in the decades after 1560. Between 1600 and 1630 the church seems to have regained the lost ground, although in this area too an endless flood of legal cases would continue until the Revolution, evidence of the centuries-old battle between peasant obstinacy and ecclesiastical greed. The actual level of the tithe was once again a matter of innumerable local variations, in terms both of the proportion taken and the crops and land liable to pay; in practice it was predominantly a levy on cereal production, at an average level nationally of about one eleventh. The general practice was to 'farm out' the collection on six- or nine-year leases, and once again these offered fat pickings for those prosperous élites, urban and rural, who were already deeply involved in exploiting the peasantry. It is imposible to say how much money stuck to their fingers, but in some cases it may have approached 50% of the gross return. Profits of this kind, available on both tithes and seigneurial dues where these were farmed out, were inevitably the subject of competition, but this did not necessarily reduce the margin, since many auctions were probably fixed in advance by the operation of various forms of influence.

In this area, like so many others, the bourgeoisie of the towns seems to have increased its share of the operation during the seventeenth century, although not on a dramatic scale.

From the point of view of the peasant, there was probably a perceptible increase, over the long term, in the demands made of him for rent, seigneurial dues, and tithe; in the last two instances this was chiefly through a tightening up of the machinery for enforcement. There were certainly wide variations between individual communities, and a few must have been lucky enough to experience the opposite trend; in general, however, the evidence points massively towards an intensification of the whole range of pressures by which wealth was extracted from the rural world for the benefit of the privileged minorities. In overall terms the increase was probably modest, not much more than 10%-20%, and while even this represented a very heavy burden for the peasantry, it was overshadowed by the brutal impact of royal taxation. The re-establishment of the normal system of collection under Henri IV was followed by sharp increases in the 1620s, then by the greatest twist of the financial screw ever to take place under the *ancien régime*. Between 1630 and 1648 the tax burden was roughly tripled to meet the costs of war, and the nature of the system inevitably directed this increase onto the shoulders of those least able to cope with it. A good deal of the money was never collected during these years, because of local resistance and sheer inability to pay; nevertheless, the government had set a new level for its demands, which would be maintained for the rest of the century. The financial demands of Louis XIV's last wars would bring another big increase between 1690 and 1715, which again proved impossible to collect in full, and represented at the most a 50% rise on the levels established under Richelieu and Mazarin. The effects of this process represent one of the most important phenomena of the century, and will be discussed in detail later. For the present two points need to be made; the great increase under the Cardinals had taken taxation up to virtually its natural limit, beyond which it could not be enforced without destroying the agrarian economy or the social order. This was somewhere in the region of 5%-10% of the gross national production.

Secondly, this had eliminated any margin of safety for all but the most prosperous peasants, thereby contributing powerfully to the general trend towards agrarian depression.

Attempts to estimate the evolution of gross national production cannot be more than informed guesswork for this pre-statistical age. Most historians seem to agree that over the 'long' seventeenth century, from 1600 to 1715 at least, there is no evidence for a substantial increase in production, and some reason to believe in a fall, more particularly after 1650. This situation had grave implications for the privileged classes and the monarchy, those great economic parasites whose pursuit of short-term gains had done much to create it. Not only taxation was limited by the ability of the peasantry to pay; the whole range of levies discussed over the last few pages were subject to similar restraints, so in the end everyone was competing for shares of a cake which was itself finite. The ultimate effect on the income of landowners was probably quite severe, above all because the nominal position could only be maintained by allowing arrears to pile up, especially in bad years. Both the traditional nobility and the new legal or *robe* nobility (the upper levels of the royal office-holders) must have felt squeezed by the low returns on their capital investment, and this clearly had implications for their political and economic behaviour. In contrast to the sixteenth century, the opportunities to rise in the world were far more restricted in the seventeenth; only small numbers of large merchants (heavily concentrated in a few ports), and financiers lending to the government or to great nobles were likely to make money fast under such circumstances. After the great expansion of the élites which had characterized the earlier period, changes were now largely confined to shifts within the existing privileged groups. Inevitably this produced a series of tensions and strains in society, with many people feeling themselves, and even their class or group, to be threatened with some kind of decline in wealth and status. For the monarchy the most serious effect was probably to make economic reforms excessively difficult; Colbert was to find it impossible to carry through much of his programme when the economic indices were set against him. There was a fortuitous but significant

coincidence between the great era of strong government after
1630 and the lingering economic malaise, with its linked falls
in prices, production, and population. The roots of the
government's policies lay far in the past, and were not primarily economic, so no causal connection can be made. In
terms of consequences, however, there is no doubt that the
limitations of the *ancien régime*, and the nature of the socioeconomic structures it produced, were heavily influenced by
the climate in which it reached maturity.

Industry, towns, and urban élites

The whole economic climate was clearly dominated by the
agrarian situation, since less than 10% of the working population was seriously engaged in any kind of industrial activity.
Many of these lived in the countryside, and the most important industry, the production of low-quality cloth, was largely
dependent on the rural market for its outlets. Many other
artisanal activities, such as the manufacture of farm imple-
ments, barrels, domestic utensils, or shoes, were also heavily
involved with the agricultural world; depression in the
countryside affected employment in these sectors as well. In
fact the parasitic nature of most French towns meant that
their prosperity was directly linked to that of the surrounding
area, for which they provided a variety of largely non-
productive services. The wealth brought in through rents,
tithes, taxation, and other levies did provide employment for
large numbers of domestic servants, and for artisans engaged
in the luxury trades which the urban rich patronized. In
contrast to the countryside, where the demands of the land
imposed a certain unity despite differences in wealth, the
urban artisan class was highly stratified by both occupation
and wealth. Guilds helped maintain small professional cliques,
within which a few substantial masters dominated a larger
group of journeymen; although often bitterly divided intern-
ally, these organizations generally presented a common front
to the outside world, defending their sectional interests against
any threat. The units of production were commonly very
small, and even the more prosperous masters were rarely more
than passably well off; really rich men were not to be found

in the manufacturing sector. The lion's share of the profits went to the merchants, a normal characteristic of an under-developed economy; but here again one must distinguish between the mass of small local operators, often combining trade with one or more other occupations, and the relative handful of rich and established men. Seventeenth-century merchants were far from being a large and thriving class of capitalists; most of them were only too willing to move into safer ways of securing their living, and there was a steady out-flow from the upper ranks of the mercantile group into the *rentier* and official classes. Partial exceptions can be found only in a few large trading centres, notably Lyon and the big ports, Marseille, La Rochelle, Nantes, St. Malo, and (towards the end of the century only) Bordeaux. International traders working from these focal points of French commerce could accumulate substantial fortunes, and might divert only part of their gains into land, while continuing their mercantile activi-ties through several generations. The nature of their opera-tions, however, was so limited, and the scale so small, that they had no appreciable effect on the economy as a whole.

The actual conditions of life in towns were often primitive, even squalid; sanitation was virtually non-existent, water supplies unreliable, housing cramped and uncomfortable. While there was still a real threat of invasion, civil war, or simply supposedly friendly troops on the march, the towns were constricted within their fortifications, and only the poor lived outside the walls. Fire was an ever-present danger, but the most striking disadvantage of town life was the prevalence of epidemic disease. Apart from the dreaded plague, local epidemics of more mundane kinds regularly thinned out the urban populations, so the towns would have diminished steadily in size without the regular flow of immigrants from the countryside. Infant mortality was particularly high, and was made still higher by the practice, even among the lower classes, of sending babies out to wet-nurses. By modern stan-dards the towns were not large; apart from Lyon, which probably reached the 100,000 mark around 1700, it is doubt-ful whether any provincial centre had more than 60,000 inhabitants. The population of Paris is specially difficult to estimate, but there was a rapid growth during the century which took it up to well over 400,000 by the later years of Louis XIV. The problems of public order and health in the great city were so obvious, and its political potentialities so great, that the monarchy felt obliged to intervene. Characteristically by-passing the existing municipality, the office of Lieutenant of Police was established in 1667 as a kind of *intendance* for Paris. Under two remarkable administrators, La Reynie and d'Argenson, effective measures of public hygiene were combined with the surveillance of the city by a network of police and informers. In most other towns too the government came to exercise greater control, with the *intendant* keeping a watchful eye on the municipal administration; this was part of a political evolution which will be discussed later.

With the exception of Lyon and the few big ports already listed, the dominant group in the towns was that of the judges and other royal officials; the seventeenth century was perhaps the crucial period in enhancing and confirming their power at the expense of both the merchants and the old nobility. Even a textile town like Amiens, or commercial and industrial centres like Rouen and Dijon, were ruled by such men. Most of the successful merchant families of the sixteenth century had hastened to secure their social ascent by investing in royal office and land, and their descendants formed oligarchies of a peculiarly self-conscious kind, tied together both by inter-marriage and by membership of the same prestigious and clannish institutions. Many of the officials had acquired noble status, although this was only slowly and partially accepted by the traditional *noblesse d'épée*; in this way they further con-solidated their position. Taking advantage of the difficulties of the rural world, it was these families which led the move-ment to buy up land, particularly around the towns, and they were also quick to exploit the difficulties of the older nobility. Once they had become established in this way, official families tended to remain at the same level, with a good marriage being the likeliest way of increasing their wealth and status; those whose ambitions were not satisfied were likely to leave their place of origin, migrate to Paris, and enter royal service in a different way. The great majority seem to have accepted their comfortable niches within the elaborate social hierarchies of the towns, resting content simply to maintain the family situation. This ossification of the new élites left those who had not yet reached a comparable level in an uncomfortable state, with the routes to the top increasingly blocked. The depressed trading traditions which prevailed for much of the century meant that relatively few families progressed fast enough through commerce to have much hope of forcing their way into the upper echelons of urban society. The challenge came far more from those who had seen the possibilities of enrichment through involvement in the great machine of royal finance and taxation, as local *receveurs des tailles* or as *trésoriers* of one kind or another. A secondary route to advancement lay in performing similar functions for great landlords, lay or ecclesiastical; here too money tended to stick to the fingers of those who were nominally handling it for others.

Social divisions: orders and classes

Making a fortune as a financier or tax-collector was naturally an unpopular business, but as usual society's disapproval was a matter of words rather than effective action. Such social theorists as the jurist Charles Loyseau might produce elaborate descriptions of a society of orders, in which groups were ranked by the dignity and importance of their occupations. Most members of the privileged class would have agreed with this kind of picture, and it certainly influenced their attitudes, but this does not mean that seventeenth-century society actually functioned on such principles. The system of orders may be seen as a code for describing a social structure in which inherited wealth and position was the dominant feature, and which preferred to obscure such changes as did occur behind a variety of pretences. Loyseau himself, the most famous expositor of the theory of orders, tried to argue as early as the 1600s that the judges were really superior to the military nobility; if he or his fellow-lawyers thought this would convince anyone, they were the victims of an extravagant delusion. As this example illustrates, the theory could be used to make claims on behalf of one group against another, whether it was nobles deploring the rise of *parvenu* officials, different official bodies contesting precedence, or the gold-smiths claiming superiority to the tanners. Such conflicts were commonplace in France, and could lead to lengthy legal bat-tles, ending in the king's council, or to outbreaks of fisticuffs at religious ceremonies and civic processions. These endless *disputes de préséance* were not just a lamentable display of human folly and self-importance; they reflected the value the pro-tagonists placed on concepts of honour and dignity which may now be difficult to grasp. At the same time there was a certain unreality about this frenetic defence of the existing order, since it is plain that such symbolic acts had only a limited ability to prevent change when the economic conditions favoured it. Like most forms of seventeenth-century argument, this was largely a rhetorical struggle, and those who wanted to defend a change which advantaged them normally had little trouble in producing a suitable verbal smokescreen. In practice wealth did confer social mobility; the reason society was not more fluid was primarily the success of the possessors of wealth in hanging on to it, combined with an economic situation which made rapid accumulation difficult. Even the most exclusive of orders, the *noblesse d'épée*, saw a steady trickle of ministerial and official families entering its upper ranges, right up to the level of the *ducs et pairs*, the highest-ranking nobles in France.

In such a massively unequal society there is clearly a sense in which the crucial dividing line lay between the 10% or so who owned enough property to guarantee regular and ade-quate meals, and the 90% who did not. While this is a very important distinction, however, it is not much use for detailed analysis, since it corresponds to no social division recognized by contemporaries, and came into play only intermittently, in the years of harvest failure and famine. A modest *laboureur* with a capital of 4,000 *livres* and a duke worth 4 millions both belonged to the privileged 10%, but they had nothing else in common. There was also a very important difference between the peasant who owned two or three acres and a cow, and the truly landless labourer; although both depended on working for other men, and were potentially at risk, they were so to very different degrees. To talk of a two-class society would therefore be an absurd oversimplification, albeit one containing a grain of truth. The whole notion of social class fits rather badly with the realities of life in seventeenth-century France, since it is difficult to find any 'class'—even the inevitable bourgeoisie—which can be said to have possessed a genuine class-consciousness. As a result there is little sign of people's behaviour being influenced by ideas about their class interest, beyond the natural inclination of the propertied to unite when threatened by popular violence and disorder. It is disconcerting, in this context, to find that most of the identifiable social conflicts of the period cut across any reasonable divisions by social class, with vertical solidarities proving at least as strong as horizontal ones. Contemporaries would certainly have felt more at home being fitted into orders, but the usefulness of the theory of orders is also very limited, because its categories were either too narrow or too broad. The three Estates could only pretend to a very shadowy unity, with the two privileged orders, clergy and nobility, held flimsily together only by the need to defend their privileges. The Third Estate comprised a huge and disparate amalgam of sub-categories; even if it is broken down into professional groupings, the range of wealth and status within them is such that the problem is merely pushed one stage back. Probably this society can only be understood in terms of a complex mixture of economic and status gradings, recognizing all the time that it was fissured into innumerable professional and local units, which never tired of disputing their precise ranking. When noble and clerical spokesmen tried to justify their special status by appealing to hierarchical principles, the vehemence of their protests was revealing; too many obvious gaps had opened up between the theory of a divinely instituted social order and the changing realities of life. While such defence of the old verities could not stop social change, it could certainly deflect and limit it, so that the development of both mercantile and industrial capitalism was severely hampered by the archaic status system of the country. In the process that system itself came under increasing strain, with internal divisions appearing which would beset France until the Revolution, and even beyond.

Just as the solidarity of the village community was under pressure, so were many of the other solidarities of seventeenth-century French society. The church was divided, not only by intensifying doctrinal disputes, but by the opposed economic interests of the aristocratic higher clergy and the mass of *curés* who did the real work. The nobility was losing its old cohesion, as the great magnates detached themselves from their local roots, to concentrate on their careers and contacts at court. Among those nobles who stayed in the provinces there were also major divisions; the wealthier, often also holders of royal office, came to play a leading role in town society, while the poor country squires or *hobereaux* lived on their modest properties, and found their status and exemptions under growing challenge from the tax collectors and the royal bureaucracy. The office-holders themselves were split by local factional rivalries, but above all by the emergence of the royal *commis* as the real holders of devolved royal powers, whose expansion meant the effective downgrading of existing posts. The rivalries between greater and smaller operators in the fields of trade and industry have already been briefly evoked. They were combined with endless conflicts between urban and regional interest groups, with the merchants and manufacturers of one town trying to gain advantages over those of the next. The cumulative effect of these tendencies was such that close analysis of French society often seems merely to reveal a kaleidoscopic series of internal tensions and conflicts. The reasons for this state of affairs are not easy to identify, but many of them centre on the relationship between the monarchy and the different social and political groups. Traditionally the crown was seen as the guarantor of local and sectional privilege, and the arbiter when such privileges clashed. In the seventeenth century, when the competing groups had been enormously expanded, and the change in economic circumstances was making the going hard for many of them, the fissiparous character of society was suddenly much more evident, so it was to the monarchy that men turned when they felt themselves threatened, demanding some kind of remedial action. The kings and their advisers had no clear idea what was happening, and often deplored the apparent collapse of conventional relationships and values. Their lack of a conscious policy, however, meant that the crown was drawn by its own needs for money and obedience into exploiting social divisions, and intensifying the well-worn methods of 'divide and rule'. Indeed, it was just those men most dependent on royal support—financiers, new officials, the ennobled—who created much of the *furore* among defenders of traditional social distinctions.

The nobility in society

Historians have found it difficult to produce any clear descriptive scheme for this society precisely because it was so lacking in powerful cohesive forces. There were many issues on which different social groups could have united, but in practice they rarely did so, presumably because their conception of the world was still narrow and traditional. There was a vital time lag between the greater social mobility characteristic of Europe after the sixteenth century and the evolution of men's attitudes to such change, which helped to produce the situation just described. Regarding social conflict as abnormal, men greeted it by dismayed comparisons with an idealized and semi-mythical past. They failed to evolve theories explaining it as anything but a sign of decadence, and therefore had major difficulties in accepting it, still less institutionalizing it. In France there were two linked factors which increased the difficulty of adjustment; the existence of tax privileges for the nobility, and the transmission of personal noble status to all the children of an individual noble. The tax system created intense pressure for the expansion of the privileged group, so the monarchy was constantly tempted into selling exemption for cash down, usually linked to noble status. The steady inflow of wealthy *parvenus* exacerbated the tensions within the nobility, while pushing more and more of the tax burden on the shoulders of the poor; the process also encouraged those rich men outside the nobility to continue thinking of noble values as the highest values, to which they might one day aspire. Once admitted to the charmed circle, the *anoblis* faced the same problem as the older nobility; how did they settle their children in suitable positions without either breaking the social rules or weakening the long-term position of the family? A member of the non-noble élites had a relatively wide choice of husbands for his daughters and employment for his sons; the latter could be placed in trade, lesser posts in the legal or tax system, or be sent into the church, probably as *curés*. The rules of *dérogéance*, under which a noble lost his status and exemptions if he engaged in a 'demeaning' occupation, restricted the possibilities far more in the case of younger sons of noble families, placing great emphasis on the army and the church. In both the supply of suitable jobs was limited; they inevitably became the object of fierce competition, which pushed up the costs of obtaining them, making royal patronage all the more valuable to those who could secure it.

The scramble to get jobs reflected the basic fact that few noble landowners seem to have been able to increase their wealth from one generation to the next without some special good fortune. Ultimately this was a matter of social convention; a noble was expected to live up to his income, and many persistently lived beyond it. It almost seems as if the richer the family, the less common prudence it displayed, for many of the great nobles were alarmingly indebted. New fashions in architecture, clothing, and domestic life generally gave ample opportunity for conspicuous and ruinous consumption, while for the grandees the maintenance of private fortresses and armies could swallow up even the greatest fortune. Here again the monarchy was able to exploit its position as the distributor of favours and largess, without which many of its greater subjects would have faced ruin. The other standard way of rescuing the family fortunes was through marriage with the richly endowed daughter of a financier or royal official; fine theories about the superiority of noble blood were soon forgotten when such a prize was in sight. Both royal largess and profitable marriages were commonly a way of restoring fortunes rather than expanding them, however, and they were certainly not available to all nobles. For most families a sound but not spectacular marriage in each generation might be expected to counterbalance the dowries payable to daughters, or the relatively modest cost of placing them in aristocratic religious houses. If a substantial number of children survived to adulthood there might be real problems, particularly because inheritance was governed by legal rules; these varied from region to region with the different 'customs', but many of them provided for something like equal sharing among the children, always excluding those who had entered the church. There is something of a puzzle here, for very little such sharing seems actually to have taken place, except among co-heiresses. Whatever the law might say, there was clearly great pressure within the family to maintain the inheritance intact from one generation to the next, and to limit the amount passing to daughters and younger sons. In the majority of cases convention seems to have proved stronger than legal rights, and the younger children accepted settlements on unfavourable terms; bitterly contested lawsuits about inheritance were inevitably common, but there could easily have been many more. Concentrating the property in the hands of the eldest son had the positive effect of maintaining the family position, but the negative one of making it difficult for the other children to sustain their inherited social rank. There was an obvious danger that a proliferation of poor nobles would result, and indeed there was no shortage of them; there would have been far more without the widespread tendency for them not to marry. Among the small provincial nobility in particular there was great reluctance to marry outside the class, with those who lacked the resources for a proper union often remaining within the household throughout their lives, causing no alienation of capital.

Whatever self-denying conventions were adopted, the number of poor nobles was always likely to grow; the Wars of Religion had shown how dangerous such men could be, a point which would be emphasized by the conspiracies and popular revolts of the early seventeenth century. The need for control over the nobility became one of the accepted principles of royal policy, leading to a series of efforts to define and limit the order by eliminating all those who could not produce satisfactory titles. These culminated in the great *recherches de noblesse* ordered by Colbert in the years after 1665 over virtually the whole of France. Although never properly completed, this enormous investigation deprived thousands of 'false' nobles of their privileges; a certain proportion of these were certainly men of genuine noble origins, who had no legal proof and lacked the money to buy their way back into the order. The operation as a whole was very unpopular with the nobility, who were not impressed by royal arguments that the exclusion of interlopers benefited the genuine; most nobles felt humiliated by having to justify themselves before tribunals whose members were often drawn from the new *robe* nobility, regarding acceptance by the local community of *gentilshommes* as a far better test. The *recherches* also represented a threat to the nobles' view of their own position, because they operated on the principle that the order was a 'service' nobility originating in royal grants, whereas many nobles thought of themselves as descendants of the Franks, racially distinct from their inferiors. Apart from this major investigation, the tax officials were constantly sniping at the poorest levels of the nobility, and a really poor noble might well be unable to finance the legal actions which could have protected him. The rulers of France paid lip-service to noble values, and relied heavily on the basic loyalty of the nobility to combat both internal and external threats, but their agents in the localities were putting the traditional bonds under heavy stress. The situation was not helped by the noble tendency to despise lawyers and courts of every kind, which resulted in a persistent lawlessness the bureaucratic monarchy found less and less acceptable. Under Louis XIV such events as the *Grands Jours* held in the Auvergne in 1665 (a kind of special legal commission staffed by *parlementaires*) were evidence of the government's new determination to repress noble brigandage and violence, and over the years enough exemplary punishments were handed out to produce a real deterrent effect.

The monarchy's ambivalent attitude to the nobility, which it treated as a major prop of the state and also a potential threat, was characteristic of its approach to social problems in general. There was an increasing readiness to intervene, checking the pretensions of one group or another, but never challenging the basic assumptions on which social distinctions rested. The final effect was an odd one; traditional categories and social change were kept in some kind of relation, at the cost of allowing inconsistencies and contradictions to build up within the system. The greatest inconsistency of all was in the crown's own policy, since it put a great deal of effort into trying to control changes which were largely the product of its own increasing demands on the country. From the time of Richelieu onwards, the scene was dominated by the expansion of royal fiscality, itself a consequence of the external policies of the state. Between the Cardinal's rise to power in 1624 and the death of Louis XIV in 1715 roughly two years out of three were years of war, with all its implications in terms of fiscal expedients and exactions. Under the inexorable pressures of war finance the system of borrowing and taxation developed a momentum of its own; too intricate and too interdependent for anyone to control, still less reform, it twisted and moulded the political, economic, and social structures of France into that strange set of distortions we call the *ancien régime*. In the process it also shaped men's ideas, so that almost all would-be reformers, realizing something of the magnitude of their task, thought only a powerful central authority could ever unscramble the mess, thus ensuring that the legacy of Richelieu and Louis XIV would long outlast the Bourbons.

Royal fiscality and its consequences

The figures for royal income and expenditure give some idea of the amount of torque that was being applied. The overall trends can be clearly seen on the graphs, but as usual there are a number of complications involved. The operations of seventeenth-century finance were so devious that it is peculiarly difficult to reconstruct them, and it would be rash to regard any set of official figures as more than an approximation to the truth. There was no budget in the modern sense, since a great deal of the income from taxation was diverted to other destinations before it ever reached the royal treasury, so it was possible for the amounts actually levied to be far greater than the usable funds they produced. Figures for taxation are therefore a guide to the burden on the country, not the amount at the government's disposal; an attempt has been made to index them against grain prices (in graph 2) to give a more accurate picture of the changes in this respect. The figures for royal expenditure are more reliable, but here it is difficult to find any satisfactory way of allowing for variations in real value, and nominal values have been retained; this is probably a fair compromise for the period 1630–1715, while in very rough terms the 12 millions of 1560 were the equivalent of the 42 millions of 1630. One major element in the picture can only be reconstructed in a more conjectural way, as details of loans and other borrowings are often missing from official documents; graph 6 is based on estimates of the amounts borrowed year by year, excluding some forms of forced loan. Also excluded from the previous graph are the enormous concealed borrowings represented by the sale of office and associated practices, an estimate of which appears as graph 7.

Even the most cursory glance at the graphs will reveal the impact of the two desperate periods of foreign war, 1635–59 and 1689–1713. The evolution was very similar in both cases; the crown began by selling offices on a grand scale, then found the market becoming saturated, and had to place its main reliance on loans from the financiers. These loans were at high rates of interest, and could only be obtained by alienating the taxes a year or more in advance, a process that could not continue indefinitely. Both periods naturally produced increases in taxation; under the Cardinals these affected the *taille* and a number of indirect taxes, while Louis XIV introduced new forms of extraordinary taxation payable even by the privileged classes. When the wars were over, in 1661 and again in 1716, the government tried to recoup itself at the expense of the financiers, by organizing a *Chambre de justice* which investigated their misdeeds and fined them enormous sums. In 1661, under Colbert's shrewd guidance, this worked reasonably well, and most of the accumulated debt was cleared off or had its interest rates cut drastically. The situation in 1716 was very different, because the debt had grown so large that only an insignificant proportion could be eliminated by such methods. By this date the debt has been reckoned at 2,000 million *livres*, paying interest of 100 million a year, against tax revenues (including the new extraordinary taxes) of 180 million. Louis XIV had saddled his successors with a load of debt they were able to eliminate only by the disastrous expedient of John Law's System, the French equivalent of the South Sea Bubble.

Law's calamitous schemes only confirmed what sensible men had known for centuries; the government could not be relied on to honour its debts. It was the resulting inability to borrow from the public in general which placed the state at the mercy of the financiers, allowing the latter to demand extortionate rates of interest. Lack of confidence in the government made the establishment of a central bank on the Dutch model impossible, so money had to be raised through the personal credit of intermediaries. By the later years of Louis XIV the scale of lending required was such that internal French resources were inadequate, so financiers such as Samuel Bernard were used to raise funds abroad, from sources which included the Protestant bankers of Geneva and other Swiss towns. This foreign borrowing was the latest in a long series of expedients, and as in the past the government exploited it to the point of destruction; many of the bankers eventually found themselves ruined, while Bernard himself was saved only because he had become so important that he had to be bailed out by the royal treasury. The absolute monarchy's failure to put its financial affairs in any sort of order was an ominous portent for the future, which also had immediate and profound effects on the social and economic condition of France. Desperate for money, the crown multiplied useless offices, squeezed any group of potential taxpayers to the limit, granted enormous powers and privileges to the financiers, and attacked exemptions and vested rights wherever it dared. The cumulative effect of these practices was very serious indeed. Apart from creating a complex series of rivalries and resentments, which might in the short run split opposition to the government but which would eventually provide the basis for a mounting tide of criticism, they made reform from the centre more difficult. The increasingly tangled mass of vested interests was a serious impediment in itself, but still more important was the lasting reputation the state created for itself; bitter experience taught Frenchmen that proposals for change emanating from the government were the invariable prelude to new fiscal exactions.

Attempts at economic management

Royal ministers recognized many of these problems, alongside the impossibility of raising unlimited sums from the taxpayers; there was no shortage of ingenious schemes for increasing national wealth, and thereby expending the base for taxation and borrowing. Plans to improve the state of French industry and commerce became a major preoccupation of the seventeenth century, beginning under Henri IV with the efforts of the tireless Barthélemy Laffemas and the *conseil de commerce* he organized. Many of the bright ideas emanating from this source got no further than the desk of the powerful *surintendant des finances* Sully; an eminently practical man, Sully was rarely taken in by promises of quick and easy returns, and this has led some historians to claim that he was opposed in principle to industrial and commercial expansion, a view the evidence does not really support. It may be that Sully, as the leading Protestant in the royal service, was concerned not to antagonize the Dutch or interfere with Protestant merchants at Lyon or elsewhere; he certainly had a low opinion of French abilities in some fields, and saw himself as acting realistically. Like all ministers, he was assailed by innumerable demands for intervention in support of particular interests, which usually implied damaging someone else for no very clear end. He was probably right in giving precedence to his favoured activity of improving the transport system; under his control a higher proportion of royal expenditure went on roads, canals, and port facilities than at any other time during the century. A sustained effort of this kind would have been a major contribution to economic development, but unfortunately Sully had done little more than restore the damage done during the Wars of Religion, and after his dismissal in 1611 progress was minimal.

Those who solicited Sully's protection for their schemes evidently shared the general assumption that the government should be party to any large-scale industrial or commercial development. All projectors wanted protection against rivals, usually through a monopoly or suitable tariffs, and also hoped for more direct aid in the form of subsidies. Under Henri IV a number of industries did receive help, which might also include tax exemptions and special permission for nobles to participate; they included silk production, tapestry and rug making, glassmaking, and soapboiling. Another assumption was that the state would regulate manufacture, to preserve the quality of the product and ensure its continued viability. This was unfortunate in practice, since it usually meant the organization of systems of inspection which rapidly degenerated into the levy of hush-money; the fiscal side of the operation always tended to become dominant, and may sometimes have been so from the start. The results of Henri IV's industrial initiatives seem to have been very modest, even in the relatively successful case of the silk industry, and the major manufacturing industry remained the production of low-quality cloth, which owed little or nothing to royal support. The period was more productive in ideas than in solid results, and the style of economic thought known as mercantilism was becoming fashionable. Historians no longer believe in mercantilism as a coherent system, but it remains a convenient shorthand for describing a loose collection of assumptions which underlay almost all economic thinking of the period. Crudely stated, these included the notions that the wealth of the kingdom could be increased through manufactures, whose export would sustain the necessary imports of precious metals and other scarce commodities, while measures should be taken to minimize the export of bullion and the importation of expensive luxury goods. Simplistic as these ideas were, they did show that more people were devoting their minds to economic theorizing than ever before.

Few of the initiatives taken under Henri IV were followed up under the weak governments which held power in the years down to 1624, although there was some progress with colonization in Canada, and private enterprise attempts to challenge Dutch supremacy in the East had occasional successes. When a serious commercial policy was resumed under Richelieu general economic conditions were changing sharply for the worse; Europe was entering on a long period of depression, whose first effects were most acute in the manufacturing sector. The prospects for successful innovation were poor, and royal foreign policy did little to improve them, since France's increasing commitment to war against the Habsburgs brought numerous additional problems for her foreign trade, besides absorbing any money the state might otherwise have been able to invest. In consequence Richelieu's ministry is notable for the variety of projects initiated rather than for the solid results achieved. The Cardinal himself played a leading part in these activities; after the suppression of various competing admiralty jurisdictions he took the title of *grand maître du commerce et de la navigation*, and he was a prime mover in the foundation of a series of grandiloquently named trading companies such as the *compagnie de la Nacelle de Saint Pierre fleurdelysée*. Although these creations were none too successful, they were part of a genuine policy which aimed to encourage manufactures, overseas trade, and colonial ventures. Richelieu made serious diplomatic efforts to gain the favour of local rulers and special advantages for French merchants, in the Mediterranean, the Near East, and the Baltic. He also recognized the vital importance of sea power, and has claims to be regarded as the founder of the modern French navy; among the ministers of the *ancien régime* Richelieu and Colbert stand out for their willingness to think in maritime terms. The similarities between the economic policies of the two ministers are very striking; it is not surprising to hear that Colbert frequently annoyed Louis XIV by invoking precedents set under Richelieu.

Like proposals for internal administrative reform, the economic programme was pushed into the background by the aggressive foreign policy adopted after 1630. Mazarin and the Regency government showed little interest in it, which was understandable when their main concern was to survive a series of desperate short-term crises. After 1661 Colbert had to start all over again, rebuilding the royal navy from the remnants of Richelieu's fleet, and embarking on a sustained effort to encourage and regulate manufactures, while founding new trading companies to export their products. Historians used to portray Colbert as a minister of genius, poorly supported by the king and his colleagues, whose ideas would, if properly implemented, have transformed the French economy. This view, which did recognize the seriousness of his commitment to economic advance (quite exceptional for a seventeenth-century minister), has now been largely demolished. Recent scholarship has exposed and emphasized the limitations and contradictions of Colbert's policies, and the degree to which he was the prisoner of a whole set of crippling misapprehensions. He emerges as the practitioner of a kind of *dirigisme* which never worked out as he intended; of all his enterprises, only the navy and a few luxury industries achieved any real success. The whole idea of forcing merchants into trading companies was clearly ill-conceived; the merchants would go along with such organizations only when special conditions made ordinary trade impossible, and the companies also suffered from their close association with the state, which had such a catastrophic reputation as a guardian of other people's funds. Companies were losing favour in the leading mercantile nations, the Netherlands and England, despite the exceptional successes of their East India Companies, at the very time when French merchants were being chivvied into them. Colbert's policies for the regulation of industry also involved the fatal fallacy that high quality goods would sell best; low prices were more important in most markets, and the whole apparatus of inspectors and controls worked against the necessary corner-cutting. The worst misconception of all came in the field of foreign trade, with the belief that tariffs and other forms of state intervention could exclude the Dutch middlemen to the advantage of their French rivals. Throughout the century ministers were lobbied by short-sighted enthusiasts for this type of economic imperialism, but Colbert displayed an extreme lack of judgement in listening to them, and above all in trying to rush the whole process. It is just conceivable that with large-scale government investment and a time-scale seen in decades the Dutch predominance, based on a whole range of connected skills in marketing, shipping, and finance, could have been taken over by the French. The policies actually adopted, the introduction of high tariffs and general harassment of the Dutch, backfired badly; they caused far more distress to the French than to the adaptable and mobile Dutch, while the resort to war against the United Provinces in 1672 brought Colbert's whole programme to a grinding halt.

The illusory hope of quick returns may have been fostered by the general belief, expressed by numerous pamphleteers, that France was inherently the wealthiest nation in Europe, thanks to her large population and varied natural resources. Colbert seems to have shared this view, while in other ways he was more influenced by the attitudes of the great *commis* in the central government, determined to subordinate all sectional interests to those of the crown, than by the opinions of the merchants, whom he always regarded as short-sighted and self-interested. His own background was that of a financier rather than a merchant, and his career reminds us that the royal bureaucracy was dominated by men from the inland regions of northern France. Paris was not a seaport, and the major trading centres on the Atlantic and Mediterranean coasts were far away; the commercial élite occupied a peripheral position, both geographically and politically. Even if Colbert's policies had been better conceived, they would certainly have demanded major investment by the state—but there is no sign that he himself, wearing his other hat as finance minister, was willing to find the necessary funds. The total investment over the years from 1661–72 was only a derisory 2 million *livres*, and it then stopped completely. In effect the monarchy's left hand was making a feeble gesture independently of the other and much more powerful hand, which continued to extract taxes in a damaging fashion, and to attract capital into finance or offices rather than trade. Colbert did check some of the abuses in these other areas, at least until the war of 1672, but there is no evidence that he appreciated the interconnections. He was conscious of the need to open up the internal market, through the reduction or abolition of internal tolls and the improvement of communications; his efforts in these directions were praiseworthy, but had only a marginal effect. In any case the government was largely helpless in the face of the general recession which dragged the whole economy down; although it was this situation which was primarily responsible for the problems of merchants and industrialists, Colbert's policies probably worsened them. Certainly the minister became increasingly unpopular with these groups, and there was a mounting tide of opposition to state intervention. Many of the criticisms made at the time were remarkably acute, showing that considerable expertise was available in a few major centres. Always suspicious of the merchants, Colbert seems to have been much less inclined than Richelieu to modify his policies when they were criticized, and this was one reason, together with the wider range and more effective enforcement of his programme, for the emergence of the defensive doctrine of mercantile independence known as *laissez-faire*.

By the time of Colbert's death in 1683 many of his projects were virtually abandoned, and his successors as *contrôleurs généraux* over the next thirty years adopted a much more cautious and unambitious line. This did not put an end to criticism, because the machinery of regulation remained in existence, and was now used almost exclusively for fiscal purposes, while losing any relevance to an overall economic plan. The pressures of war finance made this inevitable; they also dictated the abandonment of Colbert's ambitious naval policy, for even Louis XIV could not afford to take on the whole of Europe simultaneously on land and at sea. After 1694 expenditure on the navy dropped sharply, and the emphasis consequently shifted to privateering at the expense of the English and Dutch rather than an outright challenge to their dominance at sea. Paradoxically, it is from this period of the 1690s and beyond that one must date the beginning of a genuine upswing in France's foreign trade, which was to be sustained through most of the eighteenth century. The government was anxious to manage the susceptibilities of the merchants, as potential lenders to the state, and the appearance in 1700 of a new council of commerce dominated by big merchants was one sign of the greater flexibility produced by this situation. As the government's hold on the trading companies relaxed they became more popular, while there are strong indications that major trading families were more inclined to remain active through several generations, instead of withdrawing as *rentiers* once they had built an adequate fortune. This was particularly the case in the large ports, where the ambiguous rules of *dérogéance* were consistently interpreted as allowing nobles to engage in overseas trade; as usual, local practice and opinions were decisive in determining how the law would be enforced. Trading considerations were certainly important in the eyes of the government, and the decision to accept the Spanish inheritance for Philip, duc d'Anjou, which precipitated the last and most disastrous of Louis XIV's wars, may even have been decisively influenced by the hope of monopolizing the rich commerce with Spanish America. The steady growth of the mercantile fleet, which had been taking place since 1660, and which made such hopes at least plausible, may have owed more to Colbert than is always recognized. Apart from direct encouragement of shipbuilding by premiums on larger vessels—a policy of dubious effectiveness, given the minute scale of the payments—the expansion of the royal fleet may have had some unexpected results. Greater protection for French merchant shipping was an obvious gain, especially in the Mediterranean; the switch to privateering was not a total loss in this sense, since the commitment of France's prime rivals to major fleet operations hampered their efforts to react. More important, however, was the increase in shipbuilding and port facilities, and in the supply of experienced deep-water sailors, all of which probably encouraged the expansion of mercantile activities from the 1690s on, as the purely military demands on such resources diminished. Colonial ventures, in both Canada and the Caribbean, were enough of a success to provide French merchants with valuable footholds across the Atlantic, although here too more might have been achieved if the government's support had been less intermittent and inadequate. The trade in sugar, slaves, and furs was still to reveal its true potential by the death of Louis XIV.

It is doubtful whether Colbert would have been much gratified to know that his work made a modest contribution towards the great expansion of French overseas trade in the eighteenth century. He had aimed at far more immediate results, above all at expanding the tax base for the benefit of the crown's finances, and in this last field even the later expansion was to prove deceptive. Heavy taxation of trade itself would have been self-defeating, a point which was so obvious that even the French monarchy somehow managed to refrain from imposing crippling duties. The real hope was that a trading boom would revive the internal economy, encourage investment in both the industrial and agricultural sectors, and thereby stimulate a much wider range of economic developments. It seems clear that beyond the immediate hinterland of the ports this never happened; for a variety of reasons the effect on the economy as a whole was minimal, and it pursued its own sluggish evolution, with the beginnings of a slow improvement only evident after Louis XIV's death. Constantly undermined by the internal contradictions of royal policy, and confronted by the great inert bulk of the national economy, the well-meaning efforts to initiate a new era of prosperity inevitably became little more than a series of might-have-beens. Although relations between the government and the mercantile communities improved after 1683, there was still a large element of mutual mistrust, and trading capital never became intermixed with state finance after the fashion of the Maritime Powers. The scale of the crown's military expenditure might in any case have frightened the Bank of Amsterdam itself, and the failure to develop the basis for an equivalent institution in France compelled the continuation of the old and damaging expedients already described, most notably a tax system whose inequity and disruptive effects were recognized by the ministers themselves.

The great expansion of royal taxation had profound political and administrative consequences, which will be discussed in the next chapter. Its timing was certainly significant, for it came at just the moment when there were unmistakable signs of general stagnation. With the opportunities for social advancement through profits from the land or from trade increasingly blocked by economic recession, the attractions of involvement in the sprawling machinery of tax collection and government finance were inevitably enhanced. Whatever its risks, this was the one relatively open and speedy route to wealth and status, and the contrast between an expanding 'governmental' sector and contraction elsewhere is one of the major themes of the period after 1630. While the origins of the economic depression must clearly be sought in broad movements affecting the whole of Europe, there is little doubt that in France the government's devices for increasing its income represented a major diversion of energy, talent, and resources. It seems certain that this process hampered eventual recovery from the depression, and that it had considerable long-term effects on the evolution of French society. Perhaps the most dangerous of these was the added emphasis on parasitic exploitation of the peasantry, by state, church, landlords, and bureaucrats alike; it is the remorseless character of this exploitation which is the dominant impression left by the social and economic scene in the seventeenth century.

3

The Government of France 1598–1715

(i) *Henri IV to Richelieu 1598–1624*

Religion and foreign policy under Henri IV

While the peace settlements of 1598 must have come as an enormous relief to a country exhausted by decades of war, it was always obvious that they were far from secure. In many respects the Edict of Nantes was a prescription for continuing trouble; limited religious toleration was accepted only as a last resort, and enforcement at the local level was always difficult. The partisans of both creeds were quick to take any opportunity of advancing their position, by opening a new place of worship, packing the municipal governments, and generally exploiting any loophole in the provisions of the Edict. Their alacrity in pushing their own cause was equalled only by the ferocity with which they denounced similar practices by their opponents. This situation was probably inevitable, given the attitudes of the time; the Huguenots in particular needed to maintain their cohesion and morale by this kind of limited aggression, even if in the long run they were damaged by it. The dominance of the Catholic viewpoint at court was especially dangerous in this context, since the royal attitude was bound to be influenced by the way local incidents were represented, and here the cards were stacked in favour of the Catholics. This placed the Huguenots in something of a dilemma; they could not afford to let their position go by default, yet since what they saw as legitimate self-defence often appeared to the government as wilful trouble-making, each incident tended to worsen their image. Relations between Henri IV and his one-time supporters soon became difficult, and would have been worse without the mediating role played by Sully, whose high position in the government reassured the Protestants, while giving him enough authority to restrain them from their more dangerous enterprises. This was essentially a stop-gap solution, but it worked well enough until 1610, largely because no major issue in foreign or domestic policy brought the king into direct conflict with his Protestant subjects during these years. Such good fortune could hardly last, and one danger was already becoming apparent; the king had many reasons to need the Pope's good will, which depended very much on his taking a reasonably tough line with the Huguenots. More was at stake than just ecclesiastical affairs, for Henri was only able to remarry and produce an heir when the Pope agreed to dissolve his first marriage, while French diplomacy in the critical areas of northern Italy and Germany was deeply involved with the Vatican. Few of the Huguenot leaders seem to have under-stood the constraints under which the king operated, with the result that they were constantly over-reacting to largely imaginary threats, complicating the government's life and infuriating the king.

The government was particularly sensitive over foreign policy, since many Catholics were uneasy about alliances with Protestant states, yet the logic of the situation made them inevitable. Henri and his ministers were determined to main-tain France's position against the Habsburgs, following the traditional view of French national interest; this meant culti-vating good relations with the Dutch republic, the Protestant princes in Germany, and England. Such dealings with the heretics made it all the more necessary to avoid giving the impression of favouring the Huguenots within France if Henri were to retain any credibility as a good Catholic. The pursu-ance of a 'Protestant' foreign policy might be welcome to the Huguenots, and was in itself some guarantee that the govern-ment would respect its obligations towards them, but it was not entirely to their advantage. In any case the king found it prudent to conceal some of his activities, such as the payment of subsidies to the Dutch and other allies, so the extent of his anti-Spanish commitment was not fully known. Henri was extremely fortunate in being able to secure most of his ends through a cautious, limited, and inexpensive policy, which did not give rise to major internal disputes. He could do this because of the relative weakness of the Habsburg position after 1598; in Germany the incompetent Emperor Rudolf II was losing any authority he had ever possessed, while Spain, still vainly trying to reconquer the Netherlands, was at a notably low ebb of her fortunes. Even the cautious secretary of state Villeroy, who had experienced the dangers of Spanish intervention at the time of the League, came to recognize in the years after Vervins that, with Spain needing peace as badly as France, there was little risk in taking a tougher line when disputes arose. The situation on France's borders meant that there were bound to be innumerable occasions for friction; nothing could be less like the modern notion of a frontier than the string of partly or fully autonomous principalities which stretched from Lorraine through Alsace and Franche-Comté to Switzerland and Savoy. Their rulers tried to play off the major powers against one another to preserve their independence or even increase their territory, and this elaborate diplomatic game was further complicated by the many territorial enclaves, the theoretical rights of the Emperor, and the Prince-Bishoprics and free cities along the Rhine. For the Spaniards it was a vital area, since the campaigns in the Netherlands could be sustained only if the route from northern Italy over the Alps and up the Rhine were kept open for their troops and supplies.

Until the conclusion of the twelve-year truce between the Dutch and Spain in 1609 the French diplomats were able to exploit the vulnerability of this line of communication to gain a number of minor advantages. The truce, which encouraged the Spaniards to stiffen their attitude, coincided with a dispute over the succession in the important German principality of Cleves-Julich. Henri IV responded by preparing to take the offensive; he mustered his army, secured support from the Protestant powers, and seemed set for campaigns in both Germany and Italy in the summer of 1610. His assassination on 14 May 1610 left his exact intentions uncertain, and historians have never been able to reconstruct them conclusively.

The picture is further complicated by the intervention of the king's private life, for one of his quarrels with Spain was over the refusal of the authorities in Brussels to return the Prince and Princess of Condé, who had fled to avoid his advances to the latter. No doubt Henri did hope to settle this personal matter in any agreement he reached with Spain, and it may have been crucial in pushing him into violent action, but the most likely explanation of his moves is that he intended to teach the Spaniards a sharp lesson in Germany, then resume the negotiations for a marriage between his son and the Infanta. Whatever more grandiose ambitions the king had, his death naturally put France back on the defensive, although the Regency government was successful in a brief campaign to support the Protestant claimant in Cleves-Julich. The king's death emphasized the dangers of pursuing a policy which could be interpreted as anti-Catholic, since the assassin Ravaillac was a rather deranged zealot, who seems to have acted in isolation in the belief that Henri was an enemy of the Pope and the church. While his act horrified virtually everyone, it was an extreme expression of an outlook which did have more respectable supporters; few Catholics could be entirely happy about policies which seemed to place temporal advantage above religious imperatives. The government might have had more difficulties than it actually experienced but for two factors: the widespread belief among politically aware Frenchmen that the Habsburgs used religion as a cover for their ambition to create a 'universal monarchy', and the powerful sentiments of loyalty to the crown which Henri IV's reign had done so much to revive.

The restoration of royal authority

At first sight it is not obvious that the king's rule was well calculated to win him popularity. Apart from his rather un-edifying private life, surrounded by mistresses and illegitimate children, he showed considerable impatience with the traditional rights and protections of his subjects. He used the ill-defined powers of the royal council to override the decisions of the *parlements* and other courts, made frequent and arbitrary interventions in the affairs of towns and provinces, and increased the efficiency of the tax system. Subsequent historical writing has built up such a myth of Henri IV as a sensual *bonhomme*, interested in the welfare of his people as a whole, that it is very difficult to penetrate to the reality as it was perceived at the time. When defending his policies before the *parlement*, and implicitly before public opinion, the king was ready enough to pose as the protector of the people, but this was already a well-worn device for covering up almost any kind of measure. Writing in 1609, the experienced English ambassador Sir George Carew noted that the people were 'so infinitely opprest, as they have their mouths filled with imprecations and bitter complaints; exclaiming, that their king seeketh not to be *Roy des François*, but *des Gueux*'. As Carew recognized, such grievances were offset by an awareness that the reign had brought peace, and were not dangerous so long as the king could ensure the loyalty of his greater subjects. Their existence, however, reminds us that it was much easier to appreciate the benefits of Henri's government from the vantage point of the 1630s or 1640s than it was at the time. Although the king distributed pensions and favours shrewdly, many of the grandees also had grounds for complaint; they found their marriage alliances being dictated to them, with the intention of maintaining family rivalries which divided potential opponents of the crown, while they were denied real political power and closely watched in their provincial governorships. The only major conspiracy after 1598 was that of the king's old comrade-in-arms the duc de Biron in 1602, which cost him his head, but there were numerous lesser indications of discontent, so that no-one could suppose aristocratic rebellion was a thing of the past. The first prince of the blood, Condé, his uncle Soissons, and the numerous members of the house of Guise all experienced Henri's suspicion and disfavour; he rightly calculated that they were incapable of uniting, and that none of them had the strength or the will to rebel alone. This policy was good enough while the king lived, but these great magnates remained very powerful, enjoying the support of widespread clienteles. Permanent exclusion from power and royal favour must eventually drive them into open opposition, yet to give satisfaction to what they saw as their legitimate aspirations would have meant surrendering a large amount of royal power. There was a fundamental dilemma here, which was to persist far into the seventeenth century, underlying many of the seemingly confused political events of the period.

Apart from the obvious incompetence of most of the grandees as potential ministers, the monarchy was now able to call on a group of servants who had been steadily increasing their status and power during the past century. A limited number of families had risen through the ranks of the royal office-holders, established close links with the crown itself, and come to monopolize the major civil offices in the state. Despite their wealth and power, they had yet to be fully accepted by the old nobility; this accentuated a tendency towards intermarriage, which combined with nepotism to create a tight circle of related families. The holding of office was not in itself the key to power, for the Chancellor could be reduced to impotence by the appointment of a separate Keeper of the Seals, while a secretary of state might have no say in the affairs which passed through his own department. What was crucial was the increasing tendency of the monarchs to admit a few such men to membership of the inner council which dealt with major affairs of state, while giving individual secretaries of state control of the vital areas of foreign policy and military administration. Some of the important steps in this evolution seem to have taken place during the dark days of Henri III's reign, and among Henri IV's ministers Bellièvre (Chancellor 1599–1607, although effectively retired after 1605) and Villeroy (secretary of state charged with foreign affairs) were veterans of this earlier period. Other members of the inner circle were Brûlart de Sillery (Chancellor after 1607) and Jeannin (*surintendant des finances* after 1611), both from typical *robe* families. All these men shared certain characteristics apart from their social origins; they inclined towards conciliation, respect for established institutions and practices, and a cautious foreign policy. Their values and attitudes were not entirely in harmony with the traditional noble concepts of *honneur* and *gloire*, which carried much weight with the king himself, and they were frequently worried by his bellicosity, his generosity in pardoning enemies, and the intrigues surrounding his mistresses. In practice this latent conflict seems to have proved useful; Henri allowed his own inclinations to be tempered by the advice of the ministers most of the time, although he was always capable of brushing their objections aside. The most important minister, Sully (*surintendant des finances* 1598–1611), was a very different figure, a Huguenot nobleman whose behaviour and ideas were much closer to those of the king. It says much for Henri's basic good sense that he never allowed Sully to dominate the royal council, although he was its most influential member.

Sully's importance stemmed partly from the multiple functions he performed; apart from his control of the finances, he was responsible for the royal fortifications, buildings, navy, and artillery, and for the upkeep of highways, bridges, and canals. In all these spheres he demonstrated considerable technical ability, associated with a shrewd concern to gather information and expertise for better decision-making, and a brusque authoritarianism which certainly produced results. He was not a great innovator, but through hard work and application to detail he made the conventional machinery function again after long years of relative neglect. His most remarkable achievement was to accumulate a substantial reserve of cash in hand, which by 1610 amounted to some 15 million *livres*; this was only possible because of the prolonged peace, itself more the result of the other ministers' caution than of Sully's strongly anti-Spanish views. He does seem to have reduced corruption and peculation within the tax system, while making substantial progress towards cutting down the size and cost of the long-term royal debt, and recovering some of the alienated royal demesne. As *surintendant* Sully was largely responsible for the most significant new measure of the reign, the introduction of the system known as the *paulette*, but it is impossible to determine how far he appreciated its importance, or even exactly what his motives were. The *paulette* or *droit annuel* was essentially a device which allowed the royal officials to ensure that their heirs would continue in possession of the family offices, in return for an annual payment to the crown of 1/60th of the capital value. It replaced a much more confused scheme which permitted the transfer of offices under certain conditions, whose most notable feature was that the resigning holder must survive the transaction by more than forty days. From the point of view of the officials, the *paulette* had two great advantages: the family position was no longer threatened by unexpected death, and the cost of retaining the office was spread out evenly instead of involving the payment of heavy dues at irregular intervals. For the government there was a considerable gain in making the revenue from this source a steady and reliable one, while in the long run the system might be expected to make the officials more loyal, lessening their need for any protector other than the king.

The *paulette* came into operation in 1604, after a long series of debates in the royal council, in which the chancellor Bellièvre had opposed it bitterly. He was the spokesman for a powerful current of opinion which regarded the sale of judicial offices as an abuse, and saw that the new arrangements would entrench venality more firmly than ever. Bellièvre also argued that by making it almost impossible to appoint suitable men when vacancies occurred, they would reduce the quality of the judiciary, and make it dangerously independent of the king. These were prescient views, which have naturally impressed later historians, but perhaps there was an element of unreality about them. It is difficult to see how the monarchy could ever have ensured the appointment of the right men to the right jobs, in an age when the idea of selection by ability and qualifications had hardly been born. The existing rules were such that the crown could rarely exercise a free choice, and to regain full control would have involved the expenditure of enormous capital sums, since the creation of offices had represented a concealed state debt, with their salaries and perquisites as interest. As Richelieu would wryly observe, the evils of the system were obvious, but such abuses were part of the very structure of the monarchy; practical ministers would try to exploit venality while limiting its evils. Probably Sully's motives were of this kind, and certainly the relative straightforwardness of the *paulette* reduced the number of tricky cases in which the crown had to arbitrate. There was a simultaneous move to regularize tax-collection, replacing the officials appointed by many individual towns and provinces through the extension of the system of *élections* staffed by royal officials, the *élus*. Despite strong local opposition, this was done in Guyenne after 1603, only to be revoked by the Regency government in 1611. Sully did announce his intention of treating some other provinces in the same way, but never proceeded to action; as in so many other matters, the crown was content to make piecemeal advances when and where it could.

There is now a tendency, while conceding the value of the peace he brought to France, to treat Henri IV's reign as a time of missed opportunities, when the monarchy might have introduced major reforms. In a sense this is probably true, but one must also admit that there were many reasons why a genuine programme of reform was effectively ruled out. Above all, the ideas of the time were not favourable to innovation; any reform would have been conceived primarily in terms of a return to the past, and no satisfactory model could have been found by such means. The king and his ministers held conventional views on the relationship between crown and subjects, although they misinterpreted them when it was convenient to do so; they were not psychologically prepared to support major change, and were still fearful of a return to the disorder from which they had so recently escaped. There was also the worrying question of the succession, for the king was already forty-eight when the dauphin was born, and had survived numerous attempts on his life. Although Henri remained vigorous until his sudden end, the prospect of a regency, with all its dangers for royal power and internal peace, had been in men's minds since 1601. It is possible to find many anticipations of later 'absolutist' policies in Henri's reign, notably in his handling of the royal officials and the great nobles, although only the *paulette* marked a radical break with the conduct of his predecessors. The threat of renewed political instability was enough to ensure that the crown would avoid head-on confrontations with the powerful interest groups in French society, even had it wished for such clashes. The ultimate reason why most of the innovations of the period remained embryonic was simply that there was no war: only demands for extraordinary finance would have driven the government to take major initiatives. The first Bourbon king ruled France not according to any grand or systematic plan, but with the eye for expediency and practicality which was precisely what the situation required. To judge him fairly, his reign should be set against what had preceded it, rather than what his successors would build on his achievement.

The Regency and the ascendancy of Marie de Medici

Henri's widow, Marie de Medici, had no political experience, and her Italian origins and limited intelligence were further reasons to fear that she would prove an unsatisfactory Regent. As it turned out, the seven years of her ascendancy were far from disastrous, although this may have owed more to luck than to judgement. Marie took the obvious course of retaining the core of her husband's government, dispensing only with the unpopular and overbearing Sully (at the beginning of 1611, after some efforts to keep him on). For the next few years policy was largely determined by the three experienced ministers Villeroy, Sillery, and Jeannin. The course they pursued was rational if unheroic. Faced with the usual demands from the magnates for a greater say in the conduct of affairs, they bought them off with lavish pensions, titles, and the grant of secondary positions. Fortunately for the crown, none of the leading nobles was a popular or dominating figure, and Henri IV's deliberate efforts to maintain divisions between them had been successful; the most dangerous magnate, the Prince de Condé, next in line for the throne after the young king and his infant brother, lacked both charm and resolution. In consequence it took some time for the inevitable aristocratic discontent to mature into open opposition, and when it did so there was never much impetus behind it. Relations with the Huguenots worsened, as the government became more exclusively Catholic, while pressure was put on leading Protestant nobles to convert, but Marie and her advisers, who had been careful to confirm the Edict of Nantes, took no initiatives so violent that they would provoke renewed religious war.

Both grandees and Huguenots might have been far more dangerous if they had been able to find support from foreign powers, and here too the Regency was lucky. The German princes, anxious to retain French goodwill, were not prepared to intervene on behalf of the Huguenots; while James I of England was always ready to meddle, he was too feeble to be a real threat. Above all, Spain under Philip III and his favourite Lerma had sunk into a strange torpor, making little attempt to take advantage of the situation in France. Protracted negotiations eventually brought about a double marriage, which united Louis XIII to the Infanta Anne of Austria, and his sister to the future Philip IV. French historians once saw this as part of a pro-Habsburg policy favoured by the Queen Mother, but this appears an exaggerated view; for the ministers at least the marriages were a ploy to keep Spain quiet while the tricky few years ahead were negotiated, and spinning the discussions out was part of this process. One tenacious but ill-founded legend holds that the Papal Nuncio and the Spanish ambassador were admitted to the Regency council; in fact their dispatches suggest that they were rather poorly informed about French internal affairs, with Villeroy bamboozling them into thinking that the Huguenots were so powerful it would be very risky not to support the government. The limitations of this kind of policy would become evident as German affairs destroyed the precarious European peace, but for a few years after 1610 it was obviously the right course. Since it was also very cheap, it allowed the government to use its reserves to buy loyalty without any serious increase in taxation.

Any attempt to generalize about the political situation during the Regency is liable to smooth out the innumerable changes of balance and petty intrigues which fill the memoirs of the time. Always characteristic of court life, they were given additional force by the evident uncertainty of the Regent, and the limited power of ministers who were despised by the grandees. By the beginning of 1614 a combination of minor grievances arising out of these court squabbles, together with a general feeling among the great nobles that they were not having enough say in the government, led to a serious challenge to the Regent's authority. Condé and a number of others left court to raise troops in their local strongholds. They received little popular support, the government reacted effectively by raising its own army, and by the summer a settlement had been reached; some of the personal claims of individual rebels were satisfied, while the Regent agreed to summon the Estates General. Condé had hoped to use the Estates to further his own claims to power, but the government managed the elections so well that very few supporters of the dissident nobles were chosen as deputies. The opening of the Estates was delayed until after the formal declaration of the king's majority (as he was only thirteen, the effective power remained with his mother), and from the start the ministers seemed to have regarded the occasion as an exercise in window-dressing. The deputies naturally had other ideas which resulted in a good deal of friction, but the attempts to produce a programme of reforms ended in the presentation of some anodyne *cahiers de doléances*, which were greeted with vague royal promises, and followed by the rapid winding-up of the Estates. Much of their time had been taken up with wrangling over two issues; the relationship between the French state and the Papacy, and the venality of offices. On the first issue the Third Estate had been at loggerheads with the clergy, on the second with both the clergy and the nobles. It was plainer than ever that the structure of the Estates was radically defective, calculated to produce endless disputes between the three separate Orders; they were so manifestly useless to everyone that their disappearance from the political scene for nearly two centuries was no surprise.

The Estates were merely an episode in a long-drawn-out struggle for power; soon Condé, Bouillon, and others had left court to stage another armed demonstration, followed by a new settlement reached at Loudun in 1616, which seemed to concede most of Condé's demands for a dominant voice in the royal council. This otherwise rather insignificant revolt is important because the Huguenots rashly allied themselves with Condé, confirming the young king and many others in the belief that they were a perpetual danger to the state. Meanwhile, however, a new claimant for power was emerging, in the person of Carlo Concini, maréchal d'Ancre, husband of the Queen Mother's favourite Italian lady-in-waiting. Concini, who had already become a considerable personage before Henri IV's death, exploited his wife's favour to build up his own wealth and acquire important governorships under the Regency. Always influential with Marie de Medici, he nevertheless seems to have played only a secondary role until 1615, when his aggrandisement became a major grievance advanced by the rebellious princes. During the summer of 1616 he secured the dismissal of the veteran ministers, who were replaced by a vigorous group of the Queen Mother's personal servants; before the end of the year they had been joined by the bishop of Luçon, the future Cardinal de Richelieu, as secretary of state with special responsibility for foreign and military affairs. This palace revolution, signalled by the arrest of Condé, gave rise to yet another noble revolt, which the ministers showed every determination to crush by force of arms; by April 1617 the position of the rebels seemed hopeless, when the whole face of affairs was suddenly changed. Concini and his friends had been astonishingly blind to the need to secure the trust of the young king himself, and a gentleman of his entourage, Luynes, had persuaded Louis to break away from his mother's tutelage. The king had Concini murdered by the captain of the royal guard, the new ministers had to give way to the old, Luynes became a duke and effective master of the state, and the Queen Mother was exiled to Blois. The whole episode of Concini's power had been so brief that he remains an enigmatic figure; a self-avowed adventurer, he nevertheless impressed Richelieu as a man with serious intentions of reasserting royal authority, so there may have been more to him than his innumerable detractors admitted.

Luynes, the German conflict, and the Protestants

The new favourite was soon as detested as his predecessor; a modest gentleman from Provence, Luynes lacked both political and military experience, and used his position to amass wealth and titles for himself and his family. This was normal enough, but what made him really odious to the courtiers was his determination to monopolize the king's ear, allowing no other influence any scope at all. Apparently safe in the deep affection and admiration of the adolescent king, he could afford to disregard such envy for the moment, but he had committed himself to ruling France at a difficult juncture; too many failures would inevitably destroy his credit. Lacking any sort of personal following, Luynes had to turn to the same ministerial group as the Regent for help in finding workable policies. This was not a great success, for the death of Villeroy soon removed the ablest of the old councillors, and Sillery's son Puisieux was an inadequate replacement in charge of foreign affairs. It became apparent that France was suffering from a crisis of leadership; neither Luynes nor the grandees could supply the necessary skills, while the clique of ministerial families was now represented by tired old men or their mediocre sons. The whole problem was a neat illustration of the danger of placing excessive weight on inherited position and status, which was to be one of the recurrent difficulties of the *ancien régime*. It was almost as if there was a cyclical process, which saw one set of families establish itself, then gradually decline in ability and application until a new clique could displace it. The inadequacies of the ministers were particularly serious after 1617, because the international situation was deteriorating fast, demanding urgent attention from the French government. Existing disputes with Spain in northern Italy were absorbed into the major conflict which broke out in Germany after 1618, when the Bohemian subjects of the Habsburgs rebelled; they later elected the Protestant Elector Palatine as their new king, beginning what we now know as the Thirty Years War. With the truce between Spain and the Dutch due to expire in 1621, it was plain that the fragile European peace was about to collapse, so one major uncertainty in every statesman's mind was how France would behave. Would she follow her traditional anti-Habsburg line, supporting the Protestant powers in Germany and the Netherlands, or would the strength of Catholic feeling lead her to remain neutral, even to intervene on the side of the Emperor and the king of Spain?

The answer to this question was to be a long time coming, while the unfortunate French government, unable to make up its own mind about the policy to follow, blundered from one

irrelevant expedient to the next. This was not just a product
of incompetence, for there were great difficulties in charting a
course through these stormy waters. If France took the side of
the Protestant powers, and recent signs of Habsburg weakness
proved accurate, then Catholicism in general might suffer a
permanent setback, while the Huguenots would be encouraged
to seek external protectors. Open support for the Habsburgs,
on the other hand, risked not only restoring their power to
sixteenth-century levels, but also alienating many of France's
traditional allies. As in many ways the status quo suited France
very well, the only reasonably consistent feature of French
policy during the early 1620s was a desire to restore the pre-
1618 position; probably an impossible objective, this would
certainly have required far more vigorous measures than the
ministers dared contemplate. Luynes himself, who never seems
to have grasped the full complexity of the issues, was probably
most concerned to manage the king's susceptibilities. These
were a real and lasting problem, for Louis had been educated
into a strongly Catholic prince who was never easy about
alliances with heretics; his instinctive reaction to the crisis was
to offer support to the Emperor. The French negotiators who
arranged the treaty of Ulm (July 1620), by which the Protestant princes virtually left the Elector Palatine to be defeated
and expelled by the Habsburgs, have often been blamed, but
at least they were pursuing a more moderate line than Louis
himself, who had contemplated sending an army into Germany
to help the Emperor. In any case the government was in
serious difficulties at home, faced by a coalition of dissatisfied
grandees and the Queen Mother, and by the discontent of the
officials after the revocation of the *paulette* in 1618 and the
creation of new offices at the beginning of 1620. In exiling
Marie de Medici from the court Luynes had provided an
obvious rallying point for his enemies; he now found it necessary to permit the bishop of Luçon to act as her chief adviser,
and a go-between with the government. Faced with a typical
armed demonstration by disgruntled nobles, the king and
Luynes took the field with an army in 1620. Confronting the
king himself was more than the nobles had bargained for, so
after an ignominious rout of their forces at Ponts-de-Cé in

August they were ready enough to accept the generous terms offered them. Luynes and the king then followed the lead given by the Catholic zealots at court, marching the royal army south to settle some old scores with the Huguenots in Béarn.

This decision, apparently taken without serious deliberation, was a momentous one; it exposed the monarchy to great dangers both within and without the kingdom, and it would need years of effort to liquidate the consequences. Louis XIII had yet to learn the virtues of prudence, while Luynes was not the man to restrain or advise him, above all because the king plainly had a will of his own, which the favourite did not care to cross. The expedition to Béarn, legally quite defensible because the Huguenots there had defied royal decisions, proved something of a walk-over; by November the king was back in Paris with the Catholic church re-established in Béarn. The day after his return the Bohemian rebels were routed at the battle of the White Mountain, and the French emissaries in Germany could only stand by and watch the triumph of the Habsburgs, as over the next few months the Protestant princes abandoned all hope of resistance. The French government was desperately slow to recognize the significance of these events; in any case it had lost the power to intervene, for the use of armed force in Béarn had finally driven a large party among the Huguenots into open revolt. The king's own error had produced a similarly ill-considered response, which was far from commanding total support among the Protestants. The advocates of armed resistance had hitherto been in a minority, and although many of the towns of the Midi were now willing to follow their lead, the more exposed communities in the west and north still held aloof. Worse still, the older Huguenot grandees, Bouillon, Sully, and Lesdiguières (the virtual ruler of Dauphiné), remained loyal to the king, while many other nobles had already been converted to Catholicism. The rebels, led by the duc de Rohan and his brother Soubise, soon found that they could not oppose the royal army in the field, so it was simply a question of how long their fortresses could hold out, and how long the royal finances could bear the strain of war. They had embarked on a war they could not win, but which was of the greatest service to the Catholic cause in Europe; quite apart from absorbing the king's attention, it greatly complicated his relations with the Protestant powers, and made it more difficult for him to reconcile an anti-Habsburg policy with either his conscience or his interest. By giving some plausibility to the fears of an international Protestant conspiracy, the revolt strengthened the arguments of those who opposed all alliances with heretics, and saw safety only in a grand Catholic coalition.

The campaign of 1621 started well enough; after a reconciliation with his mother, which reduced the danger of trouble in his absence with the army, the king quickly cleared much of western France, against non-existent or half-hearted resistance. However, Luynes (now created Constable of France, amidst much derision) was an incompetent general, and he so mismanaged the siege of the major stronghold of Montauban that it had to be abandoned after three months, with heavy losses. Among these was Luynes himself, dead of camp fever in December; his disappearance was greeted with general relief, but left a void at the centre of affairs. The young king was no fool, for all his defects of personality and limited intellectual capacities, and he had already recognized some of the dangers inherent in allowing a favourite to monopolize the government. He now intended to rule through his council, to which his mother was readmitted early in 1622. Through her the ideas of her chaplain and adviser the bishop of Luçon could now reach the king, but at first it was the violently anti-Huguenot advice of the prince de Condé which prevailed, for the king was eager to return to the battlefield. The campaign of 1622 repeated the pattern of 1621; early successes followed by a check before the important fortress of Montpellier. The war was proving desperately expensive in money and blood, so the king was eventually persuaded to respond to Rohan's overtures for peace. The treaty of Montpellier (October 1622) was a heavy blow to the Huguenots, prescribing the razing of many of their strongholds, but it still left them in possession of the most important of all, Montauban and La Rochelle. Condé was so furious that he left for Italy, demonstrating once and for all his inability to sustain a major political role. In fact the crown had perhaps come out of the war better than it deserved, for the position of the Huguenots had been so weakened that most of their leaders, among both nobility and town oligarchies, were coming to the conclusion that further rebellion would be useless. As long as there were still troops and fortresses to mobilize, however, there would always be some Protestant zealots ready to turn them against the king, expecting divine intervention in favour of the righteous few. The government was soon to discover that, with such people around, only the complete disarming of the Huguenots could bring religious peace.

Meanwhile events in Europe had taken an ominous turn; the imperial cause was prospering in Germany, hostilities had resumed between Spain and the Dutch, and the long-standing disputes between France and Spain in northern Italy threatened to produce a serious diplomatic crisis. Two years of war had left the royal finances in a desperate state, which weakened French capacity to respond to these challenges; in any case the government, now dominated by chancellor Sillery and his relatives, was more concerned to exist than to take any real initiative. Louis XIII, very conscious of his prestige and dignity, was not likely to be happy with this situation for long. The most immediate problem was in the Valtelline, where French and Spanish interests clashed over control of a vital route from northern Italy to the Alpine passes. The local situation was highly confused, with the Catholic inhabitants of the valley under the suzerainty of the Protestant Grisons, among whom agents of the contending powers were always active. A seemingly endless imbroglio resulted, lasting through the 1620s and 1630s, as control of the region passed back and forth. For the French it was a matter of upholding long-established rights to a privileged position, keeping open a route which might be useful for intervention in Italy, demonstrating that France would honour her obligations to her allies, and obstructing the Spaniards The latter were determined to keep the passes open for their troops, since after Henri IV's annexation of the Bresse and Bugey area previously controlled by Savoy (1602) it was the only reliable route by which they could pass men from their recruiting and training grounds in the Duchy of Milan into Germany or up the

'Spanish Road' to Flanders. For most of the period Spain did succeed in her aim, but at the cost of repeatedly disregarding the successive treaties which purported to settle her dispute with France. The Valtelline was certainly important for its strategic position; it may have been even more crucial because Spanish conduct there was a constant provocation to France, greatly strengthening the arguments of those who urged an anti-Habsburg policy on Louis XIII. The king's annoyance at the failure of their diplomacy over this issue was the prime cause of the dismissal of Sillery and Puisieux at the beginning of 1624, a move which virtually obliged him to overcome his suspicions of the Cardinal de Richelieu (the bishop of Luçon had been promoted Cardinal in 1622) and admit him to the council. Richelieu's abilities—and ambition—were already widely recognized, he had strong backing from the Queen Mother, and alternative ministers were conspicuous only by their absence. By August 1624, having secured the disgrace of his last remaining rival, the *surintendant* La Vieuville, he could begin to install his own supporters and dependents in the central positions in the government, laying the foundations for one of the most remarkable ministries in French history.

(ii) *The Ministry of Richelieu*

The early years, 1624–30

Some astute contemporary observers saw that the appointment of an able and industrious minister might prove a turning-point in Louis XIII's reign, but it would be a long time before their opinion was clearly justified. At first Richelieu seemed as much the prisoner of the situation as his predecessors, forced into numerous switches of policy by events beyond his control. There was an ambiguity about his own position; he had come to power with the support of both the *bons français* who feared Spanish imperialism and the *dévots* who regarded heresy as the chief enemy. This was no accident, for the Cardinal himself sympathized with both positions, probably seeing no fundamental clash between them. Together with great intelligence and penetration, he possessed the fortunate ability to gloss over the numerous inconsistencies in his own attitudes; a supreme pragmatist, he carried very little ideological baggage. There is something almost laughable about the programme historians once thought to deduce from his political writings and apply to his career, for he was one of the last men to be constrained by such self-imposed shackles. The popular image of a merciless tyrant is also a gross distortion, for Richelieu's genius was as a compromiser and negotiator, although he could be ruthless when the occasion demanded. Perhaps his most remarkable success was in winning and retaining the trust and affection of the king, always a difficult and suspicious master, whose attitude was pithily summarized by La Rochefoucauld: 'He wanted to be ruled, yet chafed when he was.' There is no serious evidence that Louis ever genuinely wished to dismiss his minister, although he sometimes found it hard to resist pressure from others for him to do so. Dominated by an almost excessive sense of duty, and fully aware of Richelieu's exceptional gifts, the king repeatedly refused his offers to retire, and took his part against the intrigues of his mother and brother. On his side, the Cardinal was meticulously careful to inform the king about every detail of policy, ensuring that important decisions were taken after consulting the council and in full awareness of their implications. He put enormous effort into managing the king, watching his moods, bringing business before him when he was favourably inclined, often using third parties to sound him out or prepare him for difficult issues. Despite occasional displays of petulance, Louis responded well to this treatment; he was rightly proud of his own application to the affairs of state, and Richelieu encouraged and flattered him accordingly. With great finesse the Cardinal normally offered him a real choice; secure in the feeling that he was not being dictated to, the king was then only too glad to follow his advice.

At first Richelieu appeared ready to adopt a posture of outright hostility towards Spain. He carried through the marriage alliance with England prepared by La Vieuville (by which the king's sister Henrietta Maria married the future Charles I), agreeing to help the English and Dutch restore the unfortunate Elector Palatine in his hereditary lands. A French army invaded the Valtelline, while projects for operations in Italy were discussed with the Duke of Savoy. Meanwhile, however, the Huguenots started to give trouble again, with Soubise exploiting the king's weakness at sea to carry out a series of operations along the western coast, while Rohan raised the Cévennes. Richelieu was understandably furious at such behaviour when he was embarking on a daringly pro-Protestant foreign policy, and the threat of serious internal troubles was certainly a factor in causing him to revert to a more cautious line. One may still wonder whether Rohan and Soubise's imprudence was as important as the Cardinal found it convenient to suggest; it had soon become evident that England under Buckingham was a highly unreliable ally, the plans for intervention in Germany were little more than castles in the air, and the seizure of the Valtelline had gravely offended the Pope. The risks inherent in an aggressive foreign policy were emphasized when Spain proved her strength by the capture of the Dutch fortress of Breda (May 1625). France quickly turned to negotiation; early in 1626 the ambiguous treaty of Monçon purported to settle Franco-Spanish differences over the Valtelline, while the Protestant rebels, through English mediation, made their peace with the crown. Like Luynes before him, Richelieu seemed prepared to leave the Habsburgs a free hand in Europe, and before the end of the year he went along with the *dévot* party around the Queen Mother to the extent of concluding a defensive alliance with Spain. His intentions at this period remain surprisingly obscure; probably he had recognized the near-certainty of failure in his foreign enterprises, and decided to turn his attention to questions of internal policy. It was during 1626 that he drew up his most elaborate plans for new trading companies, convoked an Assembly of Notables to consider changes in economic and financial policy, and faced the first major conspiracy against his power. The so-called 'Chalais conspiracy' was an ominous portent for the future, as it was centred on the heir to the throne, the king's younger brother Gaston d'Orléans. For the rest of Richelieu's life this irresponsible and feckless young man was to be a constant danger; safe from reprisals himself, he would attract—and betray—a series of noble adventurers.

The relative failure of the Cardinal's first moves, admittedly masked by some very adroit face-saving, was a good illustration of his own repeated assertion that policies can only succeed when the time is ripe. The episode also underlined the dangers of trying to take the initiative, particularly serious when there were such divided counsels about the morality and wisdom of all choices. Richelieu was soon to discover the great advantages of being the counter-attacker, a position from which it was far easier to deflate internal critics by pointing to the opponent's aggression. With astonishing folly his enemies were to present him with a sequence of opportunities of just this kind, allowing him to win successes which incidentally strengthened his own hold on power. Far from working to some grandiose master plan, he was to owe his triumphs to opportunism and his dexterity in taking advantage of every chance to advance France's traditional aims. The first stroke of good fortune came in 1627, with Buckingham's bizarre and pointless decision to precipitate an Anglo-French war, into which the key Huguenot stronghold of La Rochelle was rather unwillingly drawn. The French Protestants in general showed little enthusiasm for this unwanted war, while the settlement of 1622 had greatly reduced their military power. Neither they nor the equally half-hearted English proved able to relieve La Rochelle, starved out after a fourteen month siege. By the summer of 1629, when most of the remaining Huguenot fortresses had been taken, the king was able to impose his own terms by the Peace of Alais. With an act of statesmanship it would be difficult to overpraise, for both its political shrewdness and its genuine humanity, Richelieu advised the king to confirm the Edict of Nantes, pardon the rebellion, and simply revoke the supplementary articles; the Huguenots lost their fortresses and troops, but were guaranteed liberty of conscience. The 'Peace of Grace' obtained the deserved reward, for over the next few decades the Huguenots never gave the government real cause for concern. Only in very different circumstances would Louis XIV rashly choose to undo Richelieu's work, and bring back religious strife to France.

The years 1628 and 1629, during which the Huguenots were defeated, clearly marked a watershed in the European power struggle, as the Habsburg offensive in Germany and the Netherlands reached its peak and began to falter. By 1628 the imperial general Wallenstein had reached the Baltic, where his attempts to create a fleet threatened an attack on the vital Dutch trade in the area; his menacing presence finally persuaded Gustavus Adolphus of Sweden that in self-defence as much as from ambition he should go to the help of the German Protestants. Meanwhile the Spaniards pressed slowly forwards in the Netherlands, only to be brought to a grinding halt by one of the most significant feats of arms in the century, the capture of the entire American treasure fleet by the Dutch admiral Piet Heyn at Matanzas (October 1628). The tottering edifice of Spanish war finance slid into temporary chaos, so that in 1629 it was the Dutch who were able to take the offensive. In the same year the Emperor rashly compromised his hard-won dominance in Germany by issuing the Edict of Restitution, ordering the return of secularized lands to the Catholic church. These events coincided with the appearance of a new dispute between France and Spain, arising out of the death of the duke of Mantua at the end of 1627. The heir to his territories, which included the major fortresses of Mantua and Casale, was the French duc de Nevers; having taken possession, he found himself attacked by both Spain and Savoy in support of other claimants. This was a disastrous Spanish error, which resulted largely from the familiar story of a local commander dragging his government after him; Louis XIII would have been humiliated if he had abandoned Nevers to his fate, so hostilities were inevitable. Even before the final defeat of the Huguenots the king and Richelieu had conducted a short but ferocious campaign in Savoy (March 1629), forcing the duke to revoke his alliance with Spain. It was soon apparent that this was not enough, so king and Cardinal spent much of 1630 occupying Savoy and helping Nevers. Military successes in Italy proper were fairly evenly balanced, but the imperialists and Spaniards soon realized that they were being drawn into a conflict they could not afford, in view of their problems elsewhere, and in 1631 they conceded defeat by the treaty of Cherasco. The armies had brought the plague, which ravaged both Mantua and the

Milanese (this is the setting of Manzoni's classic novel *I Promessi Sposi*); to add to Spain's woes, one of her main recruiting grounds was now rendered useless.

Opposition and the 'Day of Dupes'

The Mantuan War may have turned out to be a highly successful enterprise, but it had narrowly failed to bring about Richelieu's downfall. His moderate treatment of the Huguenots had offended his one-time allies in the *dévot* group around the Queen Mother, led by the Cardinal de Bérulle (who died in October 1629) and the *garde des sceaux* Michel de Marillac. Although recognizing the compelling reasons for supporting Nevers, they were always unhappy about the prospect that France might be drawn into an all-out war against Spain, which would mean abandoning all hope of a general Catholic crusade or of internal reforms. They could emphasize the need for the latter by pointing to the numerous signs of dissension and rebellion within the kingdom, and the ruinous state of the finances. In almost every year since 1620 the king had mustered a substantial army, costly enough in itself, while major campaigns like those of 1621–2 and 1628–30 were prodigiously expensive. Successive *surintendants* had resorted to every known financial device to meet the bills; apart from increasing existing taxes and introducing new ones, they had sold great numbers of offices, extorted large sums from existing officials, and secured loans and advances against future revenues. Richelieu had originally planned various measures to reduce abuses among the officials and put the finances on a sound footing, along with his schemes for founding trading companies and expanding the royal navy. None too convincing in any case, these plans relied on the unlikely assumption that France could avoid costly entanglements abroad for several years, at a time when a general European war was raging. The Assembly of Notables which met around the turn of the years 1626–7 to consider the government's ideas was not very helpful; since the only way out of current obligations was to find large sums of money to liquidate them, the chief preoccupation of the different groups was to ensure this was not at their expense. After the dissolution of the Assembly, Marillac was charged with preparing an enormous ordinance, clarifying and regulating virtually every aspect of the relations between crown and subjects. Nicknamed the 'code Michaud' after its draughtsman, this was an unwieldy collection of pious hopes, which inevitably contained something to upset almost everybody; all that was lacking was any plausible scheme for enforcing it. The *parlement* of Paris, already hostile on many grounds, was further irritated when the king, anxious to leave for the campaign in Savoy, enforced registration by a *lit de justice* early in 1629, without allowing time for proper discussion or modifications. Like its sixteenth-century predecessors, the *code* soon became a dead letter in most respects; after Marillac's disgrace the government openly connived at the evasion of many of its provisions by the courts, while ignoring others itself.

In the predictable absence of genuine reforms, the ministers tried to increase revenue by putting pressure on the groups which depended on the crown and were known to have capital reserves. The threat of a *chambre de justice* extracted reparations from the financiers in 1624, but this was not an operation which could be repeated too frequently, since the major financiers had become indispensable to a state always desperate for ready cash. They could only be stripped of some of their gains occasionally, whereas the crown was under no such restraints in the case of its judicial and financial officials. The long-standing practice of raising money through the sale of offices had not deprived the government of all authority over the holders, who were to some extent the victims of a prolonged confidence trick. The king retained wide if ill-defined rights to regulate the exercise of delegated powers by his officials; in practice he could severely reduce both the rewards and status of particular groups. The terms of tenure were also subject to royal control, and while the suppression of the *paulette* in 1618 had produced many difficulties, which combined with renewed internal hostilities to bring about its reintroduction in 1621, it was the custom only to grant this highly-valued privilege for a set term of years. Secure in the knowledge that the officials as a group enjoyed little public sympathy, the crown was effectively in a position to blackmail them into further payments for the maintenance of their privileges. During the 1620s a variety of methods were deployed with this aim; the introduction of new offices in existing courts and bureaux, the establishment of parallel bodies which acted in alternate years, the redistribution of functions to allow the creation of new bodies, and other similar devices. Often the government was prepared to withdraw these measures, covered as they were by the merest fig-leaf of pretended public interest, against 'indemnities' by the endangered officials. None of this was new, but the intensity with which the officials were squeezed during this period was unprecedented, leading to widespread disobedience and resistance. This was a serious matter, for the consequences could include virtual judicial strikes and delays in the collection of taxes; worse still, the 'sovereign' courts such as the *parlements* and *cours des aides* could block financial innovations and creations of office by refusing registration. Ultimately the king could force compliance with his wishes, but at a severe cost, for it was far easier to implement new legislation when it was not hampered by the continuing ill-will of recalcitrant officials. Generally it suited both sides to reach a compromise, so the outcome was a repeated pattern of exaggerated royal demands, followed by threats of resistance and negotiations, ending in substantial modifications to the original proposals.

In allowing the *parlements* and other bodies such frequent exercise of a vaguely limited power of veto over royal legislation the government was mortgaging the future as surely as by the accumulation of an immense state debt, yet there was no obvious alternative. King, ministers, and officials shared certain understandings about the nature of the state which were more effective in limiting royal despotism than any strict legalism could have been. The monarchy was generally recognized to be absolute, but its authority was tempered by respect for the rights and privileges of its subjects, which the king confirmed by his coronation oath. It was tacitly accepted that the process of judicial review, by which the higher courts monitored legislation, was a guarantee of this royal commitment; ministers overrode it with great reluctance, aware that excessive use of enforced registration was politically dangerous.

Contemporary pamphleteers found an apt phrase when they wrote of the veil that should cover the inner mysteries of the state, a concept which emphasized both the vagueness and fragility of these assumptions. In various ways the actions of Richelieu and his colleagues were to do almost irremediable violence to the traditional polity of France, but there is no sign that this was intentional; at a time of extreme strain, a determined government was inevitably driven to expose the basic contradictions of the system. Many of the difficulties stemmed from the sheer proliferation of offices and agencies, giving rise to what has appropriately been called a 'confusion of powers', in which boundary disputes between different bodies became endemic. At a higher level, the competence of the various component parts of the royal council to intervene and remove cases from the ordinary courts was never clearly defined, producing a perpetual paper war of countermanding *arrêts*. The widespread dissatisfaction of the officials made it still more difficult to rely on them to enforce royal decisions in the localities, an important point when most courts had loosely defined powers of *police* in their own sphere of action. The introduction of new taxes gave a further means of resisting the government, for popular resentment against these innovations could easily be exploited by municipalities normally dominated by officials and their relatives. By the end of the 1620s behaviour of this kind was becoming uncomfortably common, and the position was worsened by the important *crises de subsistence* and outbreaks of plague which marked the years 1628–31.

Confronted by stiffening resistance from its own servants, the government tried to use the expiry of the *paulette* at the end of 1629 as a crude bargaining weapon. The results were alarming, with a series of urban revolts in 1629–30 finding the local authorities sympathetic; notable cases were in the *parlementaire* towns of Dijon and Aix, where the rebels known respectively as the *lanturlus* and the *cascaveoux* claimed to be defending provincial liberties, and neither officials nor governor showed any zeal in repressing them. In both these cases a major cause of revolt was a renewed attempt to introduce the *élus* into provinces which had previously managed their own tax-collection, but the attitude of the officials was clearly influenced by the uncertainty over the *paulette*. Over the past few years they had also been irritated by the manner in which Marillac had tried to enforce previously disregarded rules, notably those preventing too many close relatives sitting in the same court. The *garde des sceaux* was well-known for his authoritarian temperament and his taste for drawing up systematic regulations; much of the pressure for greater control over the officials and the reduction of venality probably came from him. Over these questions, as over other matters of policy, he placed the demands of religion and morality before those of political expediency, and this was bound eventually to bring him into conflict with Richelieu. All the ministers probably agreed that it was necessary to supervise the officials carefully, not least because of the many disputes and jealousies between them. The obvious way to achieve this was through a well-established practice of sending out royal *commissaires*: individuals whose powers were defined by a special commission in the king's name. This technique had been in frequent use since the middle of the sixteenth century, although in a rather spasmodic fashion, and the *commissaires* had varying responsibilities laid on them. Some were concerned with the organization of specific financial measures, others with logistic support for the armies, others again with reducing corruption or partiality among both financial and judicial officials. Known under a variety of names, among them *commissaires départis* and *intendants*, a common feature was that their duties cut across the normal operations of the established bureaucracy, even when they were not specifically concerned to check its abuses. Often empowered to try cases without reference to the ordinary courts, the *commissaires* were naturally unpopular with the other officials; this unpopularity increased during the period after 1617, when the government reacted to widespread disobedience by making greater use of them. After 1624 the commissions of the *intendants* became more wide-ranging, and more damaging to the pretensions of the *parlements* and other bodies, although their presence in a particular province was still the exception rather than the rule.

The use of *intendants* was partly a recognition by the government that its regular administrative machinery could not be relied on under the strain imposed by war finance. Marillac and those who thought like him were gravely concerned by the evidence of a progressive breakdown of the normal process of law, and frightened by the wave of revolts in 1629-30; they also believed that Richelieu was drawing the king into foreign adventures from which it would be very difficult to withdraw. In the light of what happened in the 1630s these were very justifiable fears, and the divisions within the royal council in 1630 were more than just a clash of personalities. The king had to choose between two sets of risks; those to his authority at home if he adopted a relatively aggressive foreign policy, and those to his prestige and France's international position if he left the Habsburgs a virtually free hand in Europe. The historian is badly placed to judge between these options, since Marillac's policy was never put to the test, while Richelieu's had such complex and contradictory results that it defies any simple assessment in terms of success or failure. In the short run Richelieu was clearly right in wanting to push the Mantuan War to a conclusion, for the settlement of 1631, much more favourable than any that could have been reached in 1630, was not itself the cause of further hostilities.

The great importance of the choice, however, was that the king and the ministers saw it as a decisive option; after 1630 there seems to have been far less debate about the desirability of an interventionist foreign policy. The events of 1630 are rightly seen as a crucial turning-point in the history of the French monarchy, for when Louis XIII effectively committed his state to a major conflict with Spain he initiated a process of drastic, almost revolutionary change. Most of these changes were to be in directions the king and Richelieu would probably have approved, but they would involve running greater risks than they can have envisaged. With the advantage of hindsight it seems probable that their judgement of the international situation was faulty; the Habsburgs were already in such difficulties that they would have been very unlikely to defeat either the Protestant armies in Germany or the Dutch, even without French intervention. It is hardly fair to criticize

Richelieu on these grounds, for it would have required extra-ordinary percipience to see the true weakness of his enemies in the early 1630s. Given the very aggressive policies of the Spaniards in a whole range of disputed zones along the borders, there was no plausible middle way between inter-vention and complete neutrality, for the pro-French parties and rulers, already discouraged by the experiences of the past decade, would soon have abandoned their allegiance if they were not better supported. Although Richelieu saw that he had an excellent opportunity to reverse the run of Habsburg successes, he proceeded with great caution, avoiding open war as long as possible. Perhaps the most damaging criticism is that participation in the Thirty Years War began a sequence of military adventures which eventually cost France dear. In the light of the previous record of the French monarchy, how-ever, it may be doubted whether the victory of the *dévot* party would have meant the permanent renunciation of such policies. If one is playing the game of assigning moral responsibility, the case argued by Richelieu's own propagandists remains immensely strong: it was the obstinate determination of the Habsburgs to seek military solutions in Germany, the Netherlands, and Italy which was the ultimate cause of the war.

The moral attractions of Marillac's desire to avoid war and lift some of the burdens off the people of France have to be set against his willingness to impose Catholicism by force; after the Peace of Alais, Richelieu had some difficulty in preventing him from harrying the Huguenots through a narrowly legalis-tic application of the Edict of Nantes. It would have been difficult for the two men to remain in the royal council for long after 1629, but Marillac brought matters to a head by his intrigues against Richelieu during the following year. The Queen Mother, who regarded the Cardinal as her protégé, had been progressively infuriated by his independent hold over the king, and was easily persuaded to seek his dismissal. Louis tried to temporize and settle the quarrel, but after the court had returned to Paris his mother renewed the attack; the result was the famous 'Day of Dupes' (10 November 1630). After a violent scene between Queen Mother, king, and

Cardinal, Louis was so distressed that observers thought Richelieu had lost, and he himself shared their view. The courtiers flocked to the Luxembourg Palace to congratulate Marie de Medici, only to discover next morning that the king had opted unequivocally for Richelieu, and that Marillac was under arrest.

The road to war, 1630–42

No great changes of policy followed these dramatic events, but they made a considerable difference to the nature of the inner circle of royal councillors. The Queen Mother obstinately refused to resume her place in the council, until in the summer of 1631 she sought refuge in the Spanish Netherlands, never to return to France. The uneasy balance between different opinions gave way to a new situation, in which all major offices were filled by men who signalled their devotion to Richelieu by describing themselves as his *créatures*; with this clientele solidly implanted at the centre of affairs the council would become a docile instrument of the Cardinal's will. Opponents of his policies would in future have to express themselves in revolt or in appeals to public opinion, already awakened by a considerable pamphlet literature. Richelieu himself, who had used the latter technique since the early 1620s, was extremely quick to see the possibilities of official propaganda, employing a group of political writers for the purpose, and subsidizing an official newspaper, the *Gazette*. After 1630 a flood of pro-government treatises and pamphlets praised Richelieu as the exponent of *raison d'état*, the true protector of France's national interests, who knew how to outplay the Spaniards at their own game in order to preserve European liberties from their tyranny. Publishing in secret or abroad, a small group of opponents sounded a contrasting note, denouncing the alliances with heretics, the harsh treatment of the royal family and the grandees, the crushing weight of taxation, and the Cardinal's personal arrogance. Appealing to concepts of natural order in support of their favoured policy of alliance with the Catholic powers against the Protestants, these writers were always inclined to argue by analogy; in contrast, the best of the government supporters were analytic in their approach, seeking to establish legitimate distinctions between religion and politics. Although it produced no major contributions to political theory, this is a fascinating episode in the history of ideas, which demonstrates the very real difficulties of reconciling political practice with any general moral code. Many of the arguments employed were those familiar from the debates of *ligueurs* and *politiques*, but they were now being explored to the point where it became plain that they represented radically different styles of thought. How far the readers of this literature were impressed by one or the other view remains obscure; the extent to which the debate over the major political choices before the government was carried on in the public eye is nevertheless surprising.

Much of the anxiety over foreign policy in the early 1630s stemmed from events which were largely independent of French influence, notably the victories of the king of Sweden. By the time he was killed in battle at the end of 1632 Gustavus Adolphus had effectively destroyed all the imperial gains of the preceding decade in Germany, to change the whole aspect of the European conflict. Nominally an ally of France, his success had been so overwhelming that Richelieu was probably relieved at the news of his death, for French policy aimed to restore a balance in Germany, not to bring about a Protestant triumph. However much double-think they may have contained, the claims to distinguish between the interests of Catholicism and the ambitions of the Habsburgs were perfectly sincere, and Richelieu's *raison d'état* was not the outright Machiavellianism of which he has often been accused. In retrospect it is obvious that the theory was a precarious and temporary compromise, which opened the way to a purely secular approach to politics, but at the time it was a plausible effort to find a middle way. It was in this spirit that the French agents in Germany, organized by Richelieu's confidential adviser Father Joseph, tried to use the Catholic Elector of Bavaria and the imperial general Wallenstein as counterweights to the Swedish armies. The eventual failure of these projects pushed France towards the outright alliances with the leading Protestant powers, Sweden and the United

Provinces, which she had so long avoided, bringing her closer to open war. The final impetus was provided by the events of the winter and spring of 1634–5, when the heavy defeat of the Swedes at Nordlingen was followed by the Peace of Prague, a compromise settlement between the leading Protestant princes and the Emperor. At this moment an end to the German war might have been possible, but there could be no general peace unless Spain abandoned her futile attempts to reconquer the Netherlands, with the associated pretensions to control a land route up the Rhine. No-one thought for a moment that the Spaniards, whose fortunes had seemed to be reviving in 1634, would contemplate such a renunciation; in fact they were now anxious to force a rupture with France. The undeclared hostilities of the previous years had allowed Louis XIII to send troops into Germany, subsidize their enemies, and seize control of Lorraine, without any possibility of retaliation. Several provocative steps, including the capture of the town of Trier and its Elector, an ally of France, led to the formal declaration of war in May 1635.

It might have appeared that the intervention of France would so tip the balance of forces that the defeat of the Habsburgs would now be rapid; such ideas were probably current in Paris. This was to reckon without the conditions of seventeenth-century warfare, which were very unfavourable to quick decisions. The development of fortifications, and the relative stagnation of artillery techniques, made sieges slow and costly affairs, while the problems of supplying armies rendered long-range thrusts highly dangerous ventures. Few wars of the period were concluded by outright military victories; it was rather a matter of which combatant eventually cracked under the financial strain of keeping his forces in the field. Richelieu never seems to have fully grasped these crucial facts, while even if he had, it would not have been easy to persuade the king and his generals that they were committed to a war of attrition. Many of France's setbacks after 1635 derived from over-ambitious plans, involving the mustering of armies too big for the king to pay or supply properly. The commanders of these motley hordes often had to abandon the official plan of campaign, giving first priority to finding something for their men to eat; on other occasions desertions and indiscipline wrecked vital sieges. At the outset there was another danger in the much greater experience of the opposing troops and generals, hardened to the conditions prevailing in the Netherlands and Germany. The Spaniards, however, were also out in their strategic reckoning, believing that an offensive in northern France would be sufficient to divert French efforts from other fronts. Although the Army of Flanders advanced menacingly towards Paris in 1636, it could not sustain this pressure, and the French managed to grind slowly forward elsewhere. At a terrible cost in blood and treasure, Richelieu's policy gradually sapped the strength of his enemies, until in 1640 Spain was struck by disaster when the successful revolt of Catalonia was followed by that of Portugal. This was a decisive turning-point, but it did not bring an end to the war; Spain fought obstinately on, and at the conventional rate of siege warfare she still had considerable power to resist, if not to win. Just how long hostilities would have continued without the deaths of Richelieu and Louis XIII (in December 1642 and May 1643 respectively) we cannot know. Certainly the prospect of troubles during the long royal minority ahead was a great inducement for the Spaniards to drag things out, hoping for some change of fortune which might strengthen their negotiating position.

Noble conspiracy and rebellion

If the memory of the Wars of Religion was not enough, the manifest difficulties in enforcing the government's will under Richelieu must have encouraged France's opponents to take this kind of gamble. The frequency of revolts, by both the privileged groups and the common people, emphasized the widespread hostility to the innovations of the central power, although it was also a back-handed tribute to the determination with which these policies were being carried into the localities. For both king and Cardinal the popular resistance to tax-collection seems to have been a secondary concern; such rebellions were commonplace, merely demonstrating the well-known ignorance and irresponsibility of 'la lie du peuple', as their rulers thought of them. Royal agents were always ready to sense more sinister motivations behind such events, embroidering fantasies of treasonable conspiracies around the merest scraps of evidence. This obsession with the supposed instigators of what were often spontaneous outbursts of popular fury is a very revealing one, not only because it shows a certain contempt for the people, apparently thought too brutish to take an independent initiative. It also reflects more accurate perceptions of the extent to which the nobles still credited themselves with a special licence to employ violence against personal rivals or royal officials, of the widespread opposition to the war policy even among the upper classes, and of the fact that the really dangerous revolts were those which had clear political objectives. For the social historian the noble conspiracies and rebellions are liable to be less interesting than the reactions of the ordinary people, but he should not forget that the government was right to think the former the greater threat.

Opposition to Richelieu's government, especially after 1630, was partly a response to his monopoly of patronage and power, which he distributed among his *créatures*. More than any of his predecessors, he transported the practices of *fidélité*, so deeprooted among the lesser nobility of Poitou from which he came, into the management of the central administration. In no other age would one expect to find a secretary of state, a great personal favourite of the minister, ending a letter as Chavigny did, with the assurance that he had 'nothing else on my mind but the care to please Monseigneur, and the passion to show him by all my actions that I am his very humble, very obedient, very faithful and very obliged *créature* . . .'. Such a tone may now seem odious, but in the context of its time it expressed a reciprocal commitment of great solidity, with obedience and service standing to be rewarded by social and political advancement. As Richelieu entrenched his power, so he vastly expanded his clientele, until it was almost identified with the royal administration itself. Even the prince de Condé, the greatest nobleman in France and a notoriously difficult character, accepted such a relationship to the Cardinal, to the extent of marrying his son into his family. For Richelieu's relatives and close associates, the system meant a flood of titles, including several of *duc et pair*, of great offices, of pensions, or of bishoprics and archbishoprics. At first sight such practices may seem hard to justify; they did indeed shock many contemporaries, notably those who failed to benefit from them. The Cardinal's critics were quick to point out that only his *fidèles* had ready access to the king, and that loyalty to the minister was being elevated above loyalty to the monarch. Such criticisms were well founded, but there was another side to the picture. To a greater extent than had ever been true of royal patronage, Richelieu's favour was dependent on the highest degree of loyalty and service; administrators or military commanders who failed in their duties were liable to summary disgrace. It is difficult not to admire the skill with which Richelieu exploited the techniques previously used by opponents of the crown, making them the basis of his drive to recover power for the centre of the state. This inevitably led to a new degree of polarization, which temporarily sharpened antagonisms and resentments, but eventually gave the monarchy such a dominant position as the great source of patronage that all lesser systems were rendered marginal.

The determination to concentrate the means of buying loyalty under the government's control worsened one already difficult problem, that posed by the king's brother Gaston d'Orléans. Younger sons have usually been a severe liability in monarchical systems, and until 1638 Gaston was also the heir presumptive to the throne. His character was no help, for beneath the superficial charm he was idle and weak; always bearing the imprint of whoever had sat on him last, he was the perfect target for any ambitious malcontent, who could work through him. His relations with the elder brother, never very good, had been severely damaged by the Chalais affair of 1626, when he was accused of plotting to seize the throne. This seems very implausible, although some members of his entourage may have toyed with such ideas; for all his faults Gaston himself appears to have disapproved of plans for violent palace coups, and he would on more than one occasion refuse to give the signal for a planned assassination of Richelieu. The king's mistrust, however, combined with general political considerations, meant that his brother was excluded from any independent rôle, and granted only a modest apanage from the royal estates. Always his mother's favourite child, he naturally reacted badly to the 'Day of Dupes' and its aftermath, leaving court early in 1631 to begin a series of conspiracies and revolts which only ended with his return in 1634. During the intervening period he had drawn a number of unfortunate nobles into joining his campaign against Richelieu, among them the greatest nobleman of France outside the royal house itself, the duc de Montmorency. When Gaston took a small army into France in 1632 Montmorency tried to exploit the unpopularity of royal policies in the province of Languedoc, of which he was governor, to bring the Estates into open rebellion behind him. For all his personal popularity, the risks were so obvious that few followed him, and he was captured by the royal forces at Castelnaudary. The doctors managed to patch up his serious wounds so that he could stand his trial and be executed at Toulouse at the end of October 1632: several lesser followers of Gaston had already suffered a similar fate. Such treatment of one of the greatest figures in France, who had a fine personal record of service to the crown, caused a sensation, with endless appeals for clemency being made to the king. Louis showed no sign of yielding, and while there is no doubt Richelieu approved of this harsh attitude, it was almost certainly one which came naturally to the king. An obstinate, withdrawn man, he had a merciless, almost sadistic streak in his character; there is good reason to suppose that he played a large part in setting that style of remorseless punishment which was the grimmest side of his reign.

To complete the picture of personal difficulties within the royal family, Louis was frequently on bad terms with his queen, Anne of Austria. Naturally inclined to support the pro-Spanish *dévots*, the queen provided a centre for court intrigue and disaffection; in 1637 she was discovered to be carrying on a secret correspondence with her Spanish relatives, and her subsequent disgrace was only partly removed after the birth of the dauphin. Her influence on Louis was always slight, however, so Richelieu's special relationship with the king was much more severely threatened by the favourites who could exploit the latter's affection. When Louis's platonic affair with the pious Mlle de La Fayette allowed her and her friends to oppose the Cardinal's foreign policy as irreligious, Richelieu tried to meet this threat by producing a favourite of his own, in the shape of the son of one of his *fidèles*, the dead *surintendant* d'Effiat. The result was a disaster; the marquis de Cinq Mars, as the young man soon became, proved to be a moody and uncontrollable wastrel, who soon developed independent political ambitions. It was around Cinq Mars, much more than Orléans, that the last noble conspiracies of the reign were built in 1641–2. The secret treaty between the rebels and Spain, whose discovery led to the execution of Cinq Mars in the summer of 1642, was an act of treason shocking even by the relaxed standards of its time; perhaps this reflected the desperation of Richelieu's opponents at their repeated failures to shake the king's support for him. Similar feelings may have inspired the comte de Soissons to lead an army including Spanish troops into eastern France in 1641; his victory at La Marfée might have had serious consequences if he had not contrived to blow out his own brains at the moment of triumph (lifting his vizor with his pistol). These high-placed rebels harped constantly on the old theme of the virtuous king led astray by an evil and scheming minister, which provided some flimsy defence against the accusation of treason to the king himself, and probably they ended up by partially convincing themselves of its truth. Many nobles must have agreed, yet this did not mean that serious conspiracies were a constant feature of the political scene; under Richelieu they were concentrated in the periods 1626–32 and 1641–2. Factors discouraging such activity may have included a basic loyalty to the king, fear of harsh punishment, and Richelieu's use of the patronage system to win over many potential opponents.

Resistance to war finance; the popular revolts

In the nature of things it was only revolts led by great personages that would aim for such major political objectives as a change of ministry. All other rebellions were essentially directed to the preservation of existing rights and privileges, or the protection of local interests. Provincial nobles, royal officials, artisans, and peasants alike were increasingly jumpy as they felt the strain of a general economic recession, rapidly followed by the enormous increase in royal taxation. A great variety of particular grievances might be grafted on to the general malaise, from the rough treatment of the officials to the unfair assessment of taxes by those same officials. In view of these characteristics of popular revolts, it comes as no surprise that the great majority of such outbursts took place between the years 1630–60, and thus coincided with the period of transition to the 'absolutist' state. As this transition was itself a chaotic and disorganized process, representing the brutal acceleration of previous trends under the pressure imposed by a desperate war, it was peculiarly painful and abrupt. In the middle of these unplanned and piecemeal changes it was difficult for even their makers to understand what was happening, so inevitably the opposition too was fragmented, local, and frequently ill-directed. Among the numerous contemporary terms for describing violent resistance to the government's agents or other authorities, *émotions populaires* seems the most apt. It conveys something of both the communal excitement and the feelings of justified anger involved, while hinting at the rhythms and patterns characteristic of these episodes, which were fairly well understood by the government and its representatives. The vast majority of revolts were demonstrations, limited to symbolic minor breaches of public order; rarely punished, they frequently produced concessions by the authorities. The nature of the phenomenon as a whole can only be understood if one recognizes the extent to which revolts of this kind were tacitly accepted as a legitimate form of political action.

Many disturbances were directed against particular individuals or groups, such as the *échevins* or *consuls* who ran the affairs of the community, or the regional courts controlling financial and legal administration. In such cases there were often faction struggles among the ruling groups, which might lead them to use a popular cause to rally support among the poorer elements in local society. This could produce one of the bread riots which remained a regular feature of urban life until after the Revolution. There is no reason, however, to

doubt the spontaneity of most of these outbreaks, which frequently began among the women in the market-place; apart
from the natural desire to protect their families, the women
knew that since they were regarded as relatively irresponsible,
they were very unlikely to be punished. Bread riots played an
important part in maintaining some kind of balance between
the interests of the masses and those of the ruling minority;
without sanctions of this kind it is doubtful whether the rich
and powerful would have taken much action to keep prices
down and ensure reasonable supplies of grain. They were
largely confined to the towns, for in the countryside the poor
were too directly dependent on the bigger men for employment, while informal local charity probably functioned better.
Another regular cause of disorder and violence was the movement of troops, who habitually left a trail of rape and pillage,
leading one *intendant* to describe them as 'the plague which
will destroy this state'. At the news of their approach towns
would shut their gates and peasants abandoned their villages;
small detachments or stragglers were often the targets for
revenge after the atrocities committed by their comrades. In
this world of intense local solidarities the soldier was an out-
sider, and his own consciousness of the fact encouraged him to
treat the civilian population as his enemies. In any case the
government's failure to provide proper funds, combined with
the malversations of officers and contractors, forced the troops
to live off the country. Many of the problems were most acute
during the period of winter quarter, and ill-feeling was
increased because the authorities exploited the fear of billeting to justify special taxes. The revenues from these were
meant to replace local arrangements for supporting the
troops, but in practice they were swallowed up in the general
tax revenue, while the old abuses continued unchecked. On
the whole the government could afford to disregard troubles
connected with its armies, for the soldiers could normally look
after themselves, and the widespread hostility to them even
had a useful tendency to discourage desertion. The cumulative
effects of the troops' behaviour, however, must have contributed to the climate of fear and resentment which did so much
to generate more dangerous revolts.

All the major popular revolts of this century were fundamentally directed against the rising burden of royal taxation,
although they might have some secondary features which were
not. Many of these peripheral aspects were the consequence of
the government's efforts to overcome the widespread resistance to taxation, by making changes in the system of collection, and attacking institutions or rights which had proved to
be foci of opposition. Other causes of discontent, such as
monetary problems (particularly with the copper coins), or
Richelieu's large-scale demolition of noble fortresses, were
merely further variants on the same theme. Revolts which
proved sufficiently large and protracted to call for military
repression were preponderantly rural; in these cases it is very
rare to find evidence of hostility between landlords and tenants
(the great exception is the 1675 Breton rising of the *torrében*).
These outbreaks among the peasantry were primarily against
the activities of the tax-collectors and other officials, and
therefore merged into the general opposition between town
and country, for the hated royal agents were normally town-
dwellers. Peasant revolts frequently culminated in attacks on
the towns by peasant armies, who wanted to lynch the
gabeleurs who had taken refuge within the walls, and the
attackers might be assisted by the poorer inhabitants of the
faubourgs. The ruling groups in the towns were well aware of
the hatred that the peasantry felt towards them, and made
sure they were kept out; in numerous urban revolts the first
concern of the *garde bourgeoise* was to hold the gates, preventing
any junction between the urban rioters and the peasants.
There were certainly a large number of urban revolts, but
their concern was with the indirect taxes, such as the *aides*, or
sometimes with the forced loans, rather than with the *taille*,
and they tended to follow different patterns. Specialist groups,
like the innkeepers or the tanners, would take the lead in
exciting popular anger against those who arrived to declare
and collect new or increased taxes. On occasion it was the
local officials, in tacit sympathy with the rioters, who leaked
information or rumours; prosperous members of the community were too well aware of the danger of reprisals to
risk prolonged or excessively violent opposition. A display of

popular antagonism towards the intruders, leading to their withdrawal, was merely the prelude to negotiations in which the local leadership sought to obtain a formal pardon, alongside the abolition or reduction of the offending tax. This controlled use of revolt was possible for two reasons: the existence of the *garde bourgeoise*, a reasonably well trained and equipped militia which could normally be relied on to prevent a complete breakdown of order; and the relatively sophisticated attitudes of many artisans and craftsmen, aware that limited objectives were all that could be attained. Despite these factors, a minority of urban revolts did get out of hand, because the ruling groups were divided or irresolute, or on account of exceptionally strong popular feelings. The kind of episodes which occurred at Bordeaux and Agen in 1635, at Moulins in 1640, at Montpellier in 1645, or at Aubenas in 1670 demonstrated how anti-fiscal riots could develop into confrontations between rich and poor. Overtones of this kind were relatively common, but these cases were very unusual in that they were translated into action.

In the countryside the only authority comparable to that of the town *notables* was that of the lesser nobility, who could normally muster a force of servants and dependants, and held limited supplies of arms. Other individuals such as the *curés* and the rural lawyers and notaries, might emerge as leaders in rebellions, but they had no established following of this semi-military kind. In the rural context it was the *taille* and other associated direct taxes which provided the major issue, with incidents commonly sparked off by attempts to enforce payment rather than by the assessment itself. The enormous increase in the sums demanded in the 1630s led to a mounting problem of arrears; this in its turn made the collectors use force on an ever-widening scale. The seizure of goods and animals, the *contrainte solidaire* which made the whole community responsible for the unpaid tax of individuals, and the bilieting of troops, were all widely used in the late 1630s in an attempt to terrorize the peasantry into paying. From a situation in which relatively light taxes were levied with a degree of grudging consent, the crown's demands had created a new mood of bitter and sustained resistance, so that the money could only be extracted by the threat or actual use of force. This meant the intrusion of alien elements into the rural communities, one of whose natural reactions was to invoke the protection traditionally afforded by the local nobility. The attitudes of the nobles themselves encouraged this appeal; they had long been accustomed to run affairs their own way, with little regard for any outside authority, and a good deal of feuding and violence. They were contemptuous of the lawyers and officials of the towns, representatives of an encroaching culture of paper writs and judgements which they could rarely enforce. The nobles knew that possession was nine-tenths of the law, and acted accordingly in disputes over property or other rights; such behaviour was easily extended to cover the defence of the community against the tax-collectors. Personal violence was seldom the object of effective sanctions, while gentlemen did not expect to be punished for injuring or killing their social inferiors. This cultural background was more important in determining the nobility's attitude than any specific desire to protect their economic interests, in the form of rents and feudal dues, against competition from the taxes. In areas such as Normandy and south-west France the rural nobles were responsible for persistent lawlessness and attacks on tax officials, which had serious effects on both the government's ability to collect the *taille* and the costs of doing so.

Unruly and dangerous though they were, the nobles were also basically loyal to the king, and saw themselves more as opposing the unauthorized misdeeds of his agents than as challenging the royal authority itself. There was a basic ambivalence in their attitude; willing to encourage persistent small-scale disobedience, they generally shrank from anything that resembled open revolt. Although the nobles did not generally respond very well when summoned to aid the governor or his deputy, there were occasions when they helped to repress large-scale risings. Their failure to participate in such revolts, which was certainly very obvious, must on its own eventually have weakened the bonds between them and the local communities. The peasants could hardly have avoided feeling betrayed when their local protectors, who had previously backed them against the outsiders, suddenly deserted them in the real crisis. Such developments are very difficult to measure, but by the 1660s the first signs of local hostility to the lesser nobility were appearing, almost certainly connected with a significant decline in their power to render services to the community. Armed protection was no longer much use against an increasingly effective tax machine, even if the nobles had shown themselves more effective defenders of local privileges. Their conflicting loyalties had caused them to behave inconsistently, stirring up trouble, yet finally supporting the government. Such conduct pleased no-one, and ultimately led to an enduring loss of both prestige and power; this decline in the influence of the rural nobility was an enormous help to the expansion and entrenchment of the royal authority in the localities. Much of the power of the lesser nobles had in any case depended on their organization through the clientage systems of the great magnates, and although these seem gradually to have withered away, the manner in which they did so remains something of a mystery. One reason why the leading nobles demanded provincial governorships was to secure substantial patronage with which they could reward supporters, but this can never have gone far among such enormous followings as those of Condé, Épernon, or La Rochefoucauld. Traditional loyalties, combined with the need for self-protection in a still violent society, must have been of greater general importance than any tangible returns in offices or pensions. In this context it seems likely that the behaviour of the grandees during the Fronde, the subsequent enforcement of law and order under Louis XIV, and the centralization of patronage at court, all helped to break the ties between different strata of the nobility.

The most crucial episodes in detaching the peasantry from their traditional protectors were the major revolts, which marked the period of warfare after 1635. These outbursts habitually began in the spring, with a series of attacks on the tax-collectors leading to assemblies of large numbers of peasants at which lists of grievances were prepared. The programme which repeatedly emerged was simplistic, even unrealistic, based on the idea of returning to an imaginary golden age at least a generation back, often expressed in the

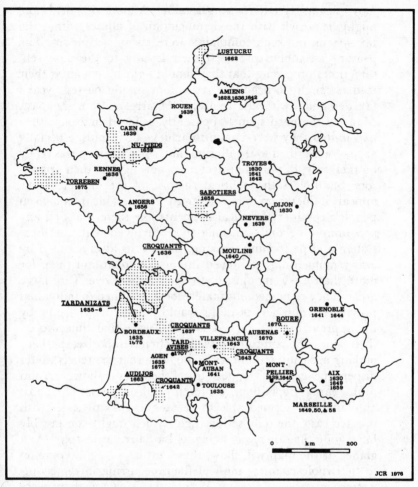

Certain urban riots and peasant revolts under Louis XIII and Louis XIV (1630–1715)

naïve slogan 'vive le roi sans la taille'. A more practical note might be struck with the denunciation of abuses within the tax system, but such complaints were always secondary. The peasant assemblies professed their loyalty to the monarch, sometimes proposing that they should fight his enemies; their leaders sought to negotiate reductions in the current year's tax demands, with the remission of arrears from the past. Many of the participants apparently believed that once they had united they were bound to achieve their ends, especially as they subscribed to the illusion that, since the king was really on their side, he would protect his people against their oppressors. Shabby as the political rhetoric of the day may now appear, it does seem to have exerted considerable influence on people's conduct at critical moments like these. Lacking any programme beyond attacking those involved with the fiscal system and petitioning the king, the revolts always ended by losing momentum; it proved impossible to sustain them for more than a few months, or to extend them over very large areas. They remained obstinately local, confined to individual provinces, while few peasants would not be drawn home by the approach of the harvest season. Aware that time was on their side, the authorities would often temporize, perhaps making misleading promises in the hope that the rebels would disperse peacefully. The need to get the taxes in, however, and to discourage repetitions, commonly led to the use of troops; regular forces seemed able to defeat the peasant levies with relative ease, the only serious fight which might conceivably have gone the other way being at La Sauvetat in 1637. As a glance at the map will show, these revolts were not common to the whole country, most of them occurring in the south-western quarter of France. Within this area too there were particular regions which gave persistent trouble, usually marked out by strong local traditions, special exemptions, difficult terrain, and similar factors. There is a certain coincidence between the areas of frequent revolt and of Protestantism, although no direct link emerges; it is at least plausible to suggest that the connection was one related to communal independence and the relative strength of the local nobility. Many of the factors found in the south-west are also true of

Normandy, scene of the great rebellion of the *Nu-pieds* in 1639, and of endemic local resistance to the tax-collectors. It is likely that these two areas bore an unfair share of the total tax burden, although it is not clear how far this was a primary reason for their greater readiness to rebel.

Confronted by these multiple forms of disobedience, by officials, towns, nobles, and peasants, and under intense financial pressure, the ministers responded with a shrewd mixture of retreat and aggression. Demands for new taxes, for loans, or creations of new offices were often withdrawn or modified, while reprisals rarely went beyond the execution of a few scapegoats from the poorest classes. Aware that it was better to get some money in quickly than to spark off a revolt by insisting that the original demands be met in full, the government was usually prepared to be flexible, provided it got something out of the final deal. This was an untidy but practical way of proceeding; no-one could tell in advance how easy it would be to exploit a particular fiscal device, so the only way of maximizing income was to maintain a rapid fire of such innovations, and accept a high failure rate. As it turned out, the ministers had judged the political dangers pretty well, and for more than a decade after 1635 the resistance, widespread though it was, never posed a major threat to the stability of the state. One reason for this was the favourable treatment given to the frontier provinces and the *pays d'états*, the areas which could most easily try to secede, or organize their opposition around respected local institutions. The main weight of taxation fell on the *pays d'élections*, where there were far fewer traditional checks on royal authority, while where these provinces had retained some kind of representative estates, as in Normandy and Poitou, they were deliberately left in abeyance. They were never formally abolished, for the regime had no desire to crush provincial liberties as such, recognizing the complex patchwork of rights and exemptions as the natural order of things. This was one of the keys to its relative success, since the oblique approach and the steady erosion of individual privileges were far more difficult to denounce and oppose than a frontal attack would have been. There were so many ambiguities and loopholes in the laws and customs which nominally regulated the crown's relationship with its subjects that it was easy for the royal lawyers to give most changes a façade of legality, and for the king and his advisers to remain largely unaware of the extent to which they were effecting something of a revolution in the government of France.

The administrative revolution; the intendants

After taxation the main source of royal income lay in the sale of offices, which was producing an average of 20 million *livres* a year under Richelieu (see graph 7). Lucrative though it was, this practice actually helped to make the collection of the ordinary taxes more difficult. The system of assessment and collection by the *élus* and the *trésoriers de France* was inherently inefficient, only performing adequately under peacetime conditions, when the overall level of taxation was relatively low; in wartime it proved slow, inequitable, and corrupt, virtually compelling some kind of remedial action. Matters became even worse when the officials were full of resentment at the creation of additional posts, the redistribution of work to allow the establishment of new *bureaux*, the failure to pay salaries, and a series of financial exactions. They felt no compunction about recouping themselves out of the funds they handled, or extending the old practices of favouring their own property and that of their associates. As the tax demands from the centre rose, so did the arrears, for the local officials, who had no interest in impoverishing their own region, performed their duties with a noticeable lack of enthusiasm. The government's natural reaction was to reinforce the traditional methods of overseeing and disciplining the financial officials, by the use of special *commissaires*. During the 1630s the presence of an *intendant* became the normal rule, where it had previously been sporadic; without any clear intention, the crown was establishing a parallel system of non-venal administrators, with tremendous potential as a tool for centralization. Once such a structure existed, it was inevitable that it would expand its power rapidly, by attracting a multiplicity of roles. By the mid-1630s the *intendants* were already functioning as the normal means of controlling troops, as indispensable sources of information for the government, as watchdogs over the officials, and as repressors of rebellion. Their efforts to rectify corruption and inefficiency in the tax system were bringing them into conflict with the *cours des aides*, while their wide judicial powers produced similar difficulties with the *parlements*. An *intendant* had a formidable job, calling for a combination of intelligence, drive, and tact; the success of the institution depended on the crown's ability to find a supply of such men. By a curious but effective compromise, the great majority of these prime enemies of the venal office-holders were the sons of officials, who had themselves bought or inherited their permanent posts as *maîtres des requêtes*. The primary function of this corps of some eighty men had been to provide the *rapporteurs* who serviced the royal council, but since the sixteenth century they had also become the normal source for *commissaires*. A neat process of self-selection came into operation; the offices were expensive and not immediately lucrative, so they were only attractive to the ambitious and able young men who wanted to make a political career, and were prepared to take some risks. In this way the government tapped a remarkable pool of talent, which did much to ensure the viability of the new system.

During the period 1635–48 the *intendants* began to develop many of the features of a permanent organization, despite the temporary nature of their individual commissions. The practice of assigning one *intendant* to each *généralité* tended to become the rule; larger units were tried, but proved unworkable, while the appointment of two *intendants*, as in Languedoc, gave rise to personal rivalries and difficulties, and was finally abandoned. Despite a rather unfavourable attitude by the central government, the office of *subdélégué* quickly established itself as an essential aid to the overworked *intendants*, who desperately needed reliable subordinates with local knowledge. There were always some ambitious local officials who were prepared to accept these unpopular positions, just as the *intendants* succeeded in finding *trésoriers* and *élus* who would break ranks with their colleagues to help uncover abuses in the tax system. Faced with the resentment of the *parlements*, the *commissaires* could often exploit local rivalries to secure the support of the lesser courts. The most important relationship of all was often that with the provincial governor, who could easily feel himself threatened by the presence of an independent agent of the royal council. If governors and *intendants* seem generally to have co-operated reasonably well, this probably reflected Richelieu's very effective (and unpopular) policy of removing unsatisfactory governors and lieutenant-governors. The brusque dismissals of such veteran governors as the ducs de Guise, de Bellegarde, and d'Épernon, the execution of Montmorency, and the use of the now docile prince de Condé as a kind of hatchet-man who could replace dissident grandees, all marked a new ruthlessness on the part of the crown. The government sometimes allowed the governors to influence the selection of *intendants*, even to install one of their own dependents, but such special concessions were rapidly withdrawn if there were any doubts of the governor's fidelity.

The most crucial developments of all were again the product of the difficulties of war finance. The widespread disorders and revolts in the south-west between 1635 and 1637 made armed force indispensable if the taxes were to be collected at all, but the ordinary troops were virtually useless for this task. Special companies of *fusiliers* were recruited, under the overall command of the *intendants*; in provinces like Poitou and Limousin they might be 200 or 300 strong. Here again a temporary expedient soon became institutionalized, and the regime would continue to extract taxation by force for the rest of the century, despite strenuous efforts by Colbert to reverse the trend. At the same time the government had begun to use the *intendants* to collect money directly, in the case of a forced loan demanded from the towns at the end of 1636. The *surintendant* Bullion was in bad odour with Richelieu at this moment, because a failure to send money to Rohan had resulted in the loss of French control over the Valtelline; frightened that he might be dismissed, or have his huge fortune investigated, Bullion was desperate when the towns failed to pay up. He ordered the *intendants* to collect the money, most of which eventually dribbled in, although the task proved a hard one. Over the next few years, since a number of attempts to introduce major new taxes failed, in the face of widespread resistance, the only way the government could keep funds flowing in was by 'farming' the receipts of the *taille* against advances by the *traitants*. By 1641–2 the *taille* itself was coming in so poorly that the whole system was on the point of collapse, so in August 1642 the ministers took a radical initiative. The power to make the *assiette*, the basic tax assessment, was transferred to the *intendants*, with overriding authority as against the established officials, the *élus* and *trésoriers*. In numerous cases the *intendants* were permitted to dismiss the *receveurs des tailles* in order to replace them by agents of the tax-farmers, the only way to be sure that the latter would continue their vital loans. It was these practices which allowed Mazarin to mortgage the revenues three years ahead, for even the weak Regency government managed to disregard the efforts of the *cours des aides* to whittle down the powers granted by the *arrêt* of 1642. The *intendants* had effectively dispossessed the old financial officials, who were reduced to a marginal and humiliating state; it was this drastic act, and their involvement with the whole system of loans and tax farming, which made them the target for so much resentment from both officials and people during the 1640s.

By choosing to confront Spain on the battlefields of Europe, Richelieu and Louis XIII had also obliged themselves to exploit the monarchy's potential to the limit, and bend the traditions and conventions of French political life accordingly. The results were more radical than anyone can have intended; in the face of this ruthless onslaught almost all the old bulwarks against royal despotism proved to be made of sand. Violent and desperate though the opposition often was, it remained too divided and localized to impose more than temporary delays on the advance of centralized power. Its lack of coherence was emphasized by the triumph of theories of absolutism, as expounded by the veteran councillor Cardin Le Bret, from the 1630s onwards; Bodin and Loyseau, earlier advocates of a 'limited' monarchy in which the *officiers* played a vital intermediary role, had no direct successors. The new political order was far from complete by the time of Louis XIII's death in 1643, but it had acquired a formidable momentum of its own, as large numbers of able and ambitious men had already come to see royal service as the best route to advancement. In many respects it exemplified the old technique of divide and rule, with the crown taking particular advantage of the anomalous position of the 'Fourth Estate' of officials which it had itself created. Although the officials had already accumulated a good deal of wealth and power, there was still a sense in which they were at a transitional stage, yet to be fully accepted by the older nobility or to feel confident that they could sustain their recent advances. Another generation or two, and the crown might have found it far more difficult to overawe them; arguably the timing of the royal offensive was crucial, for if Richelieu's policies had not been followed, the officials might have dug themselves in as major obstacles to the will of the monarchy which had created them. As it was, Richelieu's ministry marked an unmistakable watershed in the evolution of the French state, heralding the great age of royal authoritarianism.

(iii) *The Regency, the Fronde, and the Ministry of Cardinal Mazarin*

Foreign success and internal problems 1643-8

In the immediate future France was confronted by the alarming prospect of a royal minority, which might see a large-scale reversal of the trends of the previous decades, or at the worst a slide into anarchy. Louis XIII's last weeks were haunted by the fear that all his work would be undone with his death, and he tried to keep control beyond the grave by making an elaborate will, designed to prevent his widow and his brother from exercising the full powers of Regent and Lieutenant-General respectively. Having suffered from their unreliability for so long, he could have no faith in their ability to direct the affairs of state. One of the few reasonably clear points in French constitutional law, however, was that royal wills of this kind were invalid, and within four days of his death (14 May 1643) the *parlement* of Paris had accepted a declaration by the four-year-old Louis XIV that his mother had full authority to act in his name. The new Regent faced an unenviable situation, much more difficult than that of 1610; it would be more than eight years before the king reached his nominal majority, and the country was locked in a desperate foreign war. Anne of Austria hardly looked the leader for the hour, for she was lazy, proud, and none too intelligent. Despite her long residence in France she had no real understanding of French politics, a defect shared by the new first minister, Cardinal Mazarin. He too was a foreigner, an Italian who had started in the papal service and then attached his fortunes to those of Richelieu; the latter had been so impressed by Mazarin's diplomatic abilities that he recommended him as his successor. What no one could have foreseen was the personal bond which quickly developed between Regent and minister, possibly to the extent of a secret marriage. On balance this was a distinct gain for the Regency government, since the relationship provided an element of stability at the centre, and Mazarin was able to retain the services of many of Richelieu's *fidèles*, even if he could never rely on their loyalty as their original master could. A good deal was going to depend on Gaston d'Orléans, who surprised many people by playing a relatively helpful role in the new set-up. Released from the oppressive suspicion of his elder brother, Orléans proved capable of taking a degree of responsibility; he would never be a major support to the government, but nor was he any great threat.

The decision to keep Mazarin as first minister implied the continuation of the foreign policy of the previous reign, so there was little hope of any improvement in the crown's appalling financial position, or of any decrease in the taxes. Most of the abuses which had aroused such a storm of protest against Richelieu's ministry continued unchecked, although a number of his political enemies returned from exile and imprisonment. It may appear surprising that the Regency government survived at all, still more so that it enjoyed a measure of success for several years. One important reason for this was that most men of property genuinely wanted stability and firm rule, so long as it did not operate too strongly against their self-interest; conscious of the dangers of anarchy during the minority, they exercised a degree of restraint. For the great nobles the war meant prestigious military commands,

while after the disappearance of the morose and puritanical
Louis XIII the atmosphere at court became much freer and
livelier. In the end court intrigues and rivalries would become
a serious nuisance to the government, but in the short run the
feeling of release helped to keep the political scene relatively
calm. A similar kind of precarious balance could be seen in
the regime's relationship with the *parlement* of Paris, which had
traditionally played an important role during periods of royal
minority. Many of the *parlementaire* leaders, like the *premier
président* Molé and the *avocat général* Omer Talon, were basically
conservative royalists, and even their more radical colleagues
differed from them on matters of detail rather than of principle. The judges knew that their own authority was derived
from that of the crown, and had no intention of heading any
movement of opposition; when they clashed with the Regent or
the ministers, it was because they thought government policy
either unwise or unlawful. The very moderation of their
general stance made such criticism all the more powerful,
with a constant danger that some misjudgement by the government would produce a confrontation in which both sides
found it very difficult to back down. There were several
threatening moments during the early years of the Regency,
arising from the increasingly frantic search for money to keep
the war going; every clash of this kind left a legacy of mutual
distrust behind it.

In many respects the ministers were living on borrowed time,
and only great political skill could have averted a major crisis
indefinitely. Mazarin himself was adept at the game of mani-
pulating individual ambitions and buying off the aggrieved;
his affectations of humility won him tolerance, if not respect,
from potential rivals. To these latter the predominance of a
foreign Cardinal was perhaps more bearable than that of any
of their native competitors, while Mazarin's ignorance of
French internal affairs made him heavily dependent on their
advice in any case. The technique of turning opposition aside
with flattery and promises was hardly a long-term solution,
however; the government was steadily creating the impression,
among the political élites, that it was basically weak and dishonest. The prime target of criticism was the finance minister,

Particelli d'Emery, an ingenious but unscrupulous operator in the murky waters of royal finance. D'Emery was a specialist in the art of raising loans from the *traitants*, whose success in this field between 1643 and 1645 allowed royal expenditure to reach its highest levels for the whole of the long war. With genuine income from taxation static or falling, the conjuring trick could not be worked year after year; d'Emery could only borrow by paying extortionate rates of interest, and there were natural limits to the amount of credit the *traitants* could raise. D'Emery's financial policies caused widespread discontent: among the officials because their salaries were unpaid and the old abuses continued; in the *parlement* over demands for new taxes and attempts to evade the normal machinery of budgetary control; and in the country at large at the sheer weight of taxation and the way it was enforced. Although the years 1643–8 saw no really big revolts, there were plenty of smaller ones, while in a number of areas the tax-collectors had simply given up; arrears mounted steadily. After more than a decade of 'extraordinary' fiscality the royal administration may have become hardened to the normal chorus of protest, and failed to recognize that the pressure was building up to the point where an explosion could occur at any moment. The object of the whole exercise in brinkmanship was to enable Mazarin to carry through Richelieu's foreign policy by bringing the Habsburgs to their knees, an ambition which had little appeal for most Frenchmen now it was clear that Spain had lost any capacity to take the offensive.

Nevertheless the war dragged on, as leisurely peace talks began in Germany with much dispute over protocol and seating arrangements. Whatever its failings elsewhere, the Regency was lucky in war with the emergence of two young generals of genius, the duc d'Enghien (soon to be the *grand* Condé) and Turenne. Within a week of Louis XIV's accession Enghien had destroyed the Spanish army of Flanders at Rocroi, a battle which is often regarded as marking the end of Spain's military greatness. The next few years saw numerous French successes in the Rhineland and the southern Netherlands, culminating in another great victory by Condé (as he now was) at Lens in 1648, which eliminated what was left of the Spanish veterans.

In Catalonia, however, the war did not go so well, with Philip IV and his ministers obstinately refusing to accept their defeat; in the end they preferred to abandon all claim to the northern Netherlands, in order to concentrate their remaining forces against France and the rebels in Catalonia and Portugal. This decision meant that 1648 saw the conclusion of the wars in Germany and the Netherlands, leaving France and Spain to fight out their differences. The peaces of Westphalia and Münster represented a triumph for traditional French policies, bringing about a great diminution in the prestige and power of the two Habsburg empires, but they did not earn Mazarin the domestic credit he expected. Instead he was widely blamed for failing to secure a peace settlement with Spain; his critics did not realize that this was only possible if the Spaniards wanted to negotiate, whereas in fact they still cherished dreams of revenge once they were free from their other commitments. The idea that Mazarin was prolonging the war to enrich himself and make himself indispensable quickly gained credence even in circles normally favourable to the government, and intensified the political crisis which had developed in Paris during the early months of 1648.

The crisis of 1648

Exasperation at d'Emery's fiscal policies had reached the point where all his proposals for new taxes were being blocked, bringing the crown to the verge of bankruptcy. The ministers therefore put intensive pressure on the *parlement* of Paris to accept at least some new taxes; in so doing they fatally undermined the position of the more conservative judges who normally kept the radicals under some restraint. Despite tremendous efforts by *premier président* Molé to bring about some kind of compromise, the rift became progressively deeper, and the government's blusterings only served to expose its lack of real power to coerce its opponents. The longer the arguments continued, the bolder the radicals became, while the government was tempted into desperate measures which could do little but bring disaster. Above all, a crude and obvious attempt to exploit the periodic negotiations for the renewal of the *paulette* proved to be the catalyst for an unprecedented upsurge of unity among the royal officials as a whole. Even the *maîtres des requêtes* temporarily made common cause with their *parlementaire* rivals, while the *trésoriers* and *élus* had already reacted to the loss of their functions by forming *syndicats*, and these naturally took the opportunity to advance their grievances anew. In May 1648 the *parlement* added a new dimension to the crisis by calling for a joint assembly of the four Paris sovereign courts in the Chambre Saint Louis, ostensibly to discuss salaries and the *paulette*. In practice such an asembly was bound to invite wider criticisms of the administration and the ministers in alarm, quickly pointed out that the courts had no right to meet without the Regent's approval. The opposition had now built up too great a head of steam to be bothered by such legal niceties however, and the government realized that it would be wiser to allow the assembly than to be humiliated by the open defiance of its own officials. Mazarin advised the Regent to be conciliatory until the campaigning season was over, then use the troops if necessary to restore royal authority. A dubious gamble at the best of times, this plan was soon rendered useless by the rapid evolution of events in Paris and across the whole country.

The dangers inherent in wild hopes of the end of heavy taxes had already been illustrated after the deaths of Richelieu and Louis XIII, when rumours of tax remission had caused a lot of trouble. The disappointment which ensued may have played a part in generating the numerous popular revolts of the period 1643–5. These were followed by two years of relative calm; it seemed as if repression was beginning to work, and in the early summer of 1648 some *intendants* were reporting confidently that assessment and collection were going well. The picture changed with bewildering speed, as news that the Chambre Saint Louis was meeting swept across the country, closely followed by the announcement of a series of concessions by the government. The *surintendant* d'Emery was dismissed, reductions made in the taxes, and the *intendants* recalled (except for those in the frontier provinces and with the army). Intended as a tactical retreat, the process turned into an undignified rout of the *commissaires* and the financiers; the whole machinery of centralized control, so painstakingly built up over the previous decades, soon lay in ruins. Confronted by something approaching a general tax strike, the government simply lacked the power to coerce its subjects back into obedience. The enormous drop in tax receipts which resulted inevitably damaged the government's credit, and the financiers, already under attack by the Chambre Saint Louis, found the new *surintendant* La Meilleraye trying to cut their interest rates. Like the well-meaning but naïve *parlementaires*, he had failed to realize that only an idiot would lend to the French crown for less than about 20%, in view of the risks involved. Some financiers made huge fortunes, many more ended up in poverty or in prison; the government would only keep the necessary level of repayments up for a financier who still had more to lend. By the later months of 1648 there was no money to repay anyone, and the result was virtually an undeclared state bankruptcy, with the machinery of royal credit finance in total disarray. The position of the treasury over the next few years remains shrouded in mystery, for normal accounting procedures seem to have stopped, and the government lived from hand to mouth on such intermittent loans and tax receipts as it could collect. The one advantage Mazarin still had over his rivals was that some financiers, gambling on the eventual restoration of royal power, were prepared to advance further sums. These loans did enable Mazarin to hire small mercenary armies at vital moments, but they were too small to change the crown's basic plight. The rake's progress which had begun with the increase in general taxation, and continued with the exploitation of venal office, had come to its inevitable end; the resort to short-term loans during the 1640s was a despairing last fling, beggaring the crown and exasperating its traditionally minded officials to the point of open disobedience.

The ministers were now in an unenviable situation, for their inability to deal with the officials demonstrated to all the world that their power was a mere façade. Subsequent historians have enjoyed themselves pointing out all the errors and miscalculations made by the Regent, Mazarin, and others, and there were certainly plenty of these. At the same time it seems very unlikely that any policy adopted in 1648 could have averted a major breakdown of royal authority, once the opposition had found its voice. However desperate Mazarin's attempts to regain the initiative were, they at least prevented the royal position going by default, and eventually helped to expose the divisions among the other contenders for power. The Cardinal certainly started badly, when in late August 1648 he tried to capitalize on the news of Condé's victory at Lens by arresting some of the leading radicals in the *parlement*. Paris responded with its traditional form of protest, a Day of Barricades, and the government could only restore order in the capital by a humiliating climb-down. Always prone to over-estimate the importance of personal intrigues, Mazarin was aware that a clique of 'Frondeur' leaders, including Gondi (the future Cardinal de Retz) and Châteauneuf, aimed at using the protracted crisis to displace him. He therefore went ahead with his original plan, and invoked the aid of the Prince de Condé and his army. Early in the New Year the court slipped out of Paris, and the Regent denounced the *parlementaires* as traitors and enemies of the monarchy, ready to ally with Spain and imitate the rebels in England. These unwise and exaggerated accusations led even the moderate members of the *parlement* to disobey the orders for their exile and to set about organizing the defence of Paris, which was soon invested by Condé's troops. Both sides had now got themselves into a false position, from which they were anxious to extricate themselves; soon the news that a Spanish army had crossed the northern frontier alarmed everyone except a few inveterate noble conspirators. Negotiations quickly began, resulting in a compromise settlement, the Peace of Rueil (March 1649), which confirmed the reforms made by the Chambre Saint Louis the previous year.

Slide into anarchy; the Fronde of the nobles

The end of the *Fronde parlementaire*, as this first phase of the crisis has generally been known, was only an illusory relief for the government, which had lost control of the general situation. The Frondeur nobles who had taken the side of the *parlement* continued their intrigues against Mazarin, while the Cardinal's alliance with Condé was now proving a severe embarrassment.

The *grand* Condé, still under thirty, may have been an incomparably better general than his father; as a person and a politician, however, he was just as impossible. His military prestige, his wealth, and his widespread clientele made him the greatest power in the land, but they could not compensate for his lack of moderation or judgement. Over the next three years his combination of ambition, arrogance, and inconsistency would bewilder his contemporaries, spark off numerous local conflicts, and hamper any return to political stability. Financial difficulties alone would have been enough to force Mazarin to try and work with Condé, but these were now compounded by the progressive collapse of royal authority in the provinces. Once it was plain that the government, lacking both *intendants* and funds, could not intervene effectively, a whole range of previously pent-up rivalries and conflicts burst into the open. The most serious disturbances were in Provence, Guyenne, and Normandy, where governors, *parlements*, and municipalities levied troops, and armed clashes resulted. The comte d'Alais, governor of Provence, had been trying to build up a clientele in the towns and among the nobility, while taking every chance to diminish the power and prestige of the *parlement* of Aix. His inept manœuvres led to an intermittent local war, which flared up periodically between 1649 and 1652. In Guyenne the second duc d'Épernon had inherited both his father's large noble clientele and his contempt for the *parlement* of Bordeaux; here too the province was split between followers and enemies of the governor. While the governors, disposing of small forces of regular troops and a powerful following of nobles, could keep a general military superiority, they had neither the numbers nor the artillery to tackle important cities like Aix, Marseille, or Bordeaux. The resulting stalemate was probably worse for the government than an outright victory for either side, if only because the confusion made normal tax-collection impossible. There were also repercussions on court politics; Condé supported his cousin d'Alais, while siding with the *parlement* of Bordeaux against d'Épernon.

The movement of troops around Paris and in the provinces led to considerable devastation, which added to the suffering caused by one of the most serious and protracted harvest crises of the century. The years 1648–52 saw high grain prices, soaring mortality rates, and outbreaks of the plague. These bad conditions were not the cause of the Fronde, but they helped to sharpen social divisions, while lower-class discontent could easily be exploited for political ends. With France slipping into anarchy, there was the threat of radical movements developing among the lesser bourgeoisie of the towns, as they had at the time of the *Ligue*. The only cheering thing about the situation was the strange inability of the Spaniards to take advantage of it beyond recovering Catalonia; their feeble attempts to intervene probably did the government more good than harm. The Regent and Mazarin were caught in a complex maze of difficulties, needing to evade the reforms and controls imposed by the *parlementaires* in 1648–9 if they were to keep the war going, yet in the meantime lacking the strength to overawe the various noble factions. They tried to escape from this trap by playing off the factions against one another, and in the process set off a series of intrigues which need to be followed almost day by day to be fully understood. Alarmed by Condé's growing power, and by his unpredictability, Mazarin soon formed an alliance with the Frondeur group led by Gondi and Châteauneuf, with Condé, his brother Conti and his brother-in-law Longueville all arrested and imprisoned in January 1650. A new series of provincial revolts, the most important again being in Guyenne, followed this *coup d'état*; Mazarin spent most of 1650 trying to crush them, until another compromise settlement in October brought the fighting to an end. Over the next few months the Cardinal missed whatever chance existed of reconciling himself with Condé, so when the Princes were released in February 1651 it was because they had formed an alliance with the Frondeurs against Mazarin. Ever since 1648 the Parisian presses had been pouring out pamphlets, the so-called *Mazarinades*, attacking the minister and the Regent, and calling for the exclusion of foreigners and churchmen from the government. All parties could agree on one point at least, that the Cardinal must go, so he withdrew into voluntary exile at Cologne. The coalition of his enemies promptly fell apart, amid a tangle of conflicting personal fears and ambitions, while the nobles and some clerics demanded the convocation of the Estates-General. This last proposal was finally evaded, but the preliminary assemblies met to elect deputies and prepare *cahiers de doléances*; where these survive they demonstrate the widespread desire to reverse recent trends, and return to some idealized earlier age. The provincial nobility called for a great diminution in the numbers and privileges of the officials, with the abolition of venality and the *paulette*. Most obnoxious of all, in their eyes, were the financiers and their associates, repeatedly described as leeches sucking the life-blood of the people. For all their obvious lack of realism, these noble *cahiers* do convey much of the bewilderment and bitterness created by the policies of the Cardinal-Ministers.

The final and most destructive phase of the civil war began in the autumn of 1651, after the king's formal majority had been declared. Condé, who had already left court, allowed himself to be drawn into a futile revolt, lacking any plausible rallying-cry. At last clear lines began to appear between royalists and rebels, and the government was able to appeal to both straightforward loyalism and war-weariness. From his base at Bordeaux Condé tried to extend his control over Guyenne and the neighbouring provinces, but soon found the military exchanges going against him. Even the premature return of Mazarin from his exile could not do more than delay the inevitable; in a last desperate gamble Condé left Guyenne for Paris, where he arrived in April 1652, and joined forces with a rather lukewarm Orléans. The royal forces under Turenne were too small to invest the capital, and in any case had to cope with threats from the Spaniards and the duke of Lorraine, in a campaign of marches and counter-marches which wasted the countryside south of Paris. In the city itself Condé received a mixed reception, for the municipality and the *parlement* had little stomach for revolt, and his own conduct during the siege of 1649 was remembered against him. He could only overcome the passive resistance of the bourgeoisie by allying himself with a popular movement, which soon seized control after a major riot. Despite the resemblances to the *Ligue*, the new movement was far inferior to its predecessor

in idealism or staying power, while Condé himself was pro-
foundly uncomfortable in the role of a demagogue. With the
help of a second and shorter withdrawal into exile by Mazarin
the Parisian Fronde collapsed, Condé retreated to join the
Spaniards, and the young king re-entered his capital in
October 1652, summoning Mazarin back to the council. Even
now Bordeaux held out, for a more organized and durable
popular regime than in Paris had been established there. The
Ormée of Bordeaux was essentially a union of the small bourgeoisie and the people against the municipal oligarchy and the
parlement; once in power, however, its leaders had little positive
to offer. They abstained from any serious effort at social
revolution, while making an alliance with Spain and eventually seeking help from Cromwell. The rebels in Bordeaux
did not surrender until the late summer of 1653, but their
resistance was only a needless prolongation of a struggle which
had been decided the previous year. The prolonged period of
dearth and high prices from 1648 to 1652, and the growing
dislocation of ordinary life, had been capped in the rebellious
areas by the general move of the Frondeurs after 1651 to raise
taxes on their own account. For all but the small groups of
leaders the great anti-fiscal hopes of 1648 had been succeeded
by a desire for peace and stability at almost any price. The
bons bourgeois, who had previously observed a wary neutrality,
now showed themselves to be massively hostile to further
rebellion, and cut the ground away from under the feet of the
Frondeurs.

Historians have repeatedly stressed the strangely negative
and futile character of the Fronde, and there are few grounds
for questioning this view. The government's position was so
weak from 1649 onwards that the way was wide open for any
institution or group to assert claims to power, yet not even
Condé and his supporters made a wholehearted attempt to do
so. The *parlement* of Paris was so frightened by the experiences
of 1648–9 that it quickly reverted to its normal moderate
royalism, while the contending parties in the provinces, although they often acted in response to news from Paris, were
dominated by purely local considerations. In any case the
king's youth, although a major cause of the troubles, was also

a kind of barrier between the Frondeurs and the monarchical principle itself. It was easy to oppose the government as personified by Anne of Austria and Mazarin, while protesting one's basic loyalty to Louis XIV himself; virtually all the Frondeurs used this technique, which was in the end self-defeating. All the violence and obscenity of the *Mazarinades* cannot disguise their conceptual poverty, or their besetting tendency to seek solutions from the past. The Fronde cannot really be described as a failed revolution, since it never began to develop revolutionary aims; one of the government's most tactless moves was to accuse its opponents of resembling the English regicides. There were certainly moments when the court seemed in danger of even greater embarrassment, notably during the summer of 1652, when effective co-operation between its adversaries might have spelt disaster for the small royal army south of Paris. Presumably it was these moments Lavisse had in mind when he wrote that only the fidelity of some officers in the *vieux régiments* saved the monarchy during the noble Fronde, but it is difficult to agree entirely with this judgement. The anarchy might have forced an unfavourable peace settlement with Spain, or have dismantled even more of the royal administrative machine; although such developments would have left a good deal more for Louis XIV to do, they could only have been a temporary check on his power. And whatever the Fronde might have been, in practice it was a disaster, for all those who wished to limit the growing autocracy of the French crown. Like the *Ligue* half a century before, it discredited even quite moderate opponents and ideas, and made it easier for the government to identify both friends and enemies. Above all, it left an indelible mark on the young king himself, who never forgot or forgave the humiliations of his early years; Louis XIV's attitudes to the nobility, the *parlements*, and the Jansenists all reflected his memories of the Fronde. A movement which had begun with a well-intentioned, if muddled, attack on the abuses of royal power therefore ended up by making the king himself a formidable enemy of many of the traditional but ill-defined checks on his authority.

Mazarin and the last years of war

The restoration of royal control over France was a slow and imperfect process in the years after 1653, and it is possible to argue that the Fronde represented a real and serious break in the trend towards absolutist innovation set under Richelieu. It seems unlikely, however, that it had much effect on the long-term development of the state, for many of the practices it attacked were regarded by their instigators themselves as essentially temporary and undesirable. Extreme measures and abuses created simply to keep the war going could hardly have survived the peace settlement unchanged or unreformed, particularly given the king's own character. If Louis XIV and his ministers allowed many anomalies to persist and tolerated a considerable degree of local and legal independence, this was not because they had drawn any lessons of this kind from the Fronde. The royal government was essentially conservative, it innovated only under duress, and was remarkably punctilious in observing legal niceties. This was particularly the case in the period between the collapse of the Fronde and the Peace of the Pyrenees, when the ministers were still nervous of fresh internal disorders which might again threaten the successful pursuit of the war. The Spaniards, who now had Condé to help them, continued to put up a determined defence, and France was too exhausted to deliver a decisive blow; only the English alliance of 1657 finally gave Mazarin the means to conquer important new sectors of the Netherlands. These victories, and his continued inability to defeat the rebels in Portugal, at last persuaded Philip IV to sue for peace, and after many months of negotiation the Peace of the Pyrenees was concluded in the summer of 1659. French territorial gains were substantial, Artois, Roussillon, and a string of fortresses along the eastern frontier, but they were hardly sufficient to justify the appalling cost of the war, in both oppressive taxation and human life. If the foreign policy of the Cardinal-Ministers is to be defended at all, it can only be in terms of its primary aim, which was to protect a complex range of French international interests against Spanish hostility, and to eliminate the dangers from Habsburg imperialism. The true importance of the treaties of 1648 and 1659 was precisely along these lines, for they marked the final collapse of Spain's pretensions to European hegemony, and a dramatic shift in the power structure of the continent. In a sense France had emerged as the ultimate victor in a series of conflicts which had originated with the Italian Wars at the end of the fifteenth century, and it would be for the new king to take advantage of the situation.

The campaigns after 1653 had been financed by Mazarin and the *surintendant* Nicolas Fouquet through a final orgy of short-term borrowing, which had only worked because the financiers had been offered astonishingly favourable terms, covered up through all kinds of fraud. The tax system continued to function badly, and the government did not at first feel able to reintroduce the *intendants* on a general basis, although they were soon operating in some provinces in much the old style. By 1655 the situation was much as it had been before the crisis, with nominees of the *fermiers* again being substituted for the ordinary *receveurs*, in order that the government might be able to anticipate on the *taille*. As the pattern of the 1630s and 1640s was repeated, so local opposition began to manifest itself again after the temporary discouragement which had followed the Fronde. In some towns the lesser bourgeoisie renewed its challenge to the dominance of the oligarchy of royal officials, exploiting popular resentment over the involvement of the municipalities in the tax system. A revolt of this kind at Angers in 1656 led to a three-month occupation of the town by a force of royal guards under the command of the local *intendant*, and the definitive suppression of municipal elections; in future the *maire* and *échevins* were to be royal nominees. In the end this kind of determined repression would prove highly effective, but it needed time and repeated experiences to make it so, and by 1658 the government was really alarmed at the increase in rebellious activity. That year saw assemblies of local nobles in several western provinces, giving a lot of trouble to the *intendants*, a serious popular revolt in the Sologne (south of Orléans), and a dangerous faction struggle in the great port of Marseille. For much of the late 1650s there was also persistent trouble in the south-west, notably in Saintonge and Angoumois, which kept the *intendants* and their *fusiliers* busy. In retrospect it is easy to dismiss these episodes as doomed efforts to protect local rights and escape royal fiscality; at the time the government was frightened that the infection would spread. In Provence, remote from the capital and always regarded with suspicion by royal agents as a hotbed of sedition, disorder turned into defiance of the king's orders. Aware of the difficulties of ruling the province, Mazarin had concentrated power in the hands of the ambitious *premier président* of the *parlement* of Aix, d'Oppède, who was virtually fulfilling the normal role of an *intendant* in consequence of a private bargain with the Cardinal. A complex amalgam of resentments against his rule led to an uprising in Aix early in 1659, which was soon repressed by the governor Mercoeur; the leaders took refuge with their associates, the newly victorious faction in Marseilles. The latter, already guilty of several imprudent acts of disobedience, ignored royal orders to hand over the fugitives, apparently believing that they were safe against serious reprisals. With the peace treaty signed and sealed, Mazarin could afford to respond to the urgings of Mercoeur and d'Oppède, and crush the turbulent factions of Marseille once and for all. In January 1660 Louis XIV and his court entered Provence with an army; resistance was impossible, and d'Oppède was already busy reforming the municipal constitutions of Aix and Arles to ensure royal control. Marseille was treated virtually as a conquered city, occupied by the army, a length of wall destroyed, the inhabitants disarmed, and a new citadel built. The very title of *consul*, traditionally used by the elected magistrates, was abolished, and the previously dominant nobility excluded from civic affairs which passed under the control of the relatively docile merchants. In one brutal stroke Marseille lost her semi-independent status, to become a French city like all others, ready to accept the royal *intendant* in Provence as her master.

The punishment of the rebels in Provence was a spectacular warning of the government's determination to enforce its will, now that the constraints of foreign war were removed. The young king was being carefully schooled by Mazarin, introduced to the workings of the royal councils, and encouraged to see himself as the future master of the most powerful state in

Europe. As the Cardinal lay on his death-bed in March 1661 he could reflect on one of the most remarkable careers in history; for France his passing was the start of a new age.

(iv) *The personal rule of Louis XIV*

The confirmation of royal power

When the king announced his intention of not replacing Mazarin, and taking personal charge of the government, many must have thought he would soon tire of this passing fancy. Among them was the *surintendant* Fouquet, whose ambition and ability marked him out as a possible *premier ministre*. He and his friends were imprudently open about their hopes, but Louis XIV's growing hostility may perhaps be best explained by a psychological need for self-assertion, combined with the intrigues of Jean-Baptiste Colbert, who had managed Mazarin's affairs for the last decade. In September 1661 Fouquet was suddenly arrested, and the office of *surintendant* itself abolished; although many of its functions would soon be reunited under the *contrôleur général*, the style of independent financial management associated with the old office would never be resumed. The disgrace of Fouquet was the signal for a major reckoning with the financiers he had patronized, through the traditional means of a *chambre de justice*, which imposed fines to a total of 156 million *livres*, besides confiscating the property of those found guilty of criminal offences. The fallen minister was put on trial, and defended himself so well that his persecutors were seriously embarrassed; despite the king's evident wish for a death sentence, a hand-picked tribunal would only condemn Fouquet to banishment. For once Louis XIV took no account of legalities, and imposed his own punishment, imprisonment for life in the fortress of Pignerol. The whole affair showed the king and Colbert in a poor light, and was far from popular in informed Parisian circles, but what might under other circumstances have been a serious political error was soon submerged in the general élan of the new regime. Free at last from overriding military needs, the monarchy could turn back to the policies of grandeur and internal reform foreshadowed by Richelieu more than three decades before. Much of this would certainly have occurred under any but the most incompetent king, yet Louis XIV's personality gave additional impetus to the assertion of royal power. A mediocre enough man in many respects, the king had two great attributes: enormous physical vitality and an exceptionally strong will. His conventionality and intellectual limitation often turned to his advantage, helping him to play the role expected of him without any apparent doubt or hesitation. Above all, he found gratification not only in women, gambling, and war, but in the painstaking everyday exercise of power, through the bureaucratic institutions of his council. Confronted by a king whose will to rule proved implacable, and who really worked at the job, such groups or style of opposition as had survived the onslaught of the Cardinal-Ministers were quickly swept aside. After the chaotic and complex story of the previous reigns, the personal rule of Louis XIV seems almost devoid of dramatic events, a long era of stability, even dullness.

The absence of formal opposition is, of course, misleading. The 'absolutism' of Louis XIV was often little more than a façade, behind which many of the old limitations continued to operate. This was partly the doing of the monarchy itself; half-aware of the way in which his authority ultimately rested on religion and the laws of property, the king insisted, personally and through his propagandists, that he was no despot. Scruples of this kind saved Fouquet's neck, and the use of arbitrary powers of imprisonment was relatively restricted. Royal authority could achieve almost any individual end to which it was directed; what it could not do was to exercise constant control over all the multifarious layers of devolved power. It is easy to emphasize the elements of both continuity and change in this tangled situation, for they are visible simultaneously. Through a mixture of opportunity and personal drive, Louis XIV had brought to a climax an evolutionary process dating back to at least the late fifteenth century, in which a combination of factors, including literacy, printing, and greater bureaucratic sophistication, had allowed the monarchy to expand its power. The process had also been in part a reaction to centrifugal tendencies within the state, and had culminated in the triumph of the centre over the periphery. By the 1660s and 1670s there was little chance of getting away with the old trick of proclaiming one's loyalty while disregarding the king's orders and insulting his representatives. The revolts of the period were harshly treated; in the Boulonnais in 1662 hundreds of peasants were sent to the galleys, as were many of the followers of Audijos in the Pyrenees a few years later. In the latter case at least thirty were executed. When Bordeaux rioted against the *papier timbré* and *marque d'étain* impositions in 1675, the city had eighteen regiments quartered on it for the winter, and lost tax privileges worth half a million *livres* a year. The even more serious Breton revolts of the same year were followed by widespread executions and the billeting of 10,000 troops, while the *parlement* of Rennes spent the next fourteen years in uncomfortable exile at Vannes. The crown was now strong enough to impose such punishments, to deprive officials guilty of misconduct, and to repress the violence of the lesser nobles. It followed the practice, dating back at least to Richelieu's time, of treating the Parisian *parlement* and other courts relatively gently, while often meting out harsh treatment to their provincial equivalents. The apparently timorous behaviour of the Parisian magistrates during the middle and later years of the century must have reflected their awareness of the examples being made elsewhere. Petty obstructionism was another matter, and it was soon clear that if the government could no longer be defied, it could often be evaded. Impressive in comparison with the past, the bureaucratic organization of the state was still primitive, quite unequal to any demands for full-scale centralization. By insisting on personal control over all important measures, the king himself, and ministers like Colbert and Louvois, were in any case limiting the extent and the pace of their actions.

In theory the crown might have been able to undertake major structural reforms within the state, and at times Colbert may have dreamed of such enterprises. For all his limitations and personal unattractiveness, he does stand out as the one minister of the whole reign who tried to ask fundamental questions about the use to which royal power might be put;

indeed, no other minister to the end of the *ancien régime* achieved so much in the way of practical reform. On close inspection, however, it is evident that the changes he made were all limited to making the existing system function more efficiently, and that despite occasional flashes of insight his outlook was basically conventional. After the removal of various glaring abuses France remained divided by internal customs barriers and *gabelle* regions, while the direct taxes were still levied on the old principles. Colbert's special gift was for identifying the weak points and blockages within a given structure; this was the foundation of his great success, the restoration of the royal finances. Although only appointed *contrôleur général* in 1665, he had earlier taken on both the ordinary financial administration and the *intendants*, the latter having long ceased to depend on the ageing Séguier. Through the *chambre de justice* and a thorough revision of the *rentes* he was able to cancel much of the enormous debt left by the war, which he estimated at 450 millions; a good proportion of this was merely a paper debt, based on fraudulent transactions, so the true figure may have been as low as 70 million. The creation of the *caisse des emprunts* was a modest step towards improving royal creditworthiness, while Colbert did begin to buy back parts of the royal demesne and a small number of useless offices. Probably his most significant—and lasting—achievement was in the area of taxation, and above all the *taille*. Understanding that the tax must be fixed at a level which could be properly enforced, he reduced it by some 15%, making great efforts to return to the normal system of collection by the local *receveurs* and to stop the use of troops. Unfortunately the agrarian depression probably cancelled out the effects of the decrease, and the troops never disappeared completely, particularly in the south-west. Nevertheless, persistent attention to detail helped to bring the *taille* in more regularly than for years, to check official peculation, and to diminish local resistance. Colbert also grasped the important point that if arrears piled up, they became a major cause of trouble; those from 1647–56 were officially abandoned at the birth of the dauphin in 1662, those of 1657–62 were later quietly forgotten, but no comparable backlog was allowed to

accumulate again. The minister's general policy was to increase the relative importance of the indirect taxes, which fell
on the privileged as well as the poor, and were fairly simple to
collect. Such proposals had previously stirred up widespread
opposition, so it was a sign of the crown's enhanced authority
that comparable events were now rare, although the changes
damaged the interests of the political classes.

The maintenance of a level of tax revenue previously seen
only in wartime enormously enhanced royal power. The
money made possible the building of Versailles, the expanded
system of patronage and pensions, the creation of a navy, and
the remodelling of the army by Le Tellier. Between 1655 and
1675 the royal army was transformed from a motley collection
of privately raised forces, with only a small core of permanent
royal troops, into a passably well disciplined and organized
body of nearly 100,000 men even in peacetime. The soldiers
were still mercenaries, and an element of private enterprise
remained, but in essentials the War Ministry had achieved a
degree of control unprecedented in early modern Europe.
Much attention was also paid to the problems of equipment
and supply, while the building of barracks reduced the difficulties of winter quarter. A great school of military engineers,
of whom Vauban was the finest example, improved French
siege tactics, and lined the frontiers with strong new fortresses.
Such military strength was a dangerous toy to place in the
hands of a king ambitious for the *gloire* that could only come
from victorious warfare; at the same time it was an impressive
guarantee for his authority at home. The French crown had
succeeded in establishing the classic extortion–coercion situation, with heavy taxes supporting a repressive force capable of
meeting any likely challenge, and of compelling payment of
those same taxes. Once a regime has reached this point, it
takes a massive convulsion to bring it down, or even to shake
its hold on power. In its new form the army was also a great
source of patronage for the crown, providing career prospects
for thousands of lesser nobles, although only the lucky few
would rise very far.

One element in the monarchy's triumph over an older, more
diverse tradition of political life had been the way in which

ministers, most notably Richelieu, had succeeded in associating the government with new ideas. The central concept had been that of order, in politics, society, and culture, an order which only divine right monarchy could ensure. During the first decades of Louis XIV's rule the formula still seemed highly effective. It was expressed in the great artistic productions of a 'classical' age, and in many of the measures of practical reform introduced by Colbert and other ministers. The codification of sections of the law, the legislation to protect forests, the programme of economic regulation, along with the military and financial reorganization already discussed, all fitted the overall pattern. The foundation of the *Académie des sciences* in 1666 was Colbert's work, but he found it easy to convince the king of the merits of an institution which combined the support of 'progressive' ideas with the imposition of royal order on their exponents. For a brief moment in history the monarchy ruled not only men, but ideas; the opposition seemed as weak in the latter field as in the former. In 1669, with the 'peace of the Church', even the obdurate Jansenists came to terms with the new order. Intellectual fashions are fickle, however, and from the 1680s onwards the government found itself confronted by a rising tide of criticism and hostility. The link between monarchy and culture had been superficial and ephemeral, for each responded to its own inner dynamics and these were now taking them apart. In addition, the order which had once seemed so desirable felt more like a strait-jacket to the new generations which had never known any other state. As the king himself grew older he lost touch with the life-style of the fashionable world, while a series of disastrous political misjudgements cast increasing doubt on the wisdom and morality of his rule.

The pursuit of glory; Louis XIV and his neighbours

For Louis XIV, as for his mentor Mazarin, the great business of government was the conduct of foreign affairs, seen as much in dynastic as in national terms. The Peace of the Pyrenees had left France with a considerable residue of unsatisfied or controversial claims to territory and influence, notably in the Netherlands and the Rhineland. Aware of the

weakness of the Habsburgs, the king and his councillors set out
to realize these pretensions, under cover of a remarkable
smokescreen of specious legal arguments. Often brilliantly
executed, this policy had unforeseen and ominous implications, not least because it became a kind of addiction. Under
all the ostentation of Louis's reign there seems to have been a
lurking sense of insecurity, which emerged as an obsessive
concern for the prestige of his dynasty. In consequence
France's relations with her neighbours were marked by an
almost frenetic aggressiveness which goes far to explain their
tendency to gang up against her. While almost all the individual decisions which produced this effect can be rationally
defended, the cumulative impression they made on Europe
was a calamity. Trapped within his own narrow and egotistic
vision of the world, the king was almost totally devoid of one
ability essential to a statesman, the capacity to put himself in
his opponent's shoes. His system of government could not
correct this blindness, because Louis himself was the co-
ordinator; a group of ministers giving their advice in the
council were no substitute for a first minister, specifically
responsible for overall strategy. Conciliar government of the
kind Louis practised was all too liable to lose sight of the wood
for the trees, and probably advantaged those ministers who
advocated firm, authoritative policies. It was dangerously easy
to give advice of this kind when the king took ultimate responsibility, and significantly the first major ministerial disgrace
after Fouquet was that of the moderate Pomponne between
1679 and 1691. While too little is known of the inner politics
of the council, it seems likely that during one vital decade, the
1680s, Louis unintentionally allowed Louvois to have his way
on almost every issue. Only after the minister's sudden death
in 1691 did the king realize what had been happening; his
reaction was sharp, but it was too late to undo the damage.
By this date France had embroiled herself in a war against a
great European coalition, in which the most she could hope
for was the maintenance of the *status quo*. If the anti-French
alliances of his later years proved both durable and implacable, the king had only himself to blame, for the cement that
held them together was the fear and hatred born of his own

earlier policies. Like Spain before her, France had proved incapable of the restraint which might have made her predominance bearable by the other powers of Europe.

The complexity and length of the wars makes even a summary narrative impossible, but Table 1 attempts to convey the most important facts in brief. It is immediately obvious how the military balance steadily tipped against France, and how all the wars, with the partial exception of the War of the Spanish Succession, began with acts of aggression by French troops. Only the brief War of Devolution came anywhere near achieving its objectives—but at the cost of destroying the traditional alliance with the United Provinces. It was Louis XIV's attempt to punish this 'ingratitude' which produced the first major failure; when the invasion of 1672 looked certain to overrun them, the Dutch opened the dikes and literally bogged their enemies down. This was a check from which French foreign policy never fully recovered. The general war which followed brought an end to most of Colbert's reforms, while the peace settlements at Nijmegen in 1679 gave France border territories which could have been much more cheaply won. At this point it would still have been possible to draw back, but Louis and his ministers completely failed to learn any lesson from their setback, persuaded themselves that it had actually been a French triumph, and went on to commit a series of massive blunders. The use of the legalistic fiction of the *réunions* to annex Luxembourg, Strasbourg, and much of Alsace between 1680 and 1684 was a brutal affront to German opinion, which was capped by the extraordinary cynicism of French policy towards the new Turkish menace. Even at the time, the actions of the king's agents told their own story; Louis hoped that the Turks would destroy the Emperor's power, leaving him to pose as the saviour of Christendom, perhaps even to install the Bourbons on the throne of Charlemagne. This megalomaniac dream was brusquely interrupted by the rout of the Turks outside Vienna in 1683, followed by the recapture of Hungary by the Emperor Leopold I, which enormously increased the power and confidence of the Austrian Habsburgs. Already locked in a bitter dispute with the Pope, and now discredited

TABLE 1: *LOUIS XIV's MAJOR WARS 1661-1715*

Wars	Immediate causes	Major battles or sieges	Allies	Opponents	Peace Treaties
Devolution 1667-8	French claims to part of Spanish inheritance in Netherlands: French invasion		None	Spain	Aix-la-Chapelle, 1668. Gains: 12 fortified places in Spanish Netherlands
Dutch War, 1672-9	French invasion of United Provinces	Maestricht (taken 1673) Philippsburg (lost 1676) Cassel (victory, 1677) Ghent (taken 1678)	England (1672-4) Sweden (1675-9)	United Provinces Spain (1673-9) The Emperor (1673-9)	Nijmegen, 1679. Gains: Franche-Comte, Haiti, more towns in Spanish Netherlands. Losses: commercial concessions to Dutch
Nine Years' War (War of the League of Augsburg), 1689-97	French invasion of Palatinate, to support various claims in Germany	Philippsburg (taken 1688) Fleurus (victory, 1690) Beachy Head (naval victory, 1690) Namur (taken 1692) La Hogue (naval defeat, 1692) Neerwinden (victory, 1693) Namur (lost 1695)	None	United Provinces England The Emperor Spain Savoy Brandenburg Bavaria	Ryswick, 1697. Losses: most of territories occupied by *réunions* (but not Strasbourg); most of Lorraine
Spanish Succession, 1701-13	French acceptance of Spanish inheritance for Philippe of Anjou: occupation of Barrier fortresses: recognition of 'James III' of England.	Chiari (defeat, 1701) Blenheim (defeat, 1704) Ramillies (defeat, 1706) Turin (defeat, 1706) Oudenarde (defeat, 1708) Lille (lost 1708) Malplaquet (drawn, 1709) Denain (victory, 1712)	Spain Bavaria	United Provinces England The Emperor Savoy Brandenburg Portugal	Utrecht, 1713; and Rastadt, 1714. Losses: partition of Spanish empire, exclusion of Spanish Bourbons from French throne. Many Barrier fortresses to be garrisoned by Dutch, Dunkirk defences demolished. Some colonial territories and 30-year *asiento* for slave trade to

by his covert assistance to the infidel, there still seemed one way for *le roi très chrétien* to demonstrate that he really was the 'eldest son of the Church'. For more than a decade the government had been putting increasing pressure on the Huguenots, whittling away their remaining privileges, while obtaining many conversions through bribery or coercion. In 1684 a policy of general conversion by force—the billeting of troops—was put into effect, and by the autumn of 1685 so many Protestants had abjured that the king thought it was the moment to revoke the Edict of Nantes.

The enormous popularity of the Revocation among Catholic Frenchmen at the time cannot disguise the fact, subsequently admitted by even the king's defenders, that it was both a crime and a blunder. The lack of respect for elementary human decency with which it was carried out discredited the regime abroad, while the mass of *nouveaux convertis* presented the Catholic clergy with problems they never really solved. There had been a reasonable hope that the more moderate pressure of earlier years would have eroded the Protestant church to vanishing point, whereas the Revocation actually ensured its survival as an 'underground' phenomenon. The direct economic damage may have been negligible, but at least 250,000 emigrated, taking many valuable skills to France's competitors, alongside a bitterness which was easily transmitted to their hosts. It did not need the crass folly of some bishops, blurting out their hopes of new Catholic crusades elsewhere, to rouse the fury of Protestant Europe and deprive Louis of old or potential allies. The Revocation went far to undermine the position of James II in England, while it impressed neither Emperor nor Pope. Even Louis realized that he had better leave Alsace alone, so the much-vaunted One Faith never extended to all his subjects. It was all part of a policy of force and terror which only temporarily masked the way the initiative was passing to France's enemies; bombarding Genoa and the cities of the Spanish Netherlands in 1684 was a poor riposte to imperial victories against the Turks. By 1688 the hostility of the Emperor and the Pope was posing serious problems for French influence and French clients in western Germany, so Louis rashly decided on a pre-emptive strike to uphold his various claims by force. He was aware of William of Orange's designs on England, but the Prince disguised his intentions exceptionally well, perhaps because he was none too sure of them himself. He gained an unexpected benefit from Louis's German policy, which provided the perfect excuse for him to assemble a large army at Nijmegen, poised to intervene on the Rhine or in England. It was impossible for the French to guard against all eventualities, and the most astute statesman could hardly have foreseen the speed with which James II would crumple up. By the late summer, when the position in England still seemed fairly stable, Louis had effectively lost any chance of helping James, because the only naval forces he had equipped that year were in the Mediterranean. Once William took the decision to invade, he could be in England before the French could get a fleet or an army anywhere near the Channel. That winter, as William secured a bloodless triumph in England, the French troops laid waste the Palatinate and other areas of western Germany, with the aim of creating an empty and inhospitable zone in front of the screen of French fortresses along the Rhine. War atrocities of this kind were not new, but this time the orders had been given from Paris, and had been attenuated rather than exceeded by the commanders on the spot. Far from cowing the German princes and the Emperor into ratifying all France's recent gains, the events of 1688–9 united Europe against a monarch whose will to dominate threatened all his neighbours.

The Nine Years War proved the value of Vauban's fortresses and the army created by Le Tellier and Louvois, but the military operations did not decide the outcome. The financial strength of London and Amsterdam enabled the allies to outlast French resources, finally exhausted by the terrible harvest year 1693–4. The Peace of Ryswick (1697) was a first great humiliation for Louis, with the loss of most of his conquests since 1679. At last the old king began to recognize the realities of the situation; in future he would try to avoid war, spare his people, and reach some kind of *modus vivendi* with the other powers of Europe. All these good intentions foundered on the rock of the Spanish succession, partly because old habits of aggressive imperialism died too hard. For years the various potential claimants had been anticipating the death of Charles II of Spain without a direct heir, and by 1697 their prime concern was to find some compromise which would avert another war. Neither the Bourbons nor the Austrian Habsburgs could accept that the whole inheritance should pass to the other, but the only generally acceptable claiment, the young prince of Bavaria, died in 1698. Louis's diplomacy at this period showed him in a chastened and constructive mood, willing to negotiate a further partition treaty in co-operation with the Maritime Powers. Unfortunately the Spanish court was determined to avoid the partition of the empire, an impossible ambition which helped to plunge Europe into yet another war. When Charles II finally died in 1700 his will made Louis's grandson Philippe d'Anjou his heir—on condition there was no partition. Louis finally decided, very reasonably, to accept the will: he saw the dangers, but for some obscure reason, almost went out of his way to maximize them. At the beginning of 1701 France still had an excellent chance of winning the consent of the Maritime Powers, provided certain concessions and guarantees were given. The Emperor could not seriously challenge France without the support of his wealthy allies, and there was great opposition to renewed war in both England and the United Provinces. It took a disastrous series of provocative acts by France to give the war party in both countries the upper hand; once again Louis had failed to anticipate the most predictable reactions of other people. He was now to reap what he had sown, for once hostilities had begun all the rancour and hatred accumulated over the past decades impelled his enemies to push their advantage home. The war proved long and terrible beyond all expectation, with the military genius of Marlborough and Prince Eugène helping the allies to win a series of crushing victories. France was only spared a major invasion because the delays imposed by Vauban's fortress barrier in the north-east gave time for the ministry in London to change, so that England finally pulled out of the coalition. The treaties of Utrecht and Rastatt did not impose substantial territorial concessions on France, because the claims of the victors were met at the expense of the Spanish empire, but the scale and importance of the defeat could not be hidden. Louis XIV had the misfortune to live long enough to see the consequences of his own errors, with the destruction of French claims to preponderance in Europe.

The costs of war; finance and government

The ultimate objection to Louis XIV's foreign policy is not just that it was immoral, nor that it brought death or misery to millions of people, but that the potential gains were never worth the risks involved, let alone the eventual cost. There is a striking disparity between the enhanced power and organization of the French state, and the ends to which they were put, a motley combination of dynastic pride, outdated religious antagonisms, and piecemeal frontier annexations. The wars of the Cardinal-Ministers had been equally terrible in their way, but at least they had been motivated by a conviction of overriding national needs and national danger. By comparison most of Louis's wars seem almost gratuitous; the partial exception is the War of the Spanish Succession, a conflict which more supple diplomacy should have been able to prevent or limit. The financial consequences for the monarchy were shattering, yet this did not mean that France as a whole was a ruined country at the end of the reign. Great though the hardships had been, recovery was remarkably quick; not even Louis XIV could impose sufferings on his people to compare with those of the 'great winter' of 1708–9, or destroy agricultural wealth on the scale achieved by the great bovine epidemic of 1714. The French peasantry somehow absorbed the savage blows of royal fiscality and natural disasters, kept the land under cultivation, and maintained the flow of wealth which supported monarchy and privileged orders alike. The tax demands of the 1700s may have led to the partial abandonment of some villages, and to a resurgence of violent resistance, but they were probably less damaging to the social order than the expedients used by the *contrôleur général* Pontchartrain in the 1690s. Potentially a great minister, he was forced to waste his talents on the introduction of a singular range of abuses, including debasement of the currency and the widespread sale of offices, titles of nobility, and tax exemptions. Many of the offices were both absurd and vexatious, impeding the conduct of normal life, while the conversion of elected municipal offices into venal hereditary posts meant the destruction of the last vestiges of independence in the towns.

All these devices, along with massive borrowing and periodic defaulting on interest payments, were still insufficient to cover military expenditure; the harvest crisis of 1693–4 made the position dramatically worse, compelling a new initiative. At last the crown taxed the rich, through the *capitation* tax of 1695, levied on a crude sliding scale. The twenty-odd millions it brought in were far from eliminating the deficit, however, and the king's pledge to abandon it after the conclusion of peace meant that it ceased soon after the treaty of Ryswick. The debt of 1697 remained intact as hostilities resumed in 1701, and the *capitation* returned with them, although the privileged increasingly managed to evade payment by diverting the tax to their inferiors. Offices had now become virtually unsaleable, so Pontchartrain's successors Chamillart and Desmarets had to find other sources of extraordinary revenue. The issue of paper money resulted in the predictable débâcle, while the *intendants* were ordered to resume the old practice of imposing arbitrary *taxes d'office* on the wealthier *roturiers*, always suspected of evading their full obligations. The *gabelle* and other indirect taxes rose to unprecedented levels, accompanied by a massive increase in smuggling and other forms of evasion. In 1710, aware that the *capitation* had ceased to function properly, Desmarets supplemented it by the *dixième*, which was to prove a more durable levy on the rich. None of this could prevent Louis XIV from dying amidst a virtual state bankruptcy; some optimistic calculations by Desmarets in 1715 showed a peacetime deficit of about 50 million *livres* on expenditure of 120 millions, despite the continuation of the extraordinary taxes. The figure for the total debt depends partly on the method of calculation, but it has commonly been reckoned at well over 2,000 million *livres*.

The lack of significant direct opposition to these various forms of exaction demonstrated the extent to which the monarchy had reinforced its power since 1660. Far the most important resistance came from the Huguenots of the Cévennes, where the revolt of the Camisards (1702–5) proved a major embarrassment. The fanatical determination of the rebels and the appallingly difficult terrain tied down substantial forces of regular troops; it was the diplomacy of Villars, as much as the efforts at repression, which finally brought the rebellion to an end. The only other serious popular revolt was that of the *Tard-Avisés* of Quercy in 1707, provoked by the introduction of a *contrôle des actes* charge for extracts from parish registers, which the peasants saw as a version of that longstanding fear, a tax on births. The peasant bands were quickly dispersed by royal dragoons, cutting short a revolt which in earlier times might have caused far more trouble. Whatever their feelings about the *capitation*, the lower nobility did not participate, doubtless well aware of the watchful eyes of the local *intendant* and his subordinates. After a period of fairly modest development under Colbert, the *intendants* expanded their role further from the 1680s onwards; they found it necessary to make much wider use of *subdélégués*, and to establish permanent local offices, although the latter were always insufficient to deal with the work-load. During the 1670s and 1680s the government, increasingly conscious of its own strength, was drawn into a steady extension of its intervention in the minutiae of social life. Problems such as those of the poor, the vagabonds, the gypsies, of prostitution and public hygiene, all became the object of renewed campaigns of regulation. The principle of the Paris *lieutenance de police* was extended to other towns, in close co-operation with the *intendants* and the municipalities, and backed by a constant flow of edicts and *ordonnances*. At times the government's maxim appeared to be 'if it moves, regulate it'. Inevitably the whole cumbrous mass of legislation proved largely self-defeating; the agencies for enforcement were immediately overburdened, so that in this area as in many others the regime proved to have bitten off more than it could chew. All the efforts of the next century would never succeed in getting the machinery working properly, while the government was blamed for failing in the responsibilities it had taken on itself. That the attempt was made at all was a sign of the subjection of almost all those local institutions previously charged with general duties of *police*. In 1665 the *parlements* and those other courts previously entitled 'sovereign' were brusquely renamed *cours supérieures*, while in 1673 the rights of remonstrance were so reduced that they lost all political importance. Although general legislation was still hard to enforce properly, it was now possible to issue an *arrêt du conseil* dealing with a specific issue and have it obeyed. The government snuffed out nascent troubles by exiling or imprisoning individuals who showed signs of being trouble-makers; a few tiresome officials were even deprived of their positions. When criticism of government decisions was heard from the localities, it often came from the *intendants* themselves, as they became increasingly concerned to protect their *administrés* and ease their own multifarious burdens.

The traditional techniques of distributing titles and pensions, much used by earlier governments, were expanded and refined to make obedience attractive as well as prudent. The clienteles of the great magnates seem to have been declining in any case, partly because of the disillusionment created by the feckless conduct of *les grands* during the Fronde, partly because the court monopolized the attention and fortunes of the leading nobles. The importance of royal patronage in the army, the administration, and the church made it imperative for the magnates to be in good odour at court, drawing them to reside there. This process was virtually complete before the final move to Versailles in 1682, which was more a symbol of the crown's triumph over noble dissidence than its cause. Despite the legend, the establishment of the court at Versailles coincided with the close of the great period of artistic patronage, mistresses, and displays of magnificence. The enormous palace was the background for the gloomy years of defeat, the pious rigour of Mme de Maintenon, who secretly became the king's second wife in 1684, and the bitter arguments over religion. The strange decision to isolate the court in a formalized structure was more in the Spanish tradition than the French (most French kings had allowed remarkably easy access to their person) and had some very unfortunate consequences. Divisions soon began to widen between the court nobles and their much more numerous country cousins; other factors aside, the morality of the court, always dubious, was completely undermined when several thousand people were cooped up together at Versailles, with gambling and adultery as their main distractions. The king himself became a remote figure, who no longer travelled about the kingdom as his predecessors had done. His heirs would be brought up in the stifling atmosphere of the court, learning to accept noble values and attitudes as a matter of course. The nine nobles out of ten who never went to Versailles inevitably came to feel themselves increasingly distinct from the monarchy and its gilded courtiers.

Recent Anglo-American historians, perhaps reacting against earlier hostile prejudices, have been inclined to stress the extent to which Louis XIV's regime was generally on the side of reform and economic development. While this is a valid reassessment of governmental intentions and instincts, it must not be allowed to hide the self-defeating nature of most of the policies actually followed. Like many other organizations, the royal government genuinely wished to impose standards on others, yet was unable to keep them itself. Respect for the public good, for fiscal propriety, and for the long-term rather than the immediate, were virtues all too often disregarded by the crown itself on grounds of *raison d'état* and overriding need. The picture of Louis XIV as a reforming monarch is necessarily based on his actual management of affairs, rather than on clearly formulated overall policies; the absence of the latter points up the lack of the conceptual framework indispensable for wide-ranging and successful reform. In practice it is almost impossible to disentangle the genuinely progressive elements from the need to enforce public order and secure more taxes, while traditional ideas continued to dominate critical policy choices. The ministers coped with points of detail in a determined and well-intentioned fashion, recognizing the need to secure the general good at the expense of private privilege. Unfortunately they retained great respect for privilege as such, tried to avoid clashing with it directly, and would have liked to freeze French society in a static and outdated mould. The fundamental and damaging ambivalence of their attitudes reflected the inevitable time-lag between a changing world and men's perception of the problems it threw up. The kind of reforms they tried to impose from the centre were naturally superficial, as in the case of the efforts to interest the nobility in trade and industry by relaxing the rules of *dérogéance*. Chipping away at the more vulnerable aspects of noble and corporate privilege had the effect of alerting those concerned to the danger they ran, without being enough to check the growing social distortions caused by such privilege. Conservative opponents were able to portray themselves as victims, blaming the government for their problems even when it was not responsible. It has often been said that eighteenth-century France needed an enlightened despot; perhaps it would be more plausible to suggest that Louis XIV was the French version of that curious creature, but that he came too early. The ideology of enlightenment had yet to be properly formulated, economic conditions were peculiarly difficult, and perhaps an honourable failure was all anyone could have achieved.

The growth of religious and political opposition
The same desire for order and control that dominated royal political and social policies was evident in the religious sphere. The assault on the Huguenots was not the end of Louis XIV's intervention in spiritual matters, for there were heretics within the Catholic church as well as outside it. The king's ignorance of theology, and his limited conception of religion, gave a certain power to his advisers in this area, but also complicated their task. It was never easy to make Louis XIV recognize the awkward realities of religious problems, in dealing with which he fluctuated between obvious uncertainty and the use of excessive force. Between the vague and anachronistic claims of the Papacy, and the dubious evasions of the secular power, there was every opportunity for clashes in which both sides were the losers. The more Pope and king tried to define and establish their respective authority, the more insoluble questions they raised, and the more they rendered convenient old compromises unserviceable. Within the French church the king's repeated interventions against the old bogy of Jansenism stirred up rivalries between parties, institutions, and

religious orders, which helped to broaden the appeal of Jansenism as an opposition doctrine. In both respects an inept and heavy-handed policy ended in a humiliating reversal. The long quarrel with the Papacy, which began over the minor issue of the *régale*, then deepened with the great assertion of Gallican independence by the Four Articles of 1682, culminated in an impasse which even prevented the appointment of new bishops. The king belatedly discovered that the Pope could cause him serious diplomatic problems which outweighed the other issues at stake, so the 1690s saw the abandonment of most of the troublesome royal pretensions. At this point Louis, increasingly swayed by Mme de Maintenon and her clique of *dévot* councillors, became embroiled in that series of controversies which helped provoke a major resurgence of the Jansenist quarrel. To outside observers his attitudes to the Jansenists seemed just as antiquated as those to the Protestants; at Rastatt in 1714 the French negotiators, following their instructions, asked Prince Eugène about Jansenism in the Empire, but he merely expressed astonishment that any monarch should involve himself in these irrelevant theological disputes. Still the king floundered on; in the last months before his death, exasperated by the agitation around him, he accepted the proposal of his more extreme advisers that he should convene a national council of the French church to settle the doctrinal issues once and for all. Fortunately for the church, the old king disappeared from the scene before he could carry out his design, which could only have provided another chance for the opposing parties to tear one another limb from limb.

The religious appeal of Jansenism will be discussed in the next chapter, but one of the most striking features of the great controversies of the end of the reign was their association with a range of other secular criticisms of the government. One of the great obstacles to the attempt to eradicate Jansenism was the sympathy the movement found among the *parlementaires* and other members of the high *robe* class, traditional Gallicans who were hostile to both the ecclesiastical hierarchy and the Jesuits. Many other groups were looking to these guarantors of established custom and legality, as the natural leaders in any attempt to undo the oppressive legacy of the old king, once death had removed his formidable presence. A different current of reforming ideas was associated with the circle around Louis XIV's grandson, the duc de Bourgogne, whose prominent members included archbishop Fénelon and the duc de Saint-Simon. These aristocratic critics naturally wanted to restore much lost power to the nobility; they dreamed of dismantling much of the bureaucratic system, reinforcing social distinctions, and breaking open the tight circle of ministerial families which monopolized high office. The reactionary and impractical nature of many of these plans should not entirely obscure the way in which Fénelon, in particular, appreciated the extent of the miseries Louis had brought on his people, and wanted to make kings aware of their moral responsibilities. The fact that both the duc de Bourgogne and Fénelon predeceased the king prevented these schemes from getting a real trial, which was perhaps as well, but in a less organized way this kind of thinking was to be influential in the early years of the Regency. A similar recognition of the sufferings of the people, and of the poor state of the French economy, was one element in the work of some more pragmatic critics, including Boisguilbert and the great Vauban, who proposed radical changes in the tax system. Together with the vocal opposition of the commercial world to Colbertian mercantilism, these varied attacks on the manner and purposes of Louis's rule represented a major shift in opinion, which was particularly important because it affected so many people in positions of influence or power. Faced with the immediate problems created by the great wars, the ministers could not afford to listen too hard, but they were clearly aware that the issues under discussion were real and serious ones. Inevitably the 1700s saw a certain weakening of the government's grip on the country, as criticism spread, and external commitments absorbed more and more energy. Although it is impossible to chart the decline of the king's own capabilities accurately, the last decade of the reign found him allowing more power to pass into the hands of ministers and advisers, with a consequent loss of central purpose. Louis XIV plainly lived too long for the good of his dynasty or his kingdom, yet to the last his sheer presence kept the would-be reformers at bay, while the administration continued on its well-worn paths.

Historians have often been tempted, noting that little more than seventy years separate the death of Louis XIV and the Revolution, to see some of the causes of the latter in the 'disequilibrium' the Sun King's absolutism created in French political and social life. There are considerable objections to reading history backwards in this way, while in some respects the 'administrative monarchy' was to reach its highest pitch of efficiency during the years of economic and population growth between 1720 and 1760, the great age of enlightened *intendants*. No *ancien régime* monarch had much influence over the long- and short-term cyclical movements of the economy, or could have checked the evolution of literature and ideas, all of which played a vital part in the eventual breakdown. Yet one must admit that many of the problems which the eighteenth-century kings failed to solve were the direct legacy of Louis XIV. He had cowed and crushed opposition, but he had allowed the complex structure of privileges, exemptions, and bureaucratic confusion to survive; the technique of by-passing obstructions to royal power, so successful in the short run, left behind a series of obstacles, none of them very considerable in themselves, but whose combined power to resist was enormous. After the experience of his reign, there was a general determination never to be treated in the same manner again, and the Regency opened in a mood of full-scale reaction. Victims of Louis's persecutions had already shown that they could hit back, most notably Pierre Bayle, whose sceptical writings constituted a subtle but deadly assault on the values by which the king had lived. Perhaps the most devastating testimony of popular feeling is the epitaph noted down at the end of 1715 by a simple parish priest in the village of Saint-Sulpice, near Blois:

'Louis 14, King of France and Navarre, died on September 1st of this year, scarcely regretted by his whole kingdom, on account of the exorbitant sums and heavy taxes he levied on all his subjects. He is said to have died 1,700,000,000 *livres* in debt. These debts were so great that the Regent has not been able to lift those taxes which the King promised to remove three months after the peace, the *capitation* and the *dixième* on all property. It is not permissible to repeat all the verses, all the songs, or all the unfavourable comments which have been written or said against his memory. During his life he was so absolute, that he passed above all the laws to do his will. The princes and the nobility were oppressed, the *parlements* had no more power; it was obligatory to receive and register all edicts, whatever they were, since the King was so powerful and so absolute. The clergy were shamefully servile in doing the King's will; he had hardly to request a grant to be given more than he asked. The clergy has become horribly indebted; other bodies were no less so. Only the moneylenders and tax-collectors were at peace, living joyfully with all the money of the kingdom in their possession . . .'

If this was what his people really felt about him, as all the evidence suggests, then Louis XIV had gone far to undermine his own earlier achievements, and to damage the future of his dynasty.

4

Belief and Culture

Poised between the great ages of the Renaissance and the Enlightenment, the seventeenth century has never acquired its own equivalent label. This is not surprising, for the period was pre-eminently one of confusion and transition, representing a major watershed in the development of European civilization. The exploratory and uncertain character of much thought of the time stimulated great literary and theatrical achievements, while working against the establishment of grand syntheses. The perennial tension between tradition and innovation reached a high point in the century which saw the notion of progress challenge the longstanding belief in the steady decay of the world, debates over the relative merits of Ancients and Moderns, attacks on the orthodox doctrines of Hell and eternal punishment, and the emergence of a rationalistic Deism often associated with the new science. In a peculiarly irregular and jerky fashion the intellectual world was trying to come to terms with the range of knowledge and ideas released by the rediscovery of Antiquity and the invention of printing. Big advances in education and literacy had expanded the circles interested in such matters, and capable of contributing to them, giving intellectual activity a new pace and intensity. There are signs, however, that literacy was spreading much more slowly by the end of the seventeenth century, and that a kind of frontier was being established between the élites and the masses, a related if not identical set of lines separating distinct economic, social, and cultural worlds. There is an obvious contrast between the environment of the peasantry, normally static and closed, and that of the prosperous urban classes, relatively mobile and receptive. Groups like the lesser rural nobility, the artisans, and the wealthier peasants occupied intermediate positions; culturally as in other respects they provided some modest links across a widening gap. The one apparently solid organization bringing all social categories together was the church, which played a central role in nearly all the developments and controversies of the century.

The structure of the church

By a striking irony it was the later years of Louis XIV's reign, the period when scepticism first became a major threat to the faith of the educated, that witnessed the high point of the Catholic reform at parish level. The religious revival among the élites seems to have been above all the affair of the generations born between 1590 and 1640; by the time these men and women had reshaped the church to give it new and more demanding tasks, it was for their successors to carry the resulting burdens. Most of the limitations and partial failures of the great reforming movement can be related to this time-lag between conception and execution, which was itself largely the product of the institutional scale and complexity of the church. Very like the state within which it existed, the church had the greatest difficulty in imposing some internal order and consistency on its own members, and was encumbered by an incoherent yet elaborate structure inherited from the past. Supreme authority was divided uncertainly between Pope, king, and the Assembly of the French clergy; the Assembly, dominated by the bishops, met at least every five years. This situation made it inevitable that the church as a whole would never have a clear and undisputed policy, whether in theological or pastoral matters, and left great latitude to individual bishops. In practice even their authority was far from complete; it was rare for a bishop to appoint to even half the parishes in his diocese, while his cathedral chapter and the other privileged interest groups were frequently hostile to him almost as matter of course. French bishops did have unusual discretion in respect of both doctrine and pastoral practice, however, because the king and the *parlements* had consistently blocked official acceptance of the decrees of the Council of

Trent. This did not represent hostility to reform as such, but resulted from numerous incompatibilities between the decrees and the Concordat which protected the 'Gallican liberties'. Each diocese could therefore have its own ritual, catechism, and synodal statutes, which any bishop might recast or replace, just as he might approve or forbid the use of particular books and manuals. It was as easy for a bishop to introduce his own idiosyncratic views in such ways as it was difficult for him to impose any real unity on his diocese in the face of all the techniques of obstruction open to those who differed from him. Since there were over 120 bishoprics, and nearly 30,000 parishes, to whose *curés* one must add an uncounted mass of *vicaires* and unattached priests, the texture of religious life was rich but extraordinarily diverse. The size of the system, and the range of opinions within the church, may have made such diversity inevitable; the resulting disputes and debates nevertheless absorbed an enormous amount of energy which should ideally have been put to more constructive ends.

The monarchy was frequently troubled by the internal divisions of the church, and naturally reacted by trying to increase its own indirect authority in religious affairs. This had to mean enhancing the power of the bishops, who were in effect royal nominees, their appointments normally being rubber-stamped by the Pope. It also happened to accord with the Council of Trent's emphasis on episcopal power as the only answer to the church's structural problems. At the beginning of the seventeenth century the choice of bishops seems to have been made rather haphazardly within the normal framework of royal patronage; Richelieu predictably imposed his personal control, and after his death bishoprics and other high positions in the king's gift were distributed on the advice of a small group of churchmen, whose most constant member was the king's confessor. From the 1660s to about 1700 the other major influence was that of the archbishop of Paris, for although his see did not confer primacy within the French church, having only become an archbishopric in 1622, the holder inevitably had great potential leverage at court. Whoever made the effective choice, the men appointed conformed to a pattern which changed very little over the century. The great majority were noblemen, many of them very young, although there was also a significant group of widowers who took orders relatively late in their career, including some ex-*intendants*. The *robe* nobility, especially the ministerial families, exploited their connections and perhaps their superior education to secure a disproportionate number of bishoprics in comparison to the much more numerous *épée* nobles, but roughly half of all appointments still went to the latter group. It was possible for less well-born clerics to become bishops, and about a quarter of those chosen were not noblemen; even these, however, were almost always sons of well-established *bourgeois* families, marked out by personal talent, influential protectors, or special service to the crown. The rich and prestigious sees invariably went to those of high social rank, and in this respect, as in so many others, the church mirrored the society within which it existed. It was the First Order in name only; lesser clerics were expected to give precedence to nobles, outside the limited context of religious ceremonies, and the church was essentially a vast reservoir of wealth and power, colonialized by the privileged strata of society. Clerical celibacy ensured a steady flow of vacancies open for competition, and the rules of inheritance made the dispatch of younger sons into the church an attractive way of preserving the family patrimony.

Giving preference to the highly-born did not necessarily imply the selection of scandalous or irreligious bishops; although such individuals certainly existed, they were not very common. From a mixture of genuine conviction, conformism, and an element of role-playing, the higher clergy generally applied themselves to their duties, and tried to uphold their professional prestige. Ambition and arrogance were more characteristic faults than incontinence or idleness, and while absenteeism was a besetting problem, it often arose from the demands of royal service. Ecclesiastics were employed as ambassadors, in various administrative capacities, and as military leaders. This last function had become almost normal under Richelieu, with such prominent figures as Cardinal de La Valette and Archbishop Sourdis, but disappeared during the personal rule of Louis XIV, as bishops came to be envisaged in a more straightforwardly clerical light. From this period on their 'external' role was only of regular importance in those *pays d'états*, such as Languedoc and Brittany, where they had traditional influence in the Estates, or in such strategically important cities as Strasbourg. Louis XIV's financial problems made him anxious to manage the Assembly of the clergy, and he secured substantial assistance in return for various concessions to the episcopate, notably the Edict of 1695, which considerably strengthened the bishops' authority over their diocesan clergy. Such measures reflected the incredible number of petty squabbles over jurisdiction and practical control which beset the hierarchy at the local level. The canons of the cathedral chapters were probably the most tiresome element within the secular clergy; their comfortable sinecures were usually the preserve of the local nobility, their self-defensive reflexes were abnormally well-developed, and it was an exceptional bishop who enjoyed good relations with them. Canons, archdeacons, or well-connected *curés* might also catalyze the resentments of the parish clergy as a whole, and it was not unknown for their intrigues to end with violence and disorder at a diocesan synod. The exercise of proper supervision over the mass of the secular clergy, the most difficult and fundamental of the church's internal problems, could easily lead to the frictions and misunderstandings which lay behind such unseemly episodes, and were more commonly concealed beneath a merely formal obedience, a peculiarly intractable kind of resistance. All these conflicts betray the dangerous lack of instinctive common feeling between the bishop and his subordinates; his social origins, his wealth, and sometimes his court connections, combined with the repressive authority he was required to exercise, helped to maintain the divide. A few saintly and ascetic bishops did manage to inspire their clergy, but for the most part improvements at the parish level could only be achieved by a long and sustained process of discipline and education. Despite its institutional defects, the Catholic church did prove capable of generating such a reform movement in France during the seventeenth century, with profound results.

The formative decades of the Catholic reform

The counter-reformation had been slow to make an impact in France, largely on account of the disruption caused by the Wars of Religion, which produced more fanaticism than serious reform. By the end of the wars, however, a new spirit was becoming evident among the bourgeoisie and sections of the nobility, precisely the same groups as had provided the central core of Protestant support. In many respects the reform movement was strikingly similar to the earlier forms of Protestantism, with a shift towards a more individualistic conception of religion, a revival of the notion of a godly élite, and a rejection of some of the superstitious and magical elements which still survived in popular belief. Such reformers were inevitably concerned about the corruption and worldliness associated with the church's role as a great property-owning corporation, and saw better pastoral care as a prime need. They believed in education as the means towards greater lay participation in the church, which would result in a deeper personal commitment by the faithful. The impetus of the new Catholicism came largely from these ideas, which owed much to great Italian reformers such as St. Charles Borromeo. The first half of the seventeenth century produced an impressive list of major religious leaders, including such famous names as François de Sales, Pierre de Bérulle, Vincent de Paul, and Jean-Jacques Olier. In their different ways these men all expressed an outgoing and missionary Christianity, keenly aware of human deficiencies, yet basically optimistic about the possibilities of individual salvation. They were convinced of the need to reform the secular clergy, and the method chosen was above all the creation of new organizations, such as the Oratory, the Lazarists, and the company of Saint-Sulpice. Unlike the old regular orders, these new foundations were designed for pastoral work, conducting missions in towns and countryside, and providing teachers for seminaries. These same activities were a central concern of the Jesuits, and the celebrated society had quickly established itself as a powerful force in France, in the face of hostility from many Frenchmen who saw it as a tool of the Pope and the king of Spain. The society survived these antagonisms partly because the

monarchy recognized its utility, with the post of royal confessor normally being filled by a Jesuit, and partly because its
colleges, providing the best secondary education available,
turned many parents and pupils into strong supporters. For
missions and preaching the Jesuits had effective rivals in the
reformed Franciscans known as Capucins, and numerous
other new or reformed orders also took a share in such tasks.
The older-established regular and mendicant orders, which
had reached a very low ebb in discipline, spirituality, and
public esteem, gradually experienced something of a revival,
although here there was often prolonged resistance to the
introduction of a stricter regime, and the traditionally inward-
looking nature of the establishments often limited their importance for the Catholic reform movement as a whole.

The renewal among the regulars was much quicker and
more extensive in the case of the feminine religious houses
and orders. Here too there were remarkable and inspiring
figures, among them Mme Acarie, who introduced the Carmelites to France, Jeanne de Chantal, founder of the Order
of the Visitation, Angélique Arnauld, the reforming abbess of
Port-Royal, and Louise de Marillac, associated with Vincent
de Paul in the foundation of the Sisters of Charity. Many less
celebrated women contributed their part, either by helping
the foundation of local houses of the major orders, or by creating their own local congregations. The Carmelites were a
closed order, distinguished by their piety and strict discipline,
while the Visitation and the Ursulines, also technically closed,
specialized in girls' education. The Sisters of Charity and their
imitators, on the other hand, were not nuns in the old sense at
all, but went out into the world to nurse and teach. In view of
the constraints society placed on their activity, it was inevitable that many of the feminine orders should be less aggres-
sively missionary than those of the men, and not surprising
that many nuns were drawn to mysticism. Religious establishments of every kind were founded at such a rate during the
years 1600–50 that their total number more than doubled; in
many towns it trebled. Clearly this pace could not be sustained,
and there was a sharp drop in the expansion after this time,
associated with a gradual change in attitudes. In the 1660s

Colbert and the king both deplored the excessive numbers of unproductive regular clerics, and most foundations were now for specifically useful purposes, educational or charitable. The economic base of the expansion had been fragile; devout enthusiasts naturally took the line that a modest endowment was enough, and that God would eventually provide whatever was lacking. The propertied classes were generous, but it was difficult to keep a flow of donations going, especially when other establishments were constantly appearing in competition. Houses which began with a group of young women were particularly vulnerable, for as the proceeds of their modest dowries were consumed new funds could only come from gifts or new recruits who increased both numbers and costs. By the end of the century the government was obliged to investigate the finances of many smaller houses, eventually closing down or amalgamating a fair number of them. Municipalities had long become cautious about allowing further creations within their walls, unless they were likely to prove both useful and solvent. However real these difficulties were, they represented a check rather than a serious decline; if the achievements of the later generations were to be less spectacular than those of the heroic age of expansion, there was still a great deal of effective consolidation. Even those institutions which slipped back from the high ideals of their founders generally maintained a respectable level of devotion, while the charitable organizations laboured valiantly against overwhelming problems.

The church gained in many ways from the extent to which it recruited among the upper classes of society; wealth, influence, and a vital element of clerical self-confidence all depended heavily on this link. The fact that benefices were commonly seen as careers for younger sons, and feminine religious houses as a cheaper alternative to marrying off a daughter, did not have disastrous consequences. Most children seem to have accepted such parental decisions with resignation (some, of course, faced opposition to their entry into religion), and there were compensations for both sexes. Women might well have been relieved to escape the often brutal world of seventeenth-century marriage and child-bearing, and masculine ambitions could be realized at least as successfully within the church as in any other career, Richelieu's meteoric ascent being the most notable example. Lack of vocation could lead to troubles, including scandalous sexual misconduct, and the more aristocratic nunneries (especially those of the Ursulines) occasionally suffered from outbreaks of what contemporaries identified as demonic possession; communities of young women excluded from their families in their teens were obviously vulnerable to attacks of mass hysteria with a strong sexual undercurrent. Here too fashions changed, for whereas the possession of the Ursulines of Loudun in 1633–4 caused the burning of the *curé* Urbain Grandier, and made the abbess Jeanne des Anges a celebrity as a 'saint', later episodes at Louviers, Auxonne, and Toulouse were met with growing scepticism by the authorities. The emphasis was shifting from the mysticism and fervour of the earlier decades, strongly influenced by the great Spanish saints Teresa of Avila and John of the Cross together with their numerous followers, to the more pragmatic tasks of bringing order to the clergy as a whole, and taking religion to the people. The first half of the century had been the great age of the religious orders, the second was to be that of the seminaries.

The training of the secular clergy

Until this period there had been no formal system of education for the secular clergy, and the small proportion of university graduates among the *curés*, heavily concentrated in the towns, frequently left rural parishes in the hands of a *vicaire*. Some control was supposedly exercised over ordinands, but the primary qualification required after the Edict of Orléans (1561) was financial: property worth a minimum annual sum, generally 100 *livres*. After 1600 this seems to have been fairly widely enforced, but the tests for professional competence remained notional. Most clerics still learned their trade—for this was how they and their parishioners commonly saw it—through apprenticeship to an existing priest, very often a relative. After ordination they might become *vicaires* while awaiting the reversion of a benefice, to be obtained through ties of family or favour; the widely dispersed rights of presentation, and the various means by which an existing holder could resign in favour of a named successor, contributed to this situation. Quite apart from the formal property qualifications, *cures* were bound to become the preserve of the relatively privileged, since they conferred some modest prestige and provided a secure if rarely very lucrative income. Far from being humble peasants, the great majority of *curés* were the sons of small to middling bourgeois, sometimes of lesser nobles. Where a large proportion did have rural origins, as in parts of Normandy, they were the sons of prosperous *laboureurs* monopolizing some unusually profitable positions, and across the whole country this rural élite was another source of clerics. The *curé* was often not a native of the area where he served, and certain areas were well-known exporters of clergy; the Massif Central supplied incumbents for the poorer parishes of the adjoining plains, while Normandy had a reputation for producing avaricious expatriate priests. Whatever their social or geographical origins, however, there is no doubt that the parish clergy normally underwent a certain acculturation, provided they lived in their parish and established some community of feeling with their flocks. Even at the beginning of the seventeenth century, when clerical abuses and ignorance were widely condemned, many *curés* evidently enjoyed the esteem and trust of their parishioners. The religion such men purveyed was probably fairly heterodox, since there was really no mechanism for correcting the local variations built up over time, and popular tradition was much stronger than the occasional episcopal attempts to repudiate it.

One must be careful not to generalize from a few striking examples or the blanket condemnations of contemporaries, yet there are good reasons to suppose that a majority of the secular clergy was guilty of serious infractions of the rules. It was not exceptional around the middle of the century for one priest in four to be officially rebuked during his career, and there is evidence to suggest that the majority of offenders were never detected. If a *curé* was popular with his parishioners, they were quite likely to conceal his misbehaviour, even if it included keeping a concubine and a family. Tolerated in many cases, such moral failings aroused scandalized protests when a priest was disliked for avarice and absenteeism. These were the major faults in the eyes of most laymen, and were probably given a sharper edge by the restoration of the tithe system in the early decades of the century. Meanwhile bishops and archdeacons were gradually increasing the range and frequency of their visitations, discovering in the process the dilapidated state of churches and the inadequacies of the parish clergy. Reforming bishops soon saw the relevance of the Tridentine call for diocesan seminaries; virtually unknown in 1600, these existed in the great majority of dioceses a century later. This was a vital step, for at last the authorities could impose a degree of uniformity on the lower clergy, although as usual there were many limitations. Seminaries needed funds, to pay the teachers and help poorer students, and these were not easy to raise. Bishops contributed out of their own pockets or converted existing benefices, but the process was extremely laborious, and early foundations were often small and impermanent. Bordeaux only acquired a successful seminary, able to supply most of the local needs, in 1682; in Paris there were seminaries for intending bishops, but the diocesan institution was not established until 1696. Training was limited in duration, with most students resident for only six or nine months, and inevitably concentrated on the basic rudiments. Reforming bishops recognized this to be only a beginning, so they tried to organize more continuous systems for clerical instruction. Probably the most important were the diocesan conferences, groupings of ten or so parishes whose incumbents were supposed to meet for a few hours every month to discuss practical or theological points. The conferences date from the end of the century; it proved very difficult to enforce attendance, while there was a danger that they might act as centres for Jansenism or similar troublesome opinions. Visitations gave an opportunity to single out persistent offenders, who were sometimes deprived, but more commonly the *officialité* court sent them for a three- or six-month spell in the seminary. Coupled with an upswing in the general educational level of clerical recruits, these innovations do seem to have brought about something of a revolution in the state of the parish clergy over the century. Gross misconduct became rare, residence was now the norm, and the *curé* was much less likely to go along comfortably with the views of his flock.

The priests and the people

There were naturally considerable variations between dioceses, depending on the local situation and the personalities of the bishops, but almost everywhere the same basic process can be seen, even if it was not at a regular pace. Among the clergy the Catholic reform had achieved an unprecedented penetration to parish level; it remained to be seen how this would affect the relationship between *curé* and people. The ultimate purpose of the whole great effort was to build a more godly society, in which the *curés* must necessarily be the pivotal group who transmitted the new purified religion to the masses. Specialized orders might help by providing missions, teaching, or charitable services, but the hard everyday slog, village by village, had to be the task of the resident priests. They were confronted by a rich and virtually autonomous peasant culture, whose conception of religion differed sharply from that of the bishops and seminary teachers. While generalizations are bound to give an over-schematic and simplified picture, the dominant characteristics of this popular belief appear across the whole country, local variations being of a secondary nature. It was essentially magical and semi-Manichean, set in an animistic universe, and found expression in innumerable rituals designed to procure specific benefits or ward off the threatening forces of evil. Many of the rituals were superstitious adaptations of Christianity, such as the use of consecrated hosts, holy water, and special prayers; others might involve pilgrimages to historic shrines, whose pagan origins were only lightly camouflaged. Some of these practices were approved by the church, others forbidden, but no prohibitions seem to have had much effect on their widespread use. They were deeply rooted in a coherent world view which posited a constant struggle between good and evil forces, personified by God and the Devil, or sometimes split up among a range of ambivalent saints, semi-independent deities who must be placated. Misfortune was not simply accidental; it might be a divine punishment, or it might result from the ill-will of an

enemy. The belief in malevolent witchcraft found a natural
place in this scheme of things, although it was not invoked
automatically, any more than most of the other available
supernatural explanations. The very looseness and flexibility
of the system made it peculiarly durable, partly because they
allowed the individual to take a very common-sense attitude.
French peasants did not commonly go around in terror of the
supernatural forces which permeated their mental world; they
took practical steps to guard against these dangers, just as they
did for other natural threats. Among men, in particular, popular and official religion might often be the subject of a similar
earthy scepticism, emphasizing the worldly motives of both
curé and magical healer, and tending towards a fatalistic
hedonism.

The villagers as a whole, and not just the irreligious minority, often appear as interested spectators rather than participants in the battle between good and evil. Provided they
fulfilled their basic obligations by avoiding or confessing
mortal sin and attending divine service, they felt they had
played their part and that the rest was up to the professionals.
When things went wrong they expected the church to intervene on their behalf, organizing processions and the display of
relics, anathematizing marauding beasts or insects, and generally deploying a whole arsenal of semi-magical remedies for
the everyday problems of both village and individuals. If the
curé refused to provide such services, unofficial rivals were
always ready to step in. Local wizards and wise women were
to be found everywhere passing on herbal or magical remedies
for the illnesses of men and animals, finding thieves or lost
property, and if necessary identifying the source of a spell or
bewitchment. The profound hostility of the clergy to these
unwelcome competitors was of little effect in bringing them
under control; no suitable legal machinery existed, and witnesses were extremely reluctant in any case. The *curé* also
found his own position hopelessly compromised, since many
quite orthodox practices were tinged with magic, and he was
under steady pressure to extend his use of the supernatural
powers widely attributed to him. It should not be thought that
the popular religion was exclusively, even predominantly,

concerned with immediate worldly advantage, however. Individual views doubtless varied, but for almost everyone belief in the afterlife was unquestioned, and the church's role as the agency for salvation therefore bulked very large in their minds. For all but a few extreme free-thinkers, exclusion from Christian burial was a terrible prospect, and even the poor often left money for the saying of masses to help their soul on the right path. The depth of popular feeling was revealed in the popularity of shrines where babies who had been born dead were supposed to revive for long enough to receive the indispensable sacrament of baptism, without which they could never enter heaven.

In theory this concern with the world to come should have given added strength to the system of confession and absolution, the obvious means for the *curé* to keep a tight hold on personal morality. To refuse absolution and exclude parishioners from the sacraments was to make a public example of them, quite apart from any supernatural importance attached to the sanction. The hierarchy also looked on the confessional as a coercive instrument, and bishops ordered greater strictness, with insistence on effective repentence, restitution of wrongs, and reconciliation. Books of 'cases of conscience' multiplied and made their way into the libraries of many *curés*, while the seminary teachers emphasized this aspect of pastoral work. Unfortunately the world of moral rectitude envisaged by the handbooks was too remote from reality, particularly in economic matters. Here the worst offenders were the prosperous, whom the *curé* could rarely afford to confront, particularly as they could always find a compliant confessor in a nearby town. While regular confessions every Easter may have had some modest utility, they were crammed into a brief period, so that they had to be summary, and a wise priest would avoid the kind of rigorism which could only alienate the penitents and build up animosities against him. Another problem arose over leading questions, which confessors were advised to avoid in case they put new sins into people's minds, although it is hard to see how one could get very far without such a technique. It was also possible for the individual to gamble on cheating, by only admitting to serious offences in a deathbed confession which allowed no time for penance or restitution. Apart from these practical difficulties, the whole system needed to be handled with great delicacy if it were not to encourage a very mechanical, formalized conception of religious practice, which was the opposite of what the great reformers had sought. The ideal of turning the ordinary parishioner from a passive into an active member of the church proved impossibly ambitious, and was always being submerged by other considerations. Above all, the church was constantly tempted into a repressive stance, which was really a soft option and evaded the main problem. There was a permanent tension between the desire to build a godly society, in which communal good behaviour was the vital index, and the search for a more personalized and individualized religion. By its very nature as an institution, and because of its limited manpower, the church was bound to stress the first at the expense of the second. The resulting concentration on securing greater outward conformity amounted to a surrender in the face of the obduracy of the old beliefs. Only the surface changed, and the frustration of many clerics was summed up by the *curé* who quite justifiably described his parishioners as 'des idolâtres baptisés'.

To do better than this would have required an educational revolution which was beyond the capabilities of either church or state in seventeenth-century France. Most parishes had schools, but they rarely functioned outside the winter months, and were far from educating everyone to even a basic level; many peasants saw little virtue in formal learning in any case. The spread of literacy might not be much of an advantage to the church, for the seventeenth century saw the appearance of a popular literature hawked around by the pedlars, whose emphasis on miracles and legendary heroes was in line with popular rather than official thinking. This *bibliothèque bleue* contrasted with the formal and abstract nature of the catechism, the primary agency of religious instruction, which obstinately remained a text which was learned by heart more often than it was understood. It was easier to attack the outward manifestations of popular religion, for instance by removing unauthorized images and shrines from the churches and banning traditional ceremonies. This went furthest in the towns, where the clergy were best able to enforce their decisions and could expect support from municipal authorities who shared their dislike for the disorders associated with the more emotive and communal side of faith. Clerical puritanism directed against the public dances and the farces of travelling players was naturally linked with equal rigour towards religious practices, so by the early eighteenth century many of the local processions and ceremonies had been suppressed. Many bishops saw nothing but abuses in profane realities, and spoke of leisure activities only to condemn them; the *curés* in their turn often attacked all distractions. Their dislike of the *cabarets*, the village drinking-places which tempted men away from divine service, was understandable, particularly when it arose from concern about the implications for families. There was, however, a less healthy tendency to get obsessed with the struggle against profanation of religious life, to the exclusion of even relatively harmless amusements. A tactless *curé* could find himself at loggerheads with his parishioners over the removal of a venerated shrine, attempts to close the *cabaret* at certain hours, or the prohibition of village dances. If he tried to get official backing, he was liable to come up against the anticlerical prejudices of the lawyers, while the bishop was rarely prepared to get involved in endless local confrontations. Some prelates acquired reputations as *dénicheurs de saints* through their campaigns against local shrines, but it was the *curés* who had to make the decisions stick.

The priest had a vital social role in the rural community where he automatically ranked as a *notable*. He was an agent of government charged with making public announcements from the pulpit, issuing *monitoires* which ordered witnesses to testify before the courts, and replying to questionnaires sent out by the *intendant*. He recorded baptisms, marriages, and deaths in his parish register, organized informal charity, mediated with outsiders such as lawyers and tax-collectors. Until the later years of the seventeenth century, when clerical education and discipline had been so vastly improved, *curés* were often found playing a leading part in popular revolts; the Catholic reform may have been an important factor in taming

these outbreaks, if only because where the *curé* had partici-
pated, he had seemed to confer some semi-official approval.
There was a danger that in both his secular and his religious
capacities the priest would be a rather ambivalent figure,
often having to perform unpopular duties which emphasized
that his loyalties were divided. The potential split was deepest
in spiritual matters, where the *curé* was expected to impose a
degree of liturgical and theological precision which meant
little to his flock. In practice most individuals must have
worked out some kind of compromise, but this does not disguise the polarization between an official religion dominated
by the values of the educated élites, and the beliefs of the mass
of the people. The first was rational, orderly, and individualistic in its basic tendencies, while the second were chaotic, in-
consistent, and communal. It was this unbridgeable gap which
limited the effectiveness of the reform movement at parish
level, despite its undoubted success in transforming the church
as an institution, and cleaning up many longstanding abuses.
It is noticeable that some of the most successful popular
religious organizations of the time were the *confréries*, parish
groups which arranged feasts and funeral ceremonies for their
members. Their emphasis on sociability and provision for the
afterlife gave them the kind of natural footing in popular
feeling which the church as a whole too often lacked.

The situation was different in the towns, where the *curé* had
to fit into a much more complex social context. Here parishes
were often much bigger, an unfortunate demonstration of the
inflexibility of the ecclesiastical structure, and there were
numerous rival authorities to contend with, municipal and
clerical. The regular orders offered alternative facilities, which
attracted the wealthy and influential, causing a good deal of
friction with the parish priests. There was a tendency for
clerical efforts to be concentrated on the relatively prosperous,
who usually showed the most response, and from whose social
categories the *curés* normally came. The *faubourgs*, where most
of the poor lived, were precisely the areas that were under-
provided with priests, so the mobile population associated
with the social problems of illegitimacy, prostitution, and
begging was commonly left to its own devices. Much of the

pastoral effort in the towns was undertaken by associations of pious individuals, drawn from both clerics and laity, and from both sexes. Between about 1630 and 1660 there was an attempt to organize a national reform movement of this kind, under the auspices of the Company of the Holy Sacrament, founded by a group of devout nobles. Working in secret the Company and its local offshoots tried to perform a kind of *vigilante* function, denouncing offenders against the moral code to the appropriate authorities. The government was always suspicious of any secret operations other than its own, and Louis XIV ordered the dissolution of the Company; local cells survived, however, along with similar independent groups. Interest in this rather unattractive form of moral espionage seems to have waned after the end of the century, perhaps because it had so little effect on the problems it aimed to control, while the general morality was becoming somewhat freer. The charitable organizations which followed the model set by Vincent de Paul were far more effective, but they too found it hard to sustain their effort when the visible returns were so limited. The municipalities, delighted at the thought of getting rid of some of their more tiresome responsibilities, were always ready to hand them over to voluntary groups of this kind. The increase in the numbers and wealth of the more traditional regular orders had its less fortunate side; they could easily become the focus of anti-clerical feeling, particularly if they obstructed plans for civic improvements. Their unpopularity in the rural world, as tithe collectors and landlords, was general and helped to deepen the antagonisms which too often existed between them and the secular clergy.

The Jansenist quarrel

The effects of the Catholic reform as a whole were so wideranging and ambiguous that they defy any simple summary. By 1715 the church had made enormous advances, compared with the position a century earlier, and reform had not lost all impetus, but something of the previous self-confidence had ebbed away. The removal of abuses had produced one unforeseen consequence; they could no longer be used to explain the shortcomings of popular Christianity, and a further reforming drive was called for, although it was none too clear exactly what it should consist in. The nagging uncertainties fostered by this situation may help to account for the deepening quarrels among the devout themselves, which became acute from the middle of the century onwards. Until around 1640 the most serious disputes had seemed to be those with an organizational or political bias, notably the struggles between secular and regular clergy, and between Gallicans and 'ultramontane' supporters of papal authority. The ideas of *dévot* leaders may have diverged on important points, but they still felt themselves to be a minority united in their campaign against worldliness and corruption, as well as against the Huguenots. The breakdown of this loose alliance was signalled by Richelieu's imprisonment of the abbé de Saint-Cyran in 1638, on the grounds that he was a dangerous heretic who was building up a following, and the posthumous publication in 1640 of the *Augustinus*, a massive treatise by Saint-Cyran's friend Cornelius Jansen, bishop of Ypres in the Spanish Netherlands. There were political overtones, for Saint-Cyran was a disciple of Bérulle and had supported the *dévot* faction in 1630, while Jansen had published a violent pamphlet against French intervention in the Thirty Years War. From the start Jansenism showed the hostility to the government which was to be one of its enduring characteristics. Like Protestantism, it looked to the past for its inspiration, and Saint-Cyran at least dreamed of a return to the primitive church, once claiming that all that had happened in the church for several hundred years was nothing but filth. The *Augustinus* set out to be a definitive statement of the theological position of St. Augustine, whose enormous prestige gave additional force to the implied attack on most recent moral theology. The Jansenists developed the arguments of Augustine's anti-Pelagian writings (opposing the idea that salvation results primarily from the acts of the believer) into a predestinarian system which had much in common with Calvinism; original sin had corrupted both human nature and the world to the point where unworthy men could be saved only by a special intervention from God, a predetermined gift of grace. This harsh view clashed head-on with the teachings of the Jesuits, the most dynamic exponents of the optimistic views which had appeared dominant since the Council of Trent. There were differences among the Jesuits themselves, and much wider ones between them and other theologians, but the majority opinion was clearly that some element of free will entered into the question, and that salvation was to be obtained by a combination of one's own efforts and divine grace.

To modern eyes the Jansenist position is liable to appear so antipathetic that it is hard to understand its appeal, particularly when it included such doctrines as the eternal punishment of unbaptized infants. As this example shows, it was a system of thought which took premises to their logical extremes, preferring absolute conclusions to compromises. It tried to cut through the contradictions in which more moderate clerics found themselves entangled, by a rejection of the world and its prudential values, and a denial of man's ability to determine his own fate. This was all done with a remarkable application of logic, carried to its final extreme in Pascal's demonstration that reason itself indicated its own limits, and that humanity could only abandon the attempt to penetrate the hidden mind of God. These ideas could appear as an accurate description of a world in which sin and impiety were rife, and there was also a curious way in which good works were dismissed only to return by the back door. If man was so damaged by the Fall, then he could only achieve a Christian life-style through grace, and the performance of works, although of no direct importance, was a sign that one belonged to the elect. In this way predestinarian doctrines produced a powerful internalized drive for good behaviour, since to succumb to temptation was to raise awful doubts about one's prospects of salvation. To belong to such a sect was to share in a communal sense of being singled out, and to obtain a degree of certainty which belied the nominal arguments about the unpredictable and fearful nature of God's will. These feelings may be most comprehensible in modern terms if one compares the Jansenists to those modern political groups dominated by ideology, which have taken over so much of the moral fervour once concentrated in the church. Of course the recent proliferation of such groups has weakened their impact, whereas in seventeenth-century France they could only exist in the religious sphere; the nearest approaches in political terms were the *dévots* of the 1620s and the circle of Fénelon and the duc de Bourgogne in the 1700s, both largely religious in their motivation. The relatively small size of the intellectual world also helped to make such coteries effective, and the Jansenists had the further advantage of a solid basis of support among the Parisian élites, notably the *robe* class.

The positive factors bringing converts to Jansenism were probably less important than the negative ones, which made it the focus for a great deal of varied criticism of the clerical establishment. The Jansenists gained enormously from the widespread unpopularity of the Jesuits, who displayed a remarkable ability to polarize opinion; their strength in Rome and at court aroused envy, which the unwise conduct of many of their members could only encourage. Individual Jesuits were always prone to make violent and ill-judged attacks on their opponents, in sermons, pamphlets, and treatises full of vulgar invective. The Society made no secret of its aim to dominate the church, or of its belief in its own superiority. Above all, the Jesuits had formulated their own plan for the church of the future, in which a range of pious rituals would be combined with a flexible moral teaching to make obedience attractive and easy. Almost the first great adepts in mass persuasion techniques, they wanted to adapt Christianity to the world, and in the process they were obliged to develop their own modernizing theology. They had understood the basic need of a mass church for a system of doctrine which had something to offer all believers, but this could never be entirely squared with the theology of the primitive church, essentially framed to meet the needs of a persecuted minority belief. The Jesuits were always being drawn towards assertions about free will and the salvation of all believers, which their superiors had periodically to dampen down and which were increasingly attacked as semi-Pelagian by their opponents. In a modified form their doctrines would eventually triumph, but only after more than two centuries of bitter disputes, many of them provoked by the tactlessness and arrogance of the Society itself. The most startling manifestations of the new style were found in the works of the casuists, where the attempt to introduce some flexibility in the application of Christian morality produced a system open to the wildest abuses. Some Jesuit moral theologians seemed ready to justify anything, including theft, duelling, and regicide, as if they could not resist demonstrating their dialectical prowess. In its more reasonable form, this casuistry was designed to allow a confessor to educate his penitents gently, leading them slowly towards a stricter moral standpoint; but however acute the psychological insight behind it, the system was bound to shock more traditional thinkers. One reason for the aggressiveness of the Jesuits towards their opponents may have been their consciousness of the degree to which they had exposed their flanks, and they were quick to exploit every weapon against the new Augustinians, in whom they recognized their mortal enemies. Their efforts to stifle Jansenism helped to entangle the issue with the institutional quarrels of the church, and like the persecutions undertaken by the secular authorities probably ended up by creating more sympathy for the intended victims.

Within a few years of Saint-Cyran's death in 1643 his disciples had begun to shift their ground; the great figures of the new generation, Antoine Arnauld and Pascal, made open attacks on the pastoral ideas of the Jesuits. Jansenism became virtually synonymous with a moral rigorism which rejected the laxism and worldliness of the new theologians, and tended to move away from the rigid predestinarian position of its founders. Already by the 1650s Arnauld and others were evolving a compromise position based on that of Aquinas, which allowed them to accept papal condemnations of some of Jansen's arguments with relative equanimity. Abstruse doctrinal disputes were soon submerged beneath quarrels of parties, in which both sides adopted dubious methods, while accusing the other of bad faith. The condemnation of five propositions from the *Augustinus* by the bull *Cum occasione* in 1653 proved of little service to the Jesuits, even when it was backed up by the obligation to sign a formulary signifying acceptance of the papal ruling. Such clumsy attempts to enforce uniformity would repeatedly backfire, since equivocation was all too easy, and the kind of persecution inflicted on the Jansenist nuns of Port-Royal outraged public opinion. The intrigue which deprived Arnauld of his position as a Doctor of the Sorbonne in 1655 had even worse consequences, for it induced Pascal to write his celebrated *Lettres provinciales*, in which he poured ridicule on the theology and casuistry of the Jesuits. There was an obvious paradox in the character of a movement which preached resignation and the rejection of a fundamentally corrupt world, while demonstrating a remarkable capacity for organization, intrigue, and publicity. Some Jansenists felt that Pascal had taken the wrong turning, but there was no denying that he had beaten the Jesuits at their own game, and his success played a great part in determining the future character of Jansenism. Later writers were always trying to repeat Pascal's achievement, but their satires on the opponents of Jansenism were clumsy and ineffective by comparison; they made the movement more enemies than friends, and created numerous crises. While these errors often helped the Jesuits, they were acutely embarrassing for the authorities in France and Rome alike. There was no real answer to the Jansenist charge that to condemn their position was to condemn St. Augustine, for even if they sometimes misinterpreted their hero, his teaching plainly could not be reconciled with the doctrines of the Jesuits. The dispute had exposed a truth so awkward that it could not be officially admitted; the church's own tradition and the writings of the Fathers were full of internal inconsistencies. In theory the Pope should have been able to lay down an official line, but the Curia realized that this could only be done at the price of splitting the church down the middle, so Rome tried rather unsuccessfully to compromise and avoid final pronouncements.

From the viewpoint of the Jesuits and their supporters, anxious to proceed with the reform and modernization of the church, the Jansenists seemed an infuriating group of niggling precisians, unable to see the wood for the trees. In many ways, however, the rigorist position had more in common with the reformist movement of the later seventeenth century than did the emphasis on devotional practices and the easy way to godliness—this was partly a testimony to the effectiveness of the Jansenist campaign. Already in 1657 the Assembly of the clergy, while adopting a hostile stance on matters of dogma, had reacted to the *Provinciales* by condemning the casuists, and ordering the distribution of the rigorist *Instructions to Confessors* of Borromeo. The furious polemics of the 1640s and 1650s showed that Jansenism was far from attracting the allegiance of a majority of French clerics, but also revealed widespread sympathy for the call to return to the simple morality of the primitive church. The existence of a small group of Jansenist bishops was a painful thorn in the government's side, but they were less significant than the moderate Gallican bishops, of whom Bossuet was the most distinguished, who adopted an Augustinian morality while rejecting the full predestinarian system. Louis XIV himself was always a bitter if ignorant enemy of the Jansenists, and at the beginning of his personal rule he tried coercion, exiling and imprisoning numerous prominent figures. It was soon apparent that the movement was too deep-rooted and enjoyed too much influential support to be broken by such tactics; the wiser councils of the moderates prevailed, and from 1669 Jansenists were no longer openly persecuted, although the authorities discriminated against them whenever possible. It was between the 1660s and the end of the century that Jansenism spread widely among the parish clergy, greatly extending the bridgehead it had won earlier in Paris and a few other cities. This process owed something to the prolific literary output of Arnauld, Nicole, and others, but it was primarily a matter of influence in the actual training of priests through the new seminaries. The crucial role was that of the Oratory, which had remained faithful to the moderate Augustinianism of its founder Bérulle, while acquiring the direction of a sizeable proportion of diocesan seminaries. Relatively few Oratorians were outright Jansenists, and there were periodic attempts to purge the order, but again a general sympathy was probably more effective than direct support. There was a direct rivalry between the Jesuits and the Oratory, for both specialized in education, and the Oratorian colleges enjoyed great popularity in the later part of the century because they were the leading advocates of the fashionable theories of Descartes. These had also come to have a profound influence on the thought of Arnauld and his followers, causing them to emphasize the sovereignty of reason, and further integrating Jansenism into the general intellectual trends of the age.

As the years passed Jansenism became ever more diffuse and varied, a set of linked opinions rather than a coherent organized party. Its growing strength among the *curés* produced a tendency to merge with Richérism, a theory which stressed the special dignity of the parish priest, and argued that the lesser clergy should have a real say in formulating the church's policies. This naturally appealed to the Jansenists when the royal control over bishoprics meant that the episcopate as a whole was hostile to them and obeyed the orders of Versailles. There was a dangerous fusion between the doctrinal quarrels and the latent hostility between higher and lower clergy, which found expression in these alarmingly democratic notions.

The full importance of the general evolution was seen when the disputes flared up again at the end of the century, producing a massive crisis which threatened to tear the French church apart. The trouble began with an apparent diminution of the influence of the Jesuits and their friends, with the disgrace of Fénelon (the influential archbishop of Cambrai) for his Quietist and mystical tendencies, and above all with the affair of the Chinese missions. The Jesuit missionaries in China had won remarkable successes by adapting Christianity to accommodate local practices, but their enemies found this an irresistible chance to discredit them, by pointing out that they were sanctioning open paganism. The accusations shook the credit of the Jesuits as nothing had ever done before, and although the Jansenists had not been the prime instigators, they were quick to join in the outcry; coupled with the appointment of the rigorist Cardinal Noailles to the see of Paris, these events persuaded some of the rasher enthusiasts that their hour had come. The renewal of Jansenist agitation in various unwise pamphlets, the unfailing support of Louis XIV, and an opportune change of Pope enabled the Jesuits to mount a savage counter-offensive and regain most of the lost ground. The arrest of the prominent Jansenist Quesnel in 1703 gave the authorities access to his enormous and highly incriminating correspondence, which revealed the extent of the 'underground' network built up both in France and in Rome. Quesnel's doctrine was also at the centre of the storm, for his *Moral Reflections on the New Testament* was the most successful example of a new style of Jansenist literature, which aimed at carrying the battle to the faithful at large, with the production of Biblical translations and commentaries. Fénelon, who was busy behind the scenes, quickly saw the possibility of obtaining a condemnation of the work, but the first step was simply a reiteration of the old prescriptions by the bull *Vineam Domini* in 1705. The signature of a new formulary was imposed, and when the surviving nuns of Port-Royal refused to sign, they were dispersed and the convent itself razed to the ground. Such futile gestures were not going to convert waverers; Fénelon himself saw it was an error, while admitting that there was widespread support for Jansenism in the church. For some mysterious reason he and the king's violent new Jesuit confessor Père Tellier decided that the answer was to obtain a second bull from the Pope, which would in some unexplained way bring everyone to heel.

The Pope had been angered and disillusioned by the reception of the bull of 1705, so it was only after long hesitations and intense pressure from Louis XIV that he allowed himself to be persuaded to try again. The result was the bull *Unigenitus*, promulgated in September 1713, which condemned 101 propositions taken from Quesnel's work. It was a disastrous misjudgement, whose results were to weigh heavily on the church throughout the eighteenth century, and it raised the controversy to a new level of intensity. Many people who had never thought of themselves as Jansenists found that the Pope regarded them as such, for the bull effectively condemned a whole conception of Christianity which was widespread in France. The laity were to be deprived of free access to the scriptures, of the right to participate in the sacraments, and of an equal place in the unity of the church. For the Pope and the king the church was above all an ordered hierarchy, in which the primary duty was obedience to the authorities; the faithful should be content to follow the path marked out for them, without asking to understand the higher mysteries. It is easy to see why this conception appealed to the higher clergy and the crown, and why it outraged large sections of the educated bourgeoisie. The men in power wanted something impossible, the benefits of religious reform, in terms of better conduct and greater respect, without the intense feelings and difficult moral choices which had to come with them. With the advantage of hindsight one can see that both sides were largely in the wrong; the rigorous, self-denying faith of the Jansenists could never be imposed on the masses, yet it was futile to try and emasculate the far more participatory religion of the élites. The great misfortune of the French church was the involvement of the monarchy, and the resulting attempt to impose a quite unnatural uniformity, if necessary by the use of force. With every effort to define the position and coerce the disobedient, things got worse; party divisions and hatreds accumulated, yet the crown ploughed blindly on. The position of the Jesuits at court gave them influence out of all proportion to their real strength in the church, and led their enemies into dubious manoeuvres which could easily be used as evidence of their penchant for conspiracy. Louis XIV's furious assault on the Jansenists during the last decade of his reign succeeded only in arousing wide public sympathy for them, as victims of violence and injustice, and in making their movement into a major vehicle of political opposition. Hostility to the tyranny of king, Pope, and bishops meant support for the *parlements* and the lower clergy, who appeared as the spokesmen for national opinion against an overbearing and ignorant regime. This evolution also helped to devalue the purely religious aspects of the dispute; from the beginning there had been voices warning of the danger that eventually all parties would be discredited, and so it proved. The only people to gain anything from the whole great conflagration were those who were becoming increasingly sceptical of authority and received opinion in every sphere of life.

Scepticism and censorship

One source of such scepticism lay in the classical inheritance, so important at the time as the standard of thought and conduct, and as the foundation of the educational system. The stoic ideas popularized by Montaigne and Charron around the turn of the century were prominent influences on the religious thought of the time, but they also inspired the *libertins*. Although these free-thinking writers and intellectuals, such as La Mothe le Vayer, Gassendi, Naudé, and Patin, did not subscribe to any clear system of belief, apart from sharing a general hostility to superstition and credulity, their critical attitude to established pieties shocked the orthodox. The trial of the *libertin* poet Théophile de Viau for blasphemy in 1625 foreshadowed a more repressive attitude by the authorities; the censorship, as yet very ineffective, was gradually tightened, until under the personal rule of Louis XIV most unauthorized publications came from abroad. As the century progressed, greater liberty of thought was matched by more effective repression and punishment, a policy whose futility only slowly became apparent. The circles of the *libertins* overlapped with those of the amateurs of science, and the condemnation of Galileo at Rome in 1632 emphasized the potential hostility between the church and a wide range of advanced opinions. In practice there was still a great deal of toleration shown to unorthodox views, so long as their holders were not too vociferous, partly because few if any contemporaries had fully grasped the importance of the matters in dispute. Within an increasingly fragmented scholastic framework, the thought of the first half of the century remained eclectic, and there was a persistent tendency to mask the incompatibilities within it. The Fronde seems to have coincided with a serious disintegration of the façade of intellectual consensus, ushering in an era of much greater doubt and self-questioning. Jansenism doubtless played a part here, vividly illustrated by many of Pascal's writings, as did the philosophy of Descartes, for all the latter's hopes of creating a new synthesis to replace the outmoded Aristotelian structure. The early advocates of the Catholic reform, with their generalized enthusiasm for putting reason and knowledge to the service of religion, were succeeded by a generation determined to follow truth for truth's sake, and impatient of blurred compromises. This change of mood sharpened intellectual divisions, yet produced no quick or satisfactory answers to the questions it posed. Cartesianism, which was very much the fashionable school of thought by the

1660s, was never able to secure official approval, and needed all the help it could get from the continuing eclecticism of the intellectual world, which allowed it to spread in more or less debased forms even among those who nominally opposed it. By the 1680s the government was actually trying, under Jesuit influence in particular, to enforce the teaching of the traditional Aristotelian theories in colleges and universities, partly in reaction to the strong Cartesian bias of many Jansenists and Oratorians.

Tighter censorship and control were the logical conclusion of a policy of intervention in cultural and intellectual life, which was not really contested even by those subjected to it. Royal patronage had always been keenly sought after, and ministers such as Richelieu, Séguier, Mazarin, and Fouquet had built up their own circles; the original *Académie Française* was little more than a formal scheme for distributing Richelieu's favours, and orchestrating support for the government. The establishment of an official list of pensions for writers, artists, and *savants* under Colbert was a further extension and systematization of accepted practices. The effects are difficult to evaluate; they certainly included a great deal of sycophantic adulation of the king, but individuals were encouraged to produce, and given some of the necessary facilities. The royal favour which protected Molière against the *dévots* in the great storm over *Tartuffe* also drew Racine away from the stage to the honourable but artistically sterile post of royal historiographer. Many notable figures were outside the patronage system altogether, among them La Fontaine, La Bruyère, Mme de La Fayette, and La Rochefoucauld. The amount spent on the arts in general was dwarfed by the colossal expenditure on Versailles and its satellite palaces, magnificent but soulless temples of the cult of monarchy. They remind us that, for all the cross-currents which now seem so significant, respect remained an immensely strong force in French life; no individualistic or egalitarian challenge to hierarchical principles had yet developed, and everyone still took for granted the subservience of wives to husbands, children to parents, servants to masters, and all subjects to the king. A sceptical and critical thinker like Pierre Bayle, driven into exile in

Rotterdam as a Huguenot, his brother dead in prison in 1685, had every reason to hate Louis XIV and all he stood for—yet he remained an unrepentant believer in royal authority, convinced that the only policy was to accept the king's decisions, while working to enlighten him. The *philosophes* of the eighteenth century would similarly be partisans of reforming monarchical power, and Voltaire praised Louis XIV as an indirect criticism of the indolent Louis XV. Apart from the violent pamphlets produced by alien critics, and by some groups among the exiled Huguenots, criticism of the established order under Louis XIV remained oblique and qualified. The 'pre-Enlightenment' was nevertheless a force to be reckoned with, and the printing presses of the Netherlands and the Rhineland were more than a match for the increasingly nervous censorship of the turn of the century; there were innumerable routes for smuggling in forbidden books, which predictably found a ready market.

One such book, Bayle's *Dictionary* (1695-7), with its sceptical attitude to traditional verities, and its implacable hostility to popular superstition, was probably a more destructive work than its author intended. Its articles exposed the gross inconsistencies within apparently harmonious systems of thought, and demolished a mass of pious legends. Having demonstrated the inadequacy of conventional apologetics, Bayle was left in a fideist position not unlike that of Pascal, if less lucidly expressed. His work complemented that of the ex-Oratorian Richard Simon, who set out to controvert Protestantism through the historial study of the Bible. Bossuet, who had originally encouraged Simon's work, was horrified when he saw the results, which emphasized the composite and unreliable nature of the central texts of Christianity. Simon's books were duly banned, only to appear from the Dutch presses from 1678 onwards. The adroit and worldly scientist Fontenelle kept out of trouble with the authorities, but works such as his *Histoire des Oracles* (1686) were another kind of indirect attack on revealed religion. The threat was more serious because the hitherto closed world of theology had been progressively opened to the laity, and because by far the clearest statements of atheistical ideas were to be found in the polemical writings of the theologians themselves, always ready to point out the disastrous conclusions that could be drawn from an opponent's arguments. Such carelessness betrayed a basic confidence in the solidity of Christian belief, for when Bossuet and others emphasized the crises facing the church, it was in the full expectation of emerging victorious from these new trials sent by God. They inevitably failed to recognize the importance of that sea-change in opinion which still evades precise analysis, but leads unmistakably forward to the moral licence of the Regency, and the impiety of the *philosophes*.

One of the unforeseen consequences of the sale of offices was the expansion of the circles of prosperous and educated men, with time on their hands, who were the staple of intellectual and cultural life. It was inevitable that many of the writers and artists of the time should come from this background, but its greatest importance was that it provided an informed public, capable of supporting cultural activity quite independently of the court. This development was highlighted after 1680, when Paris emerged as a major rival to the court, with the *salons* becoming more significant than the official academies, and private patrons supporting a new generation of artists. The last decades of the century saw the appearance of local academies in many provincial towns, while personal libraries became larger and more diverse, and numerous *cabinets de curiosités* demonstrated at least some general interest in science. The popularity of historical and geographical writing may be seen as evidence for a more informed view of France's relative place in the world, while fiction moved towards realism and contemporary subjects. Educational standards clearly rose over the century, notably among the bourgeoisie and the *robe* class; the education of nobles generally remained more practical, although the fashionable academies in Paris provided some additional polish. Louis XIV's encouragement of elegant manners was part of a much wider trend, stretching throughout prosperous society, which saw the evolution of values of *politesse* and *honnêteté*, expressions of a far more refined style. How far this surface change affected basic attitudes it is hard to judge, but some historians have detected shifts in the treatment of children, with greater recognition of their individual needs, and more consideration given to their wishes over the choice of marriage partners. The relationship between men and women may also have undergone some modification, although it was in the upper ranks of society that the domination of adult males was most entrenched, through the property law and social conventions alike. One of the most important phenomena at this level was the growth of a national consciousness; French had become the universal language, and communications between Paris and the provincial centres were rapid and extensive, encouraged by safer travel and the pull of the capital. From the early years of the century it was common for important provincial families to send their sons up to Paris to finish their education, and the personal friendships formed at the colleges could be an important political factor in later years. It was among these élites that the celebrated artistic productions of the century were known and appreciated, whether it was the plays of Corneille, Molière, and Racine, the fables of La Fontaine, or the popular tales recast by Perrault.

Patterns of popular literacy, crime, and marriage

The developing assurance and sophistication of polite society emphasized the lack of such changes among artisans and peasants, except where external interventions forced their introduction. In many areas language itself divided popular and privileged culture, for millions of southerners and Bretons spoke quite distinct languages, totally incomprehensible to a stranger from the Île de France. Here the ruling classes were bilingual, but all official records and almost all books were in French, a powerful discouragement to the spread of popular literacy. The cheap books of the *bibliothèque bleue*, produced in ever increasing numbers from the presses of Troyes, circulated almost exclusively in the 'literate' north and east, and had no equivalent in the minority languages. The church itself never really met the demand for service-books, catechisms, and devotional guides in the vernacular, although many *curés* and missionaries recognized them as a first essential. Where the popular literature did penetrate, it tended to confirm existing attitudes and values, for it was basically escapist, ranging from tales of legendary heroes to folk tales, astrological predictions, and magical remedies. Much of the local culture was transmitted from one generation to the next by oral means, especially through the *veillée*, the winter practice of assembling in barns or stables, where groups of families would gather for warmth, the women sewing or spinning, everyone talking, singing, and engaging in a variety of games and amusements. These were also important opportunities for young people to find marriage partners, an operation frequently carried out by gestures more than speech, and therefore misunderstood by educated observers, always prone to accuse their inferiors of brutality and insensitivity.

Contempt for peasant customs was apparently general among the ruling minorities, and by the end of the century had been extended to include a patronizing attitude towards the rural *gentilshommes* and clergy. This was just one aspect of the élites' self-portrayal as *les gens honnêtes*, marked out by prosperity and education, and by their capacity for self-control; in contrast the great mass of mankind, lacking any sense of honour, needed to be coerced into orderliness by laws and the making of examples. Although the law was most interested in questions of property rights, and the courts were particularly severe on domestic thefts by servants, the number of cases of personal violence might well have encouraged this view. Their frequency is all the more striking because village communities, rightly suspicious of the costs and uncertainty involved, showed a distinct reluctance to go to law at all, and might react against an individual who took such an initiative by a general refusal to testify. This was far from absurd, for the animosities aroused by a legal case could divide a village for generations, however trivial the original issue. Peasants were very generous with mutual assistance within certain limits, but these definitely excluded taking sides in other people's quarrels, or giving damaging evidence on behalf of anyone who was not a relative or close associate. One is left with the impression of a world of timid, fearful men and women, whose disputes were normally restricted to formalized, largely verbal, modes of expression, but too often broke out into sudden displays of violence. Even at this stage some intermediary, commonly the *curé*, would probably be preferred to a lawsuit; if the courts were involved, the *curé's* willingness to issue a *monitoire* was often decisive, for this could provide an excuse for witnesses to come forward, once they were threatened with excommunication if they remained silent. (The situation was very different among the poor of the towns, where communal solidarities had largely broken down, denunciations were commonplace, and the courts were available on the spot.)

Marriage was one of the rare instances where outside pressure did bring about considerable changes in local practice over the century. The church waged a long and eventually successful war against the *fiançailles*, virtually a form of trial marriage, with cohabitation beginning after a formal betrothal, but well before the ceremony proper. By the middle of the seventeenth century the *fiançailles* were disappearing fast, but this did not mean the end of all such problems. In the 1700s premarital conceptions accounted for an average of around 10% of first births, partly because of religious and social pressures for marriages of reparation, which kept the rural illegitimacy rate low. There is an important statistical point here, for historians have persistently exaggerated the sexual restraint of peasant society (often—and very implausibly—ascribed to Christian morality) through counting conceptions out of wedlock against *all* conceptions. Almost by definition pre-marital conceptions led to first births, while few unmarried mothers had more than one illegitimate child, so the figures are much more relevant as a proportion of first births only. There were areas of extreme rectitude, but in many others 15–20% of first babies were conceived out of wedlock, and obviously factors such as sheer luck, infertility, and primitive contraception must be allowed for in any guess at the total scale of 'illicit' sexual activity. Clearly it was sufficiently common to worry many clerics, and this helps to explain their hostility to occasions of *fréquentations*, including traditional pilgrimages and feast-days, and the pressure for the segregation of the sexes in schools and the church, efforts which probably achieved some slow effect towards the end of the century—although such marginal changes were of little real value. In the towns (where unmarried mothers from the countryside often took refuge) illegitimacy rates were certainly higher, and there may also have been more successful concealment. Those involved often ended up among those girls whom sheer poverty drove into prostitution, a rare social problem in the countryside, but an inevitable consequence of the establishment of regular garrisons and barracks in many towns. One of the preoccupations of the urban associations of devout ladies was to find ways of helping and reforming these unfortunate victims of society.

The church also had to grapple with another long-term problem over marriage, which arose from its own exaggerated hostility to consanguinity. The prohibited degrees were so widely drawn that in the immobile rural world, where so many people were related, they were constantly being infringed, and there was a heavy demand for dispensations. One of the standard ways of obtaining them was through a claim of 'scandalous commerce' involving sexual relations, so a sympathetic *curé* trying to help his parishioners might find himself in the position of virtually inciting them to commit sins he normally denounced. The retention of clerical jurisdiction in this area also brought about a conflict with the royal government; the state wanted to increase parental authority and prevent elopements, whereas the church insisted on the binding effect of the sacrament, almost regardless of the circumstances. This difference of emphasis arose chiefly because marriage was seen in essentially economic terms, involving some exchange of goods even among the poor, and the establishment of a tiny stock of household equipment. Hostility to unauthorized marriages was a defence of parental authority, family reputation, and property rights all at once, against which clerical scruples about ritual or sexual pollution counted for relatively little. Even the church predictably failed to insist that a substantial property-owner who seduced his servant should marry her; the new offence against the social order would have been greater than the original breach of the moral code. Similarly, dispensations from the prohibited degrees were fairly generously accorded to nobles who claimed they could only find socially acceptable partners among their cousins. Popular society had its own independent forms of moral constraint, most vividly expressed by the *charivari*, the noisy but generally harmless harassment of newly-weds where outsiders, a large age gap, or remarriage were involved. In the villages such activities were organized by the *jeunesse*, the young unmarried adults whose numbers were increased by the tendency to late marriage. The *charivari* was a feeble instrument for preventing such marriages, which were mostly an inevitable consequence of the haphazard pattern of mortality; its real importance was rather that it socialized the new generation by making them the mouthpiece of village conscience. In the towns the rather similar activities of the Abbeys of Misrule (which organized annual processions, ceremonies, and farces) had undergone important changes, since the Abbeys had become professional or neighbourhood groupings including men of all ages. The authorities naturally disliked all such forms of communal disorder, although real violence occurred only rarely, usually when the 'victims' over-reacted. The frequency of both ecclesiastical and municipal prohibitions suggests that the struggle was a hard one; in the country-side it was never finally won, but in many towns the 'law and order' decades under Louis XIV saw the end of ancient traditions of licensed irreverence.

Witchcraft

Another practice which came to an end under Louis XIV was the official persecution and burning of witches. Like most other European countries, France had seen witchcraft develop during the sixteenth century from occasional local episodes to a major preoccupation of the courts. There was probably a sharp increase in prosecutions during the 1580s and 90s, which may have been connected with the disturbances and hardships of these decades. While it is impossible to establish even the approximate numbers involved, there are reasons to suppose that they were still relatively small; on the evidence currently available the likeliest guess is that no more than a few thousand people died for the crime of witchcraft between 1560 and 1670. Lurid accounts of witch-hunts, or such exceptional affairs as the Devils of Loudun, distort the true nature of the phenomenon, which was essentially sporadic and local. Most peasants believed in witches as a matter of course, just as they credited the *curé* and the local wizard with supernatural powers—indeed, a fair number from both these professions were convicted as witches. The witch was an individual who could cause misfortune through wishing one ill, or performing some elementary ritual magic. There was a tendency to associate these undesirable capacities with social isolation, whether it was that of old women dependent on local charity, or of forest-dwellers, shepherds, and itinerants in general. Such suspicions were evidently widespread, and only a tiny fraction of those reputed to be witches can ever have been brought before the courts—this was in line with the wider peasant distrust of the justice handed out by urban lawyers. Reluctance to use the courts emphasized the marked contrast between the stability of peasant beliefs, and the shifting attitudes and frequent disputes among those who ruled. To take a witch to court was also construed as an extreme measure, which amounted to seeking his or her death and might lead to reprisals, particularly if alien judges ignored village feeling and ruled for acquittal. In any case there were alternative measures, above all recourse to counter-magic through the agency of priest or *devin*. The latter, like the witch-doctors of African tribes, often specialized in identifying witches, who could then be confronted and forced into lifting the evil spell they had cast. When cases were brought to court the witnesses frequently revealed a long history of such episodes, making it clear that the witch's reputation was a long-standing one, and that it had taken something exceptional to produce a formal accusation; often this was a suspicion of inflicting lingering illness or death.

The identification of a witch was based on common repute, frequently supported by allegations of a family tradition, for both healing and maleficent powers were commonly believed to be hereditary. The enclosed nature of the local community, and the role of the *veillée* in relaying old ideas and stories, helped to perpetuate such conceptions quite independently of judicial procedures. Very much as in England, the witch's malevolence was normally ascribed to a justified grievance, arising out of some breach of neighbourliness by the victim, whose guilty feelings later caused some misfortune to be blamed on the witch. The refusal of requests for gifts or loans of food and equipment played an important part, but did not predominate in the same way as in England, for in France a wider range of hostile acts seems to have preceded accusations. This greater diversity is most plausibly explained by the lack of any direct attack on the old notion of charity in the French countryside, which made this less of a focal point for trouble than it was in England, although the basic psychological situation was similar. The overall level of witchcraft fears was probably related to the strains imposed by the precarious agrarian economy, which underlay most of the quarrels, and in bad years must have created acute friction over the demands from marginal members of society. There was nothing new in the popular belief itself, and over the preceding centuries most accusations must have been successfully dealt with by informal means and counter-magic, with the occasional instance where a suspect was eliminated by direct action. This probably remained true even during the sixteenth and seventeenth centuries, but the novelty was the growing intervention of the lawyers and clerics, some of whom had elaborated a vast superstructure out of their observations of popular superstitions, combined with the darker elements in the church's own traditions. The resulting emphasis on the diabolical nature of witchcraft, symbolized by the formal pact with the Devil, could become the basis for hysterical denunciations of an enormous conspiracy of devil-worshippers, committed to the degradation and destruction of mankind. Such views never commanded general assent among the ruling classes, but for a time the courts seemed willing to treat popular beliefs with new seriousness, while grafting other elements on to them. Over the years between 1580 and 1622, which saw the publication of the major works on demonology by Bodin, Rémy, Boguet, and de Lancre, the increased rhythm of trials was associated with a slow groping towards a more adequate jurisprudence in this difficult area.

From the start the *parlementaires* seem to have been cautious, doubtless influenced by their anti-clerical instincts, but the most vocal opposition to persecution came from some doctors, who were liable to explain the whole phenomenon as a mixture of ignorance, superstition, imposture, and mental illness. Few denied the possibility of witchcraft, so criticism was most effective when it took the form of challenging its plausibility in individual cases. The workings of the judicial procedure invited such a pragmatic approach, which was seen as early as 1600, when the Paris *parlement* prohibited the swimming test (in which the bound suspect was placed in water, and considered guilty if he or she floated). In 1624 the Parisian judges followed this up by instituting an automatic appeal procedure, under which all cases had to come before the *parlement* itself, and by 1640 they had decided not to impose any more death sentences. Apart from the disconcerting and scandalous affair of Loudun, which aroused a furious public debate, the main reason for this new restraint was a conviction that the nature of the evidence was so dubious as to make the whole process unreliable. The *parlementaires* did not deny that witches might exist; they simply felt that it was impossible to identify them with any certainty, or to test the kind of evidence offered against them. It took some time for the court to impose its view, but already in 1641 a spectacular example was made when three local officials, guilty of the murder of a suspected witch, were hung in the *place de Grève*. Other *parlements*, notably that of Dijon, were moving in the same direction, and this was demonstrated in 1644, when devastating hailstorms and other climatic difficulties set off a widespread popular witch-hunt. In Burgundy, Champagne, and Gascony travelling witch-finders were active, and hundreds of suspects were sent for trial, while others doubtless received more summary treatment. The *parlements* of Dijon and Toulouse reacted by ordering the arrest of the witch-finders, some of whom were summarily executed, and releasing most of the suspects. The episode must have confirmed all their suspicions of popular superstition and credulity, and the years 1640–5 mark the point at which educated opinion swung against the persecution, persuaded that the more witches were condemned, the more new cases appeared, and that subjective evidence from peasants could not be trustworthy.

There were always some clerics ready with emotional demands for fresh campaigns against witchcraft, but the only *parlement* which remained really determined to pursue witches was that of Rouen. The matter came to a head with a new outbreak of rural witch-finding in 1670, this time in Normandy and the south-west. Colbert and Louis XIV intervened to bring the situation under control, ordering the release of the accused and prohibiting further action against supposed witches. Finally in 1682 a new royal ordinance treated witchcraft solely as a matter of fraud and imposture; although occasional illegal local prosecutions went on to the end of the century, the belief had now retreated to the popular level from which it had emerged. While fear of witches was clearly a major part of the mental world of the peasantry in this period, it is misleading to think of a 'witch-craze' in any sweeping sense. Extreme doctrines like those of Bodin were never fully accepted by the ruling élites and, although the use of torture made conviction likely, the courts were very reluctant to employ denunciations obtained by such methods as the basis for further trials. Most of those who died at the stake were convicted on common repute and a mass of trivial circumstantial evidence, and a fair proportion probably believed in their own supernatural powers, if not in the diabolical pact. An important influence in both expanding and later destroying the official persecution was that of printing; the elaboration of a systematic demonology and of various tests for witchcraft had been greatly encouraged by the pooling of apparently confirmatory evidence, but later a more critical attitude to the same material, combined with the publicity surrounding certain scandalous trials, helped to spread doubt and caution. What can never be accurately measured is the extent to which the legal persecution whipped up popular fears, but the events of 1644 and 1670 suggest that it may have been having such an effect at the very moment when the authorities decided to bring it to an end. After a period when they had faltered, the rationalist and sceptical attitudes of the ruling classes re-asserted themselves, and witchcraft beliefs became merely another example of 'la sotte crédulité du peuple'.

Conclusion

The century and a half between the outbreak of the Wars of Religion and the death of Louis XIV saw far-reaching and sometimes dramatic changes in the government and society of France. From a Renaissance state very similar to her neighbours the country developed into a distinctive 'absolute' monarchy which was widely admired and copied. At the same time social and economic relationships hardened into a mould which proved peculiarly durable, so that on most fronts the potential for further change was artificially restricted. Contemporaries understood these processes very imperfectly at first, partly because their historical and comparative sense was still so primitive. By the last decades of Louis XIV's reign, however, many of his subjects were coming to feel that the king's power had not only grown excessive, but was being seriously misused. A few daring spirits looked further still, seeing the need to check, and preferably to reverse, the trend towards increasing social inequality if France were to fulfil her economic potential. The monarchy's inability to satisfy either set of critics would eventually prove to be its downfall. There was nothing pre-ordained about this failure in 1715, and the creators of the absolute monarchy cannot be held primarily responsible for the acute sclerosis which overtook it in the eighteenth century. Yet it does seem clear that there was something radically defective about the polity they built, which it would have taken a further great effort in statecraft to overcome. All the power the monarchy had amassed apparently enabled it to do no more than fight wars and repress internal disorder. This might have been a manageable situation, if virtually all the intermediate powers which could have

played a complementary role in the area of social and economic policy had not been so emasculated that they were capable
of little beyond sterile obstructionism. The crown had crushed
the pretensions of all the defenders of provincial liberties—
grandees, estates, *parlements*, and municipalities alike—yet it
could not fill the resulting gaps.

Some contemporary theorists, especially in Holland, argued
that monarchy was less absolute than democracy, since in
practice the king had to work through the aristocracy and
other established groups. In France, however, the Bourbon
kings went far to find a way through such restraints, surrounding themselves with a small élite of devoted servants, who
embodied the will of a government which extended beyond
the monarch himself. Two or three hundred families of
administrators monopolized the central agencies of power; it
was these men Saint-Simon had in mind when he attacked
the reign of the *vile bourgeoisie* (even though they were all technically nobles). Such radicalism as the new ruling class originally possessed was soon eroded, while once Louis XIV's iron
control was removed the older nobility started to infiltrate the
system which had threatened to exclude them from all real
power. It was a peculiar misfortune that the economic depression of the second half of the seventeenth century should have
coincided with this great age of dynamic royal government.
Deeply wedded to social conservatism in any case, the crown
found its options further restricted by an economic climate so
unfavourable to new initiatives. Despite Colbert's well-meaning
efforts, France's industrial, agricultural, and commercial performance lagged well behind that of her new rivals, the Maritime Powers. Obstinately continental in his outlook, Louis
XIV grossly underestimated the power of the United Provinces and England, whose enmity he so casually incurred.
The great wars between 1689 and 1713 not only pushed back
France's frontiers, and wrecked her primitive system of public
finance; they also confirmed her opponents in their domination of the wider world beyond the seas.

War was not merely the source of calamities such as these;
it lay at the heart of the crown's whole drive to obtain an
unprecedented mastery over the political structure of the

country. However much the kings believed in their ultimate sovereignty, they all recognized that they could only infringe the innumerable particular rights of their subjects when the supreme needs of the state required it. The theorists of *raison d'état* were largely employed in elaborating this slippery doctrine; it was the misfortune of the people of France that their rulers found so many chances to invoke it. The Bourbons may have been no more bellicose than their predecessors, but the stakes were rising steadily, as war itself demanded far greater resources in men and money. It is also at least arguable that the continued dominance of aristocratic values at court, even among many of the administrators, combined with the development of a national army offering career prospects, enhanced an existing tendency to favour 'hawkish' policies. Foreign affairs always took precedence; on many occasions the government made choices it knew were damaging to the social and economic fabric, solely in order to finance its wars. In the long run one of the most crucial flaws in the system was an inability to reformulate its own objectives, so that royal policies, reflecting the conventional wisdom of the past, were often self-defeating or irrelevant. Whereas Richelieu made a brilliant if brutal response to the real problems of his day, Louis XIV and his successors too often remained within the tradition the Cardinal had established. Richelieu's fame is fully justified; enormously intelligent and ruthless, he was the true founder of the absolute monarchy. There is a certain paradox in this, however, for Richelieu himself would surely have been infinitely more flexible and constructive in responding to the new conditions after 1660. Perhaps it was such a feeling which caused Michelet to denounce 'the enormity of the arrogant insanity of Louis XIV'.

This comment also reflected its author's concern for the welfare of the people; he was one of the first to recognize the dark side of the *grand siècle*. Quite apart from the devastation war brought to several frontier provinces, the terrible famines came often enough to be part of the experience of most adults. They were dramatic evidence of failures in the finely tuned balance between population and production, whose fluctuations underlay most of the economic difficulties of the period.

Smaller variations could already mean starvation for the most vulnerable, unless local charity came to their rescue, while they forced many others to incur crippling debts, tightening the stranglehold of the privileged few over the rural masses. Combined with the efforts of the royal tax-collectors, these pressures helped to turn an ominous situation into a desperate one. The exact relationship of cause and effect is still obscure, but it appears that the agrarian economy was actually going backwards, in the sense that frantic short-term efforts to increase production were having damaging long-term repercussions. One of the most unfortunate aspects of the great divide between the towns and the countryside they exploited was that those who actually worked the land had inadequate access to such capital as was available. Any advantage the peasantry gained from their ownership of a substantial proportion of the land was largely nullified by the small size of individual holdings, and the varying forms of exaction to which they were subject. It may well be that the success of other methods of obtaining funds from the peasantry diminished the incentives for landlords to push up their income from rent, by recasting tenurial arrangements or improving the land itself. The multiple involvement of the most active purchasers, the royal officials, in fiscal, commercial, and legal activities, may also have decreased their relative interest in the land as anything but a source of prestige and security.

In the face of both an agrarian and a general European depression, it would hardly have been possible for the other sectors of the French economy to enjoy great success. In both the commercial and industrial spheres the seventeenth century saw a loss of earlier dynamism. This may have been counterbalanced, to some extent, by the development of the infrastructure vital to further advances. New skills and techniques did spread, not least in the managerial and financial areas of business life, while greater specialization took place among entrepreneurs and artisans. It was an era of consolidation, not of easy profits, and this had a marked effect on society as a whole. As those who had made good before about 1630 entrenched themselves through the purchase of offices and land, those behind found it much harder to climb the tricky pathways towards the upper social levels. When society became less mobile, and many families of lesser nobles and officials had difficulty even in maintaining their positions, self-defensive attempts to impose rigid social hierarchies naturally gained in popularity. They were aided by the monarchy's persistent campaign to impose a greater degree of law and order, for the enhanced authority of the courts, coupled with more stringent legislation on questions of status, made it easier for the established families to block the pretensions of rivals and outsiders. Whether or not one chooses to place these trends in a Marxist framework, there is good evidence that the transition to a market economy and a society divided into broad socioeconomic strata, which had seemed to be getting under way in the sixteenth century, suffered a sharp setback in the seventeenth. The old order proved very tenacious, not least in its hold over men's minds, but the crucial influence was that of the government and its bureaucracy. Whereas deliberate attempts at control were normally irrelevant, the unintentional result of the enormous expansion in the wealth and power of the state was to unbalance and distort social relationships. Royal finance, taxation, and the sale of offices have been central themes of this book, not just for their importance as props of absolutism, but because they influenced the development of French society as a whole.

Strong government and a relatively stable society provided a favourable environment for a higher civilization, which fed on the great advances in printing, literacy, and education. Here again the benefits were very unevenly spread; the main effect on the mass of the people was to cut them off from the upper levels of French culture, as their indigenous styles of behaviour and amusement became the object of contempt, even of repression, by the educated classes. For all the genuine concern of many of its members with the lot of the poor, the Catholic church came dangerously close to being another instrument that kept them in their place, while imposing alien values. The implications of cultural and religious change went far beyond this, of course, and the intellectual developments of the seventeenth century were in the long run more significant than even the triumphs of royal absolutism. The kings could tame rebellious nobles and peasants alike, but they could not destroy the independent and questioning spirit of writers and thinkers. However confused, impractical, or reactionary the opposition to the crown still was in 1715, it was a warning sign that autocratic rule would be tolerated only if it brought material benefits and social progress. The French monarchy, trapped within the numerous contradictions of its own nature and history, would find it impossible to satisfy such demands.

Looking back, it is perhaps too easy to conclude that the changes of the seventeenth century led into a blind alley, producing a state and a society so flawed that they must eventually collapse. Nations do not escape their own history so lightly, however, and the *ancien régime* is still to be found just under the surface of French life. It may be too facile to equate the *préfet* with the *intendant*, but the centralized bureaucracy often speaks with the voice of the great *commis* of the Bourbon kings. French peasants periodically revolt in ways reminiscent of their ancestors three centuries ago, while many of them consult the *devin* and fear the witch. The *notaires* still inherit or purchase their practices; Parisians and provincials continue to regard one another with mutual scorn. The coteries and cliques of French intellectual and artistic life have their ancestors in the seventeenth century, along with most of the academies which have given them a formal setting. French parliamentary democracy has generally seemed a sickly transplant, undermined by factionalism, and periodically downgraded in favour of a presidential system. If General de Gaulle's government could be deftly satirized as a modern dress Versailles, the party which supported his rule might well be seen as a vastly expanded version of the clienteles which followed the Colberts and the Le Telliers. Two survivals of the *ancien régime* stand out above all; the sense of hierarchy which pervades French society, and the national attitude towards taxation. To know something of the great age of the monarchy is to know a surprising amount about modern France.

Appendix: Graphs

Notes to the graphs

In the nature of things, none of these graphs can pretend to be more than an approximation to the truth; several of them contain a very high proportion of guesswork. They should be regarded as guides to the general trends of the period, not as a detailed year-by-year reconstruction. Apart from the chart of royal debts, a logarithmic scale is used, in an attempt to keep fluctuations at different periods in scale. Like some of the averaging methods used, the logarithmic scale is open to objections; it can appear to minimize important changes. In fact the crucial shifts show up very clearly, but if there is a bias it is towards understatement.

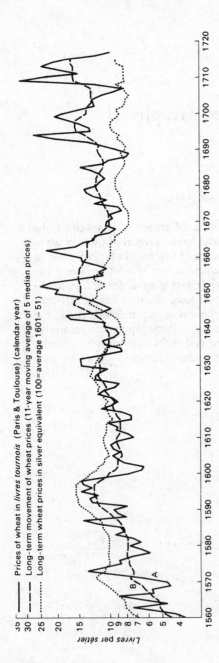

Graph 1: wheat prices 1560–1715

The concept of a national price series for wheat is almost meaningless for this period, because of local variations. This graph is computed by averaging wheat prices for Paris and Toulouse, to give some rough balance between price movements in the North and the South-West. The Parisian figures have been adjusted for the years 1589–93 in line with those of Amiens and Beauvais, to eliminate the distorting effects of the sieges and blockades of the period. Wheat prices correspond fairly closely with those for other cheaper cereals, and the major crises are clearly visible in A (the annual figures); they would show up even more dramatically if harvest years were substituted for calendar years.

The long-term movement has been plotted in B by taking the five mean prices on an 11-year moving base, then averaging them. The same figures have been recalculated to allow for debasement of the coinage, and this corrected curve appears as C.

Prices of wheat in *livres tournois* (Paris & Toulouse) (calendar year) ——
Long-term movement of wheat prices (11-year moving average of 5 median prices) – – –
Long-term wheat prices in silver equivalent (100 = average 1601–51) ·······

Livres per setier

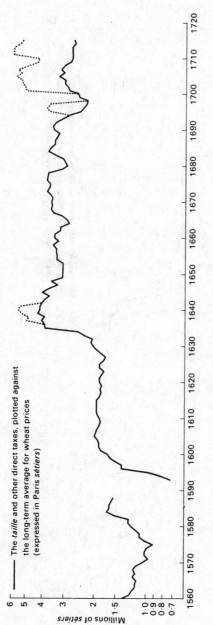

Graph 2: direct taxes in terms of wheat prices 1560–1715

Here the figures from graph 3 are combined with those from graph 1 (curve B), to show how many *sétiers* of wheat (Paris measure) would have needed to be sold to pay the assessment. The use of the 11-year moving average eliminates artificial peaks and troughs; in years of dearth the figure would otherwise appear to go down, when in fact the *taille* was an even heavier burden in such conditions, because most peasants could not afford to sell any grain at all. Low prices might theoretically have advantaged the day-labourer, but in practice they probably meant that the labour-market contracted, so that he worked fewer days, and his income fell.

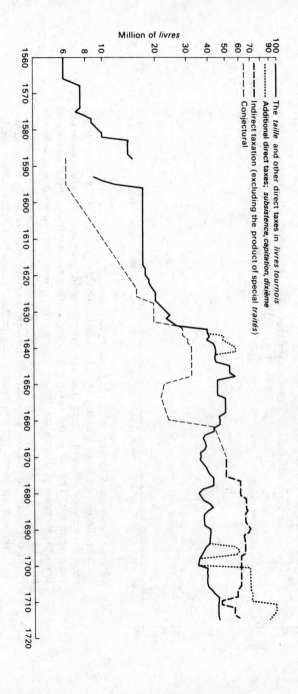

Million of *livres*

The *taille* and other direct taxes in *livres tournois*

Additional direct taxes; *subsistence, capitation, dixième*

Indirect taxation (excluding the product of special *traités*)

Conjectural

Graph 3: direct and indirect taxation 1560–1715

Here many of the figures are partly conjectural, particularly because the graph tries to give some impression of the amounts actually demanded, which were often not properly accounted. The *taille* was increased: (a) in 1637–41, by the separately levied *subsistence du quartier d'hiver*; (b) in 1695–7, by the first *capitation*; (c) in 1701, by the reintroduction of the *capitation*; (d) in 1711 by the *dixième*. The effect of these additional direct taxes is shown as a supplementary curve.

The rate of indirect taxation shown is very approximate before the 1620s, and only becomes reasonably accurate after 1660. It does not include the large sums supposedly to be raised by special taxes, the right to collect which was sold by *traités*. These were used extensively under Richelieu and Mazarin (between 1638 and 1641 the average annual yield was supposed to be 51 million *livres*), and again after 1690. Information about these operations is too scanty to allow even a reasoned guess at their practical effect.

The graph gives a reasonable impression of the general movement of taxation, with the great increases of the 1630s and the end of the century clearly visible. It cannot claim to give reliable *figures* for the total burden of taxation, another very difficult subject. Points to be borne in mind include: (a) the *taille* was increased by something between 5% and 10% in the localities, to cover certain expenses and a premium for the collectors; (b) the full sum demanded was very rarely collected, falling far short at some periods; (c) in wartime most provinces paid large sums towards the expenses of winter quarter, perhaps a 50% increase on the *taille* in some cases; (d) the indirect taxes must generally have raised more than the sum paid to the crown, to allow a profit to the farmers; (e) the towns levied their own local taxes.

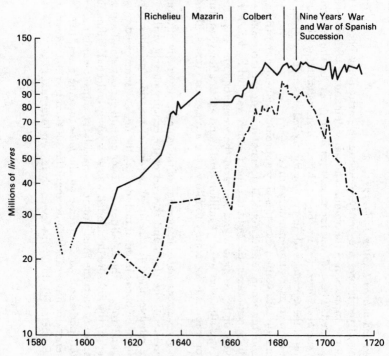

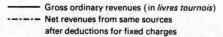

Legend (top of graph):
Gross ordinary revenues (in *livres tournois*)
Net revenues from same sources after deductions for fixed charges

Period labels: Richelieu | Mazarin | Colbert | Nine Years' War and War of Spanish Succession

Y-axis: Millions of *livres*

Graph 4: nominal and disposable royal income 1600–1715

Here the nominal income from the normal direct and indirect taxes is contrasted with the *free* income after deductions—essentially to pay debt interest and the wages of officials. While there are numerous uncertainties about the figures, they demonstrate clearly how: (a) the enormous tax increases under Richelieu simply went to finance borrowing; (b) Colbert achieved a dramatic improvement in the position; (c) the wars after 1688 made the new direct taxes (not shown here) imperative.

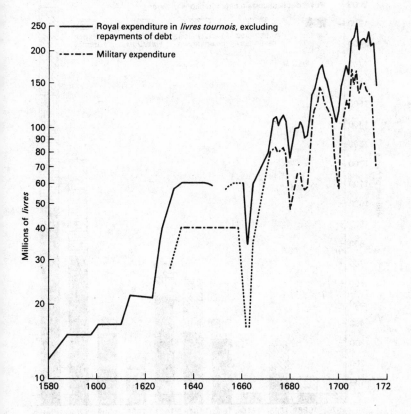

Graph 5: royal expenditure (excluding debt finance) and military expenditure 1580–1715

Figures for royal expenditure are particularly hard to interpret, because they commonly include large sums for operations concerning the debt, often merely representing paper transfers. The figures given here are for actual spending, on the army, the court, pensions, etc. Before 1670 they are very rough approximations, but from the 1630s they show how military expenditure accounted for between 60% and 75% of the total on current account.

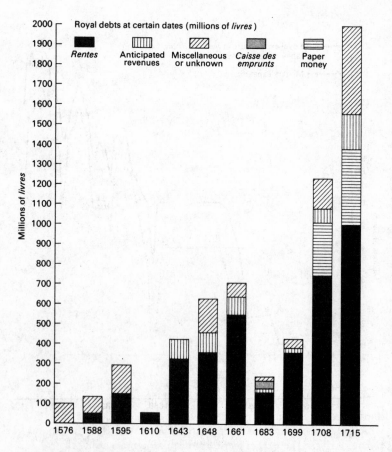

Graph 6: royal debts at certain dates 1576–1715

It is possible to compute the royal debt in various ways, and the figures are subject to serious reservations in most cases. Those of the period 1643–61 include a large element of 'fictitious' debt, which was cancelled by the *chambre de justice* of 1661–5; on the other hand, the enormous debt of 1715 was probably largely genuine. The capital value of royal offices is not included, but it can well be regarded as part of the debt; in the 1660s Colbert computed it at 420 millions, in 1715 it was at least 830 millions.

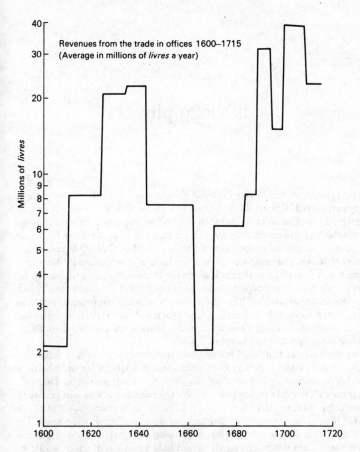

Graph 7: revenues from venal offices 1600–1715

With the trade in offices there are again doubts about the figures, and it seems certain that the crown never received the sums for which optimistic finance ministers budgeted. On the other hand, particularly in the earlier period, an unknown amount was raised through separate transactions, which cannot be shown here. In theory some 1,570,000,000 was raised from offices between 1600 and 1715, of which no more than 200,000,000 can have come from the *paulette* and other regular payments. The remainder must have been set against sales of new offices, and the enforced purchase of higher *gages* by existing officials. The graph shows averages for varying periods of years, because it is often impossible to establish figures for individual years; as far as possible the periods are chosen to coincide with changes in the level of revenue.

Bibliography

Any reasonably full bibliography of French history for the sixteenth and seventeenth centuries would be a book in itself, so this brief guide is simply a personal selection. I have included only a few important articles, but no serious student will neglect the French journals, such as the *Revue Historique* and *Annales*, or the more specialized periodicals like *XVIIe siècle* and *French Historical Studies*. Numerous contributions have also appeared in the major English and American journals. References to most of these articles will be found in the more specialized books listed below. Where complete English translations are available I have listed these in place of the original publications, but I have not included a few shortened or unfinished versions. Unless otherwise stated, French language titles were published in Paris, English language titles in London.

For the basic institutional framework, there are two works of reference by R. Doucet and G. Zeller, both published in 1948 under the identical title *Les institutions de la France au 16e siècle*. Both are valuable, Doucet's being much the fuller treatment, and are relevant to the following century as well. M. Marion, *Dictionnaire des institutions de la France aux 17e et 18e siècles* (1923) is indispensable, although far from perfect. R. Mousnier, *Les institutions de la France sous la monarchie absolue*, i (1974), is a more general work, sometimes oddly arranged but containing much of value, while F. Olivier-Martin, *Histoire du droit français des origines à la Révolution* (1948) is an authoritative summary. D. Richet, *La France moderne; l'esprit des institutions* (1974) is a short but penetrating discussion of the way institutional factors helped to shape the *ancien régime*. J. H. Shennan, *Government and Society in France, 1461–1661* (1969) is a collection of documents with a good introduction.

The standard political history of France remains that edited by E. Lavisse, *Histoire de la France*; the relevant volumes are VI to VIII (1904–8). Although some sections have dated badly, this is still a work of solid scholarship. More recently there have been analytical surveys by P. Goubert, *L'ancien régime* (2 v., 1969–73), and R. Mandrou, *La France aux 17e et 18e siècles* (1967). Mandrou's *Introduction to Modern France, 1500–1640* (1976) is an original, if sometimes rather sketchy, discussion of the environment and men's attitudes to it. Covering rather shorter periods, there are well-informed and sometimes provocative accounts by J. H. M. Salmon, *Society in Crisis* (1975), mostly concerned with the Wars of Religion, V.-L. Tapié, *France in the Age of Louis XIII and Richelieu* (1974), Goubert, *Louis XIV and Twenty Million Frenchmen* (1970), and Mandrou, *Louis XIV en son temps* (1973). Lively and well-illustrated studies of the time of *le roi soleil* can be found in J. Goimard (ed.), *La France au temps de Louis XIV* (1965), and R. M. Hatton, *Louis XIV and his World* (1972).

Perhaps the most remarkable productions of recent French historians have been the marvellously researched studies of individual areas or provinces. After the pioneer work by G. Roupnel, *La ville et la campagne au 17e siècle* (1922), describing Dijon and its hinterland, major contributions have included P. Goubert, *Beauvais et le Beauvaisis de 1600 à 1730* (1960), P. de Saint-Jacob, *Les paysans de la Bourgogne du Nord au dernier siècle de l'Ancien Régime* (1960), R. Baehrel, *Une Croissance; La Basse-Provence rurale* (1961), E. Le Roy Ladurie, *Les paysans de Languedoc* (1966), J. Jacquart, *La crise rurale en Ile-de-France, 1550–1670* (1975), and G. Frêche, *Toulouse et la région Midi-Pyrénées au siècle des lumières, vers 1670–1789* (1975). These works are fundamental to any understanding of early modern France, and of present-day French historical techniques and concerns. A similar study in an urban context is P. Deyon, *Amiens, capitale provinciale* (1967), while M. Couturier tackles a small town in *Recherches sur les structures sociales de Châteaudun, 1525–1789* (1969), and for the earlier period there is an excellent work on Lyon by R. Gascon, *Grand commerce et vie urbaine au 16e siècle* (1971).

Many of the findings of these local investigations have been summarized in two collaborative syntheses, F. Braudel and E. Labrousse (eds.), *Histoire économique et sociale de la France, ii, 1660–1789* (1971), and G. Duby and A. Wallon (eds.), *Histoire de la France rurale, ii; l'âge classique des paysans, 1340–1789* (1975). This last cannot entirely supplant Marc Bloch's classic *French Rural History* (1966), nor some of the essays by J. Meuvret collected in a remarkable volume, *Études d'histoire économique* (1972). Wine production is the subject of another classic, R. Dion, *Histoire de la vigne et du vin en France* (1959). Technical problems of money supply dominate F. C. Spooner's *The International Economy and Monetary Movements in France, 1493–1725* (Cambridge, Mass., 1972), but this is a rewarding book for those who can master its difficulties. A special number of *XVIIe siècle* was devoted to the economy (Nos. 70–1, 1966). On questions of government intervention, H. Hauser made a powerful if sometimes overstated case for Richelieu in *La pensée et l'action économique du Cardinal de Richelieu* (1944), while C. W. Cole, *Colbert and a Century of French Mercantilism* (New York, 1939), remains the most informative study of the minister. W. C. Scoville's *The Persecution of the Huguenots and French Economic Development, 1680–1720* (Berkeley, 1960) demolishes a number of myths on this controversial topic. For taxation there is the deceptively wide-ranging work by E. Esmonin, *La taille en Normandie au temps de Colbert* (1913), and an alert short summary by F. Hincker, *Les français devant l'impôt sous l'ancien régime* (1971). The central management of the finances is examined by J. Dent in *Crisis in Finance; Crown, Financiers and Society in Seventeenth Century France* (Newton Abbot,

1973), an uneven book which concentrates on the 1650s, and by R. J. Bonney in 'The Secret Expenses of Richelieu and Mazarin, 1624–61', *English Historical Review*, CCCLXI (1976).

For social history, as for economic, much of the best writing is to be found in the regional studies. To these one may add F. Lebrun, *Les hommes et la mort en Anjou (17e–18e siècles)* (1971), and J. Meyer, *La noblesse bretonne au 18e siècle* (1966); despite its title, the latter includes a very important section on the reign of Louis XIV. For the great nobility J.-P. Labatut provides a scholarly but rather limited analysis in *Les ducs et pairs au 17e siècle* (1972). D. Bitton, *The French Nobility in Crisis, 1540–1640* (Stanford, 1969), though slight, is not without interest, while a sharp insight into noble grievances comes in the documents edited by Mousnier and others, *Deux cahiers de la noblesse pour les états-généraux de 1649–51* (1965). There is an important article by P. Deyon, 'A propos des rapports entre la noblesse française et la monarchie absolue pendant la première moitié du 17e siècle', *Revue Historique* CCXXXI (1964), and another by J. Russell Major, 'The Crown and the Aristocracy in Renaissance France', *American Historical Review* LXIX (1964). At the other end of the social spectrum, there is a fascinating collection of essays by N. Z. Davis, *Society and Culture in Early Modern France* (1975), and the problem of the poor around Lyon is thoroughly treated by J.-P. Gutton, *La société et les pauvres* (1970).

The controversial subject of popular revolts was opened up by B. Porchnev, *Les soulèvements populaires en France de 1623 à 1648* (1963), a book which mixes up useful information with errors and curious interpretations. The French section of Mousnier's *Peasant Uprisings* (1971) is sometimes unbalanced by the author's polemical reaction to Porchnev. M. Foisil, *La révolte des Nu-pieds* (1970), is scholarly but uninspired; it does not supplant the long article by M. Caillard in *A travers la Normandie des 17e et 18e siècles* (Caen, 1963). Two outstanding recent works are Y.-M. Bercé, *Histoire des Croquants* (Geneva, 1974), and R. Pillorget, *Les mouvements insurrectionels en Provence, 1596–1715* (1975), which between them raise the debate to a new level, settling many earlier arguments. Bercé has also produced two shorter books, covering a wider period, *Croquants et Nu-pieds* (1974), and *Fête et révolte* (1976), while there is a good account by Y. Garlan and C. Nières of *Les révoltes bretonnes de 1675* (1975).

There has been some original and enterprising work on the history of religion, much of it employed by J. Delumeau in *Le catholicisme entre Luther et Voltaire* (1971), a good summary which is occasionally rather too sweeping. J. Bossy, 'The Counter-Reformation and the people of Catholic Europe', *Past and Present* 47 (1970), is a helpful article, while among the local diocesan studies the best are probably J. Ferté, *La vie religieuse dans les campagnes parisiennes, 1622–1695* (1962), L. Pérouas, *Le diocèse de La Rochelle, 1648–1724* (1964), and J.-F. Soulet, *Traditions et réformes religieuses dans les Pyrénées centrales au 17e siècle* (1974). On Jansenism there is a brisk and generally convincing book by A. Adam, *Du mysticisme à la révolte: les jansénistes du 17e siècle* (1968), a weighty local study by R. Taveneaux, *Le jansénisme en Lorraine* (1960), and a detailed study of a crucial period, P.

Jansen, *Le Cardinal Mazarin et le mouvement janséniste français, 1653–9* (1967). Taveneaux has also produced a useful shorter book, *Jansénisme et politique* (1965), while for the founder of the movement in France there is an authoritative biography by J. Orcibal, *Jean Duvergier de Hauranne et son temps* (1947). The links between Jansenism and the *robe* class are interestingly if unconvincingly explored by L. Goldmann in *The Hidden God* (1964), and some of the mysteries of Fénelon's conduct are unravelled by H. Hillenaar, *Fénelon et les Jésuites* (The Hague, 1967). P. Blet has clarified the official relationship between clergy and crown in *Le clergé de France et la monarchie. Étude sur les Assemblées du Clergé de 1615 à 1666* (Rome, 1959), and *Les Assemblées du Clergé et Louis XIV* (Rome, 1972). Among general books on Protestantism are E. G. Léonard, *A History of Protestantism* (1964), and D. Ligou, *Le protestantisme en France de 1598 à 1715* (1968), while the motives for the Revocation of the Edict of Nantes are explored by J. Orcibal in *Louis XIV et les protestants* (1952).

For both religious and secular culture there is an indispensable source in H.-J. Martin's *Livre, pouvoirs et société à Paris au 17e siècle* (Geneva 1969), which illuminates a great variety of topics. J. Lough, *An Introduction to Seventeenth Century France* (1954), is an elegant and deservedly popular survey with a literary bias, while A. Adam, *Grandeur and Illusion: French Literature and Society 1600–1715* (1972), gives an up-to-date view of a massively worked field. Other useful general works are D. Maland, *Culture and Society in Seventeenth Century France* (1970), and P. Bénichou, *Morales du grand siècle* (1948). The sceptical tradition is examined by R. Pintard, *Le libertinage érudit pendant la première moitié du 17e siècle* (1943), R. H. Popkin, *The History of Scepticism from Erasmus to Descartes* (Assen, 1960), and J. S. Spink, *French Free Thought from Gassendi to Voltaire* (1960). Biographies and critical studies of writers are innumerable, but three which are particularly relevant and sensitive to the historical context are D. Frame, *Montaigne, a Biography* (1965), R. Picard, *La carrière de Jean Racine* (1961), and E. Labrousse, *Pierre Bayle* (The Hague, 2 v., 1963–4). For education there is an excellent overall account by R. Chartier, M. M. Compère, and D. Julia, *L'éducation en France du 16e au 18e siècle* (1976). On popular culture there are books by R. Mandrou, *De la culture populaire aux 17e et 18e siècles* (1964), and G. Bollême, *Les almanachs populaires aux 17e et 18e siècles* (1969), and *La bibliothèque bleue* (1971). Among contributions to the study of peasant *mentalités* are a splendid microscopic work, G. Bouchard, *Le village immobile* (1972), and two books by J.-L. Flandrin, *Amours paysannes, 16e–19e siècles* (1975), and *Familles* (1976). Attitudes to death are the subject of M. Vovelle, *Mourir autrefois* (1974), towards a special kind of healing of Marc Bloch's *The Royal Touch* (1972). The standard work on witchcraft is R. Mandrou, *Magistrats et sorciers en France au 17e siècle* (1968), which may be supplemented by M. de Certeau, *La possession de Loudun* (1970), and E. W. Monter, *Witchcraft in France and Switzerland* (Ithaca, 1976).

For the condition of France around the beginning of the Wars of Religion there is still much of value in the works of L. Romier, of which the best is perhaps *Le Royaume de Catherine de Medicis* (1922). The tax position has been clarified by M. Wolfe, *The Fiscal System of Renaissance France* (New Haven, 1972). There are two important works by N. M. Sutherland, *The French Secretaries of State in the Age of Catherine de Medici* (1962), and *The Massacre of St. Bartholomew and the European Conflict, 1559–72* (1973). The massacre itself is the subject of J. Estèbe, *Tocsin pour un massacre* (1968), and A. Soman (ed.), *The Massacre of St. Bartholomew* (The Hague, 1974). Calvinist organization is examined by R. M. Kingdon in *Geneva and the Coming of the Wars of Religion in France, 1555–63* (Geneva, 1956), and *Geneva and the Consolidation of the French Protestant Movement, 1564–72* (Geneva, 1967). For the League the outstanding study remains that by H. Drouot, *Mayenne et la Bourgogne: Étude sur la Ligue 1587–1595* (1937), while the complexities of Henri IV's position are sharply illustrated by H. A. Lloyd in *The Rouen Campaign, 1590–2* (Oxford, 1973), and there is a brilliant cameo of the critical year 1588 in G. Mattingly, *The Defeat of the Spanish Armada* (1959). The best guide to political ideas remains W. F. Church, *Constitutional Thought in Sixteenth-Century France* (Cambridge, Mass., 1941); there are additional points in M. Yardeni, *La conscience nationale en France pendant les guerres de religion* (1971), and F. J. Baumgartner, *Radical Reactionaries: the Political Thought of the French Catholic League* (Geneva, 1976).

There is no satisfactory biography of Henri IV, but some of his ministers have been more fortunate. D. Buisseret, *Sully and the growth of centralised government in France, 1598–1610* (1968), is concise but thorough, while R. F. Kierstead, *Pomponne de Bellièvre* (Evanston, 1968), and E. H. Dickerman, *Bellièvre and Villeroy* (Providence, R.I., 1971), although limited, are serviceable studies. A slightly overstated case is made by J. Russell Major in 'Henry IV and Guyenne: a study concerning the origins of royal absolutism', *French Historical Studies* IV (1966). This may be the place to mention the fundamental work by R. Mousnier, *La vénalité des offices sous Henri IV et Louis XIII* (2nd ed. 1971), as well as the same author's important collected articles, *La plume, la faucille et le marteau* (1970), and his *The Assassination of Henri IV* (1973). Mousnier is also the editor of a rather scrappy collective volume, *Le conseil du roi de Louis XII à la Révolution* (1970). Other volumes including important articles are E. Esmonin, *Études sur la France des 17e et 18e siècles* (1964), and G. Zeller, *Aspects de la politique française sous l'ancien régime* (1964), while there is a collection of articles, several in English translation, edited by R. F. Kierstead, *State and Society in Seventeenth Century France* (New York, 1975).

Perhaps understandably, the period of Marie de Medici has been neglected, although J. M. Hayden, *France and the Estates General of 1614* (Cambridge, 1974), is a useful contribution, even if it overestimates the importance of the Estates. A. D. Lublinskaya, *French Absolutism: The Crucial Phase, 1620–1629* (Cambridge, 1968), is an interesting but rather wayward book, some of whose assertions are effectively attacked by D. Parker, 'The Social Foundations of French Absolutism, 1610–30', *Past and Present* 53 (1971). J. A. Clarke, *Huguenot Warrior: the Life and Times of Henri de Rohan 1579–1638* (The Hague, 1966), copes well with the career of the most committed Huguenot leader. While Cardinal Richelieu himself must run a comfortable second to Napoleon in the French biographical stakes, none of the resulting literature matches his stature; probably the best of a bad lot is the patchy six-volume effort by G. Hanotaux and the duc de la Force, *Histoire du Cardinal de Richelieu* (1896–1947). The Cardinal's relations with the other ministers after 1630 are well described by O. A. Ranum, *Richelieu and the Councillors of Louis XIII* (Oxford, 1963). Political thought and government propaganda are intelligently discussed by E. Thuau, *Raison d'état et pensée politique à l'époque de Richelieu* (1966); the overlapping book by W. F. Church, *Richelieu and Reason of State* (Princeton, 1972), is less lively, but more convincing on Richelieu's own position. An extremely clear account of the impact of Richelieu's policies on France as a whole will be found in R. J. Bonney's forthcoming book, *Political Change in France under Richelieu and Mazarin* (Oxford). There is no study of later foreign policy to equal V.-L. Tapié, *La politique étrangère de la France et le début de la guerre de trente ans, 1616–21* (1934), but some useful points are made by H. Weber, 'Richelieu et le Rhin', *Revue Historique* CCXXXIX (1968).

Unlike his predecessor, Mazarin has attracted relatively few biographers, and there is still no adequate account of his ministerial career; the 1650s have been particularly neglected. For the Fronde itself, the best account remains E. Kossmann, *La Fronde* (Leiden, 1954), although the author's rejection of all overall patterns makes it rather confusing at times. P. R. Doolin, *The Fronde* (Cambridge, Mass., 1935) retains some usefulness for the constitutional side, while there is a competent biography by J. H. M. Salmon, *Cardinal de Retz* (1969). A. L. Moote, *The Revolt of the Judges* (Princeton, 1971), is a curious mixture of real insights with perverse misinterpretations, many of which are corrected by R. J. Bonney in 'The French Civil War, 1649–53', *European Studies Review* (forthcoming). The provincial troubles in Provence and Guyenne are described in the books by Pillorget and Bercé already mentioned; the latter's discussion can be supplemented by S. A. Westrich, *The Ormée of Bordeaux* (Baltimore, 1971). A separate provincial revolt is the subject of P. Logié, *La Fronde en Normandie* (1951–2), and the reactions of a group of dispossessed office-holders emerge from the detailed work by J.-P. Charmeil, *Les trésoriers de France à l'époque de la Fronde* (1964).

The *roi soleil* receives the rather monotonous full-dress treatment he deserves from J. B. Wolf, *Louis XIV* (1968), and his government is the subject of some uneven essays edited by J. C. Rule, *Louis XIV and the Craft of Kingship* (Ohio, 1969). A higher standard is maintained in two collections edited by R. M. Hatton, *Louis XIV and Absolutism* and *Louis XIV and Europe* (1976). Foreign policy is also discussed by L. André, *Louis XIV et l'Europe* (1950), while the same author produced two standard works, *Michel le Tellier et l'organisation de l'armée monarchique* (1906) and *Michel le Tellier et Louvois* (1942). There is a good account of naval problems in G. R. Symcox, *The Crisis of French Naval Power, 1688–97* (The Hague, 1974). The administration of a frontier province is the basis of a wide-ranging book by G. Livet, *L'intendance d'Alsace sous Louis XIV* (1956). The reaction to government interference is the subject of a lively if eclectic study by L. Rothkrug, *Opposition to Louis XIV* (Princeton, 1965), and the aristocratic reaction is placed in context by A. Devyver, *Le sang épuré. Les préjugés de race chez les gentilshommes français, 1560–1720* (Brussels, 1973). The treatment of Paris is described in J. de Saint-Germain, *La Reynie et la police au 17e siècle* (1962) and O. A. Ranum, *Paris in the Age of Absolutism* (New York, 1968). As for the whole of the period covered by this book, much of the most illuminating writing is to be found in the regional and specialized studies, many of which have been listed above.

Glossary

This is not an exhaustive glossary of the technical terms used, some of which are fully explained in the text, and therefore do not appear here.

Aides. A range of indirect taxes, primarily on drink.

Assiette. Division of direct taxes between *généralités* and other subdivisions, down to parish level.

Caisse des emprunts. Embryonic state 'savings bank' created by Colbert, then destroyed by his successors' failure to meet obligations.

Capitation. Emergency poll-tax, levied 1695–7 and after 1701. Originally on a scale fixed according to profession and rank, with no exemptions.

Commissaires. Royal agents exercising administrative or judicial functions by virtue of a personal commission (non-venal and revocable).

Consuls. Name used by elected municipal councillors in much of southern France.

Cours des aides. Courts with general powers to oversee tax system (but not all new taxes), to hear appeals against decisions of lower courts such as *élections*, and try criminal cases connected with taxes. One in Paris, twelve in different provincial towns.

Dérogéance. Rule under which a nobleman who engaged in a 'demeaning' occupation, notably trade, lost his status and privileges.

Dixième. Emergency tax on income from property, introduced at end of 1710.

Échevins. Name used by elected municipal councillors in most of France.

Élections. Term applied both to the tribunals responsible for the local administration of the *taille* and other taxes, and to the areas with which they dealt. The *élus* who staffed them (venal office-holders, despite the name) carried out local visits to check that the distribution of taxes was fair. Largely supplanted by *intendants* after middle of the seventeenth century.

Fermiers. Financiers who leased the right to levy taxes from the government, in return for a fixed series of payments.

Gabelle. Salt tax, levied on varying basis in five distinct areas, a sixth group of regions being exempt.

Garde des sceaux. Keeper of the Seals: a substitute for the Chancellor, he could be granted identical powers when the latter was in disgrace.

Généralité. Financial area under jurisdiction of a bureau of *trésoriers de*

France, which later became the normal assignment of an *intendant*. There were about twenty at the beginning of the seventeenth century, but the number later increased slightly.

Intendants. Special *commissaires* sent into the provinces by the crown, who became the most important royal agents in the localities from the 1630s onwards.

Laboureurs. Prosperous peasants, wealthy enough to keep own plough-team (but in southern France merely an ordinary peasant).

Lit de justice. Ceremony in which king could personally enforce registration of edicts in the *parlement* or other sovereign courts.

Maîtres des requêtes. Officials attached to royal council, and under control of Chancellor. Most *intendants* held such an office.

Marque d'étain. Tax on pewter and tin metalware.

Officialité. Diocesan court, with jurisdiction in cases of clerical discipline and many matters concerning marriage.

Papier timbré. Indirect tax, levied by enforcing use of special stamped paper for legal transactions.

Parlements. Royal courts of appeal, also capable of performing more general administrative duties. Apart from that of Paris, there were *parlements* at Toulouse, Grenoble, Bordeaux, Dijon, Rouen, Aix, Rennes, Pau (1620), Metz (1633), Besançon (1676), and Douai (1686).

Pays d'élections. Provinces in which taxation was levied by *élus* on orders of royal council—most of France.

Pays d'états. Provinces in which taxation was levied by the local estates: Languedoc, Brittany, Burgundy, Provence, Artois were the principal instances.

Premier président. Presiding magistrate in *parlements* and other higher courts. In the *parlements* the *premier présidence* was not venal in the ordinary sense; because of the political importance of the office, the crown chose the holder with care.

Receveurs des tailles. Officials who received cash from parish collectors in settlement for direct taxes, then transmitted it to *receveurs généraux*.

Régale. Royal right to take income from vacant bishoprics until formal installation of new titularies. The attempt to extend it from its traditional area of application to the whole country provoked a major quarrel between Louis XIV and the Pope.

Rentes. A system of concealed borrowing at interest (accepted as lawful by the Church), under which fixed annual or quarterly payments were sold for cash. The crown's own credit was generally so bad that many *rentes* were nominally assigned on the municipality of Paris, the clergy, and other third parties.

Réunions. A legal device under which Louis XIV annexed frontier territories he claimed to be 'reuniting' to his heritage, after obtaining favourable judgments from a special court.

Subdélégués. Assistants appointed by *intendants*, to act for them in special matters or in certain areas.

Taille. Primary direct tax, levied in two main forms. *Taille personnelle* was supposedly proportional to the individual's ability to pay, as assessed by the local collector. *Taille réelle* (only used in Languedoc, Artois, Hainault, Flandres, Provence, and parts of Guienne) was a land tax.

Taxes d'office. Special individual surcharges imposed by the *intendants* or their agents where they suspected evasion by the more powerful non-noble taxpayers.

Traitants. Financiers who had concluded a *traité* with the crown to levy taxes, sell offices, etc. General term of opprobrium applied to financiers.

Trésoriers de France. Financial officials who staffed the *bureau des finances* in each *généralité*. Responsible for dividing up tax demands between *élections*, and for various supervisory functions. Became virtually superfluous by the later seventeenth century, as the *intendants* took over most of their functions.

Index

OXFORD

MORE OXFORD PAPERBACKS

This book is just one of nearly 1000 Oxford Paperbacks currently in print. If you would like details of other Oxford Paperbacks, including titles in the World's Classics, Oxford Reference, Oxford Books, OPUS, Past Masters, Oxford Authors, and Oxford Shakespeare series, please write to:

UK and Europe: Oxford Paperbacks Publicity Manager, Arts and Reference Publicity Department, Oxford University Press, Walton Street, Oxford OX2 6DP.

Customers in UK and Europe will find Oxford Paperbacks available in all good bookshops. But in case of difficulty please send orders to the Cash-with-Order Department, Oxford University Press Distribution Services, Saxon Way West, Corby, Northants NN18 9ES. Tel: 0536 741519; Fax: 0536 746337. Please send a cheque for the total cost of the books, plus £1.75 postage and packing for orders under £20; £2.75 for orders over £20. Customers outside the UK should add 10% of the cost of the books for postage and packing.

USA: Oxford Paperbacks Marketing Manager, Oxford University Press, Inc., 200 Madison Avenue, New York, N.Y. 10016.

Canada: Trade Department, Oxford University Press, 70 Wynford Drive, Don Mills, Ontario M3C 1J9.

Australia: Trade Marketing Manager, Oxford University Press, G.P.O. Box 2784Y, Melbourne 3001, Victoria.

South Africa: Oxford University Press, P.O. Box 1141, Cape Town 8000.

HISTORY IN OXFORD PAPERBACKS

Oxford Paperbacks' superb history list offers books on a wide range of topics from ancient to modern times, whether general period studies or assessments of particular events, movements, or personalities.

THE STRUGGLE FOR
THE MASTERY OF EUROPE 1848–1918

A. J. P. Taylor

The fall of Metternich in the revolutions of 1848 heralded an era of unprecedented nationalism in Europe, culminating in the collapse of the Hapsburg, Romanov, and Hohenzollern dynasties at the end of the First World War. In the intervening seventy years the boundaries of Europe changed dramatically from those established at Vienna in 1815. Cavour championed the cause of *Risorgimento* in Italy; Bismarck's three wars brought about the unification of Germany; Serbia and Bulgaria gained their independence courtesy of the decline of Turkey—'the sick man of Europe'; while the great powers scrambled for places in the sun in Africa. However, with America's entry into the war and President Wilson's adherence to idealistic internationalist principles, Europe ceased to be the centre of the world, although its problems, still primarily revolving around nationalist aspirations, were to smash the Treaty of Versailles and plunge the world into war once more.

A. J. P. Taylor has drawn the material for his account of this turbulent period from the many volumes of diplomatic documents which have been published in the five major European languages. By using vivid language and forceful characterization, he has produced a book that is as much a work of literature as a contribution to scientific history.

'One of the glories of twentieth-century writing.' *Observer*

Also in Oxford Paperbacks:

Portrait of an Age: Victorian England   G. M. Young
Germany 1866–1945   Gorden A. Craig
The Russian Revolution 1917–1932   Sheila Fitzpatrick
France 1848–1945   Theodore Zeldin